Theories of International Relations

Contending Approaches to World Politics

Stephanie Lawson

polity

The right of Stephanie Lawson to be identified as Author of this Work has been asserted in accordance with the UK Copyright, Designs and Patents Act 1988.

First published in 2015 by Polity Press

Polity Press
65 Bridge Street
Cambridge CB2 1UR, UK

Polity Press
350 Main Street
Malden, MA 02148, USA

ISBN-13: 978-0-7456-6423-1
ISBN-13: 978-0-7456-6424-8 (pb)

A catalogue record for this book is available from the British Library.

Library of Congress Cataloging-in-Publication Data

Lawson, Stephanie.
  Theories of international relations : contending approaches to world politics / Stephanie Lawson.
    pages cm
  ISBN 978-0-7456-6423-1 (hardback) – ISBN 0-7456-6423-7 (hardcover) – ISBN 978-0-7456-6424-8 (paperback) 1. International relations. 2. World politics. I. Title.
  JZ1242.L4 2015
  327.101–dc23
                        2014036013

Typeset in 9.5/13 Swift Light by
Servis Filmsetting Limited, Stockport, Cheshire
Printed and bound in the UK by Clays Ltd, St Ives plc

For further information on Polity, visit our website:
politybooks.com

Contents

Detailed Contents

Case Studies

Preface and Acknowledgements

The discipline of International Relations (IR) was formalized as a field of academic study in the immediate aftermath of the First World War and dedicated to addressing the causes of war and the conditions for peace in a systematic and sustained manner. It has since developed into a highly complex, multifaceted field of intellectual endeavour which, although remaining very much attuned to war and peace at an international level, now addresses a variety of issues under the general rubric of security – food and water security, energy and resource security, environmental security, gender security, and so on. Allied to these are concerns with justice and equity at a global or transnational level. These relate in turn to poverty and development, and all have a very clear normative dimension.

The academic study of these issues cannot confine itself to mere description. The task of the IR discipline is also to explain, interpret and analyse the range of events, structures and institutions, as well as the behaviour of agents, both individually and collectively, who drive events, create structures and build institutions. This task requires the conceptualization of the various dimensions of the subject matter – war and peace, anarchy and order, power and interests, justice and security, among many others. Beyond this, it requires a theoretical imagination capable of bringing together these various dimensions to tell a coherent story about why the world of international politics is as it is. In addition, most theoretical enterprises have much to say about how the world could and *should* be like and are therefore explicitly normative.

This book is organized in a fairly straightforward manner, examining the principal schools of thought, beginning with political realism in its 'classic' form and proceeding through to issue-oriented formulations of theory in the contemporary period. This is not the only way to organize a book on IR theory, but for readers coming to the subject for the first time it has the virtue of simplicity. Having said that, readers will soon find that each school of thought is itself complex and that there is contestation within schools as well as between them. At the same time, elements of different schools of thought overlap, and there has been much interaction between them. Indeed, to some extent they 'feed' off each other as they critique, and counter-critique, each other's assumptions. Another preliminary point to note is that the book does not champion any particular school of thought, or any variant within a school, but advises the reader to consider the merits and shortcomings of each one and to reflect critically on the contribution that it makes to understanding the complex world of international relations.

Writing a book such as this always incurs debts of various kinds to family, friends and colleagues. I am especially grateful to Jonathan Symons, Noah Bassil and Alan Scott for taking the time to read parts of the manuscript and to provide comments and suggestions. Many thanks are also due to Pascal Porcheron and Louise Knight at Polity Press for their support for the project and, not least, for letting me have my way with the cover illustration. Apart from its aesthetic qualities, readers will, I hope, appreciate the symbolism of Henri Rousseau's *Tiger in a Tropical Storm* for the theorization of international relations.

SL

Sydney, August 2014

1

Introduction:
Theorizing International Relations

All academic disciplines are dedicated to the task of understanding or explaining some aspect of the world, although they do so in very different ways. And they are all underpinned by bodies of theory formulated in response to particular problems or questions emerging from their particular subject matter. So the study of literature is underpinned by literary theory, sociology by social theory, physics by physical theory, politics by political theory, and so on. The study of international relations (IR), and its theorization, is a species of political studies or political science but has developed its own distinctive profile since it emerged as a specialized field almost a century ago. IR also draws on other disciplines in the humanities and social sciences, especially history, philosophy, law and economics, with social theory having a particular influence in recent years.

As an intellectual enterprise, theory is often contrasted with action or practice, sometimes in a negative sense, as reflected in the rather clichéd stock phrase 'It's all very well in theory but it doesn't work in practice'. Actually, if it doesn't work in practice, then it may not be much of a theory (whatever 'it' is) and must therefore be re-examined for errors or abandoned altogether. This suggests that theories stand to be tested in light of practice, or in competition with other theories, and succeed, fail or undergo modification on that basis. Even when theory does fail in some sense, the value of theoretical speculation should never be underestimated. Nor should 'the abstract' be set up in opposition to 'the real', as if they were completely unrelated. While theorizing is indeed a mental process rather than a physical action or event, it is intimately related to practice. It aims to make sense of actions, events or phenomena in the physical or natural world as well as the social world, of which politics is a significant part. Some go so far as to propose that theories actually create realities. At the very least, thinking generally precedes action – and, indeed, we are usually enjoined to think before we act. Whether those thinking processes

1

always result in what we might consider desirable outcomes is another matter.

As is evident from the title and contents of this book, there is no one theory of IR but rather a number of theories. Some of these are addressed very generally to questions of power, interests, conflict, cooperation, order and justice. Others have particular starting points which are more issue-oriented but which nonetheless address the same general questions in one way or another. Some have developed at least partly as critiques, either of other theoretical approaches or as a response to particular problems, or both. And, within each of them, there are different, competing strands. This introductory chapter provides some essential background to how these different approaches theorize the field of international politics, looking first at the importance of theory itself and at issues of knowledge and truth, objectivity and subjectivity, the nature of existence and reality, and the dynamics of power and interests in politics. We then consider the purpose and scope of IR as a discipline and some of the factors driving its initial theorization, as well as key historical developments, including the phenomenon of modernity and what has become the central institution of politics – the sovereign state.

Theory, Norms and Methods

'Theory' – derived from the Greek *theoria*, meaning contemplation or speculation – may be defined as an organized system of ideas devised to explain a certain set of phenomena. The phenomena about which we theorize may range from fairly simple or narrow ones to very wide-ranging, complex and controversial ones, such as those involved in theories of climate change or the evolution of species. These bodies of theory are essentially scientific, but the former in particular has generated much political controversy in the contemporary period, giving a slightly different nuance to the term 'political science'.

Because IR is a form of political or, more broadly, social *science*, it is important to consider the concept of science itself. It has been said that what makes science 'scientific' is not the nature of the phenomena under observation or study but *how* they are studied. Thus the term 'scientific' is often applied to a particular type of process or method (Kosso, 2011, p. 1). Scientific method in the natural sciences is typically described as beginning with the observation and description of phenomena followed by the formulation of a hypothesis, which is a tentative explanation of the phenomena in question, and then the testing of the hypothesis, ideally through repeated experimentation under the same conditions to confirm its capacity to make reliable, universally applicable predictions, thus constituting a 'reality' that is independent of time and place. If it stands up to such testing, it may turn from a mere hypothesis into a theory or even a law. Thus the hallmarks of scientific enquiry are the use of evidence and reason in an objective process following recognized procedures, free from the intrusion of human values, and resulting in the production of reliable, objective knowledge (Gower, 1997, p. 5; Kosso, 2011, pp. 1–2).

This is a rather idealized view of how science proceeds. In practice neither scientists nor the hypotheses or theories they produce are as objective as some might like to think. Scientists are, after all, human, and there will always be subjective elements at work in the production of scientific knowledge. This highlights the fact that, because it is a human activity, research in science is therefore by definition a *social* activity attended by all the dynamics characterizing social interaction, including cooperation, competition and conflict. Furthermore, the way in which science proceeds is often much more creative and contingent than the formal description of scientific method implies. Chance observations, unexpected reactions, accidental findings or unanticipated experimental results are as important as the more strictly methodical activities.

There has been much controversy about whether the basic methods applicable to the natural sciences can or should be adopted in the social sciences. This begs the question of whether the production of knowledge in the social sciences is amenable to the same kinds of methods as apply in the natural sciences. We can certainly generate hypotheses about a wide variety of social phenomena, and we can amass empirical data about them, but we cannot often run experiments in the social world, let alone run repeated tests over time under exactly the same conditions. Studying self-aware, sometimes rational, sometimes irrational humans in diverse social and political contexts in which a myriad of factors or variables come into play is simply not amenable to the scientific method described above. So what other methods are available?

Some social scientists make extensive use of statistical data which, on the face of it, may seem more or less objective and preclude the intrusion of the researcher's own values. However, even if the data is largely objective (which depends very much on what is counted or measured and how it is counted or measured), its interpretation is another matter. At virtually all stages of a project, subjective elements will intrude. There are also serious limits to what we can gain knowledge of through methods restricted to quantifiable data.

The use of quantitative methodology in social science research is often taken as the hallmark of *positivism*, a term coined by the French intellectual August Comte (1798–1857), who is also credited with popularizing the term 'sociology'. Comte envisaged the latter as a positive science capable of formulating invariant laws in the social sphere. Positivism is sometimes used synonymously with 'empiricism', a doctrine that holds that real knowledge – as opposed to mere belief – can *only* be gained through more or less direct observation and experience. Empiricism, however, is not engaged with theory-building as such, only with the accumulation of verifiable facts. Positivism goes beyond empiricism in that its aim is to produce and test theories while relying on empirical data that can be aggregated, usually in statistical form. The results are believed to be objective, value-free conclusions about the phenomena under investigation and ultimately to be relied on to produce valid theory and even laws of human and social behaviour.

Positivism thus conceived is opposed to theological and metaphysical modes of discovering 'truth' which had dominated in an earlier era. But Comte's stipulation that real knowledge of the social and political world could only be produced via positivism came to be regarded as far too narrow. Even the nature of empirical evidence itself is now recognized as very diverse and not always amenable to strict positivist treatment. *Qualitative* methods based on interpretive techniques are now recognized as more appropriate to the study of politics and society. Ethnography in anthropology, the collection and interpretation of artefacts in archaeology, the piecing together of archival information and other sources to produce narrative history, and participant observation in sociology, as well as case study analysis, focus group analysis, various forms of interviewing, and so on, common to a range of social science disciplines – all these are highly methodical in a qualitative sense and appropriate to the tasks they are designed to serve, but none would fit the narrower definitions of scientific method described above. Some have argued for the value of combining both quantitative and qualitative methods, thus producing an eclectic methodological framework – also known as mixed methods research – which is better suited to the task of studying complex social and political phenomena (see Teddie and Tashakkori, 2011, pp. 285–90).

The attempt to constrain the social sciences within a strict positivist framework would also seem to preclude moral or ethical issues, and yet these lie at the heart of most political questions, whether domestic or international. By definition, the very idea of an objective body of science requires that all such considerations be put aside, for science – at least in a narrow sense – is the study of what *is*, not what *ought* to be. A statement of what *is* constitutes a *positive* statement and is therefore held to be value free, while a statement of what *ought* to be is described as a *normative* statement and is value-laden by definition.

I suggest that, in the study of politics at any level, from the domestic through to the international, we need both. In other words, we need to be able to identify and describe with a fair degree of accuracy the political world as it *is*, and this is certainly where reliable methods, either quantitative or qualitative, or both, have their place in the production of knowledge. We then need to engage with *normative theory* to make considered judgements about whether or not this is the most desirable of possible worlds from some ethical point of view. This involves 'value judgements', but perfectly legitimate ones. For both social scientists and those trained in the humanities, it is not a matter of avoiding making value judgements but, rather, a matter of making well-informed judgements based on an assessment of general principles as well as the particularities of any given case.

Normative issues in politics are not so different from the ultimate concerns of many scientific endeavours, which are often (although certainly not always) directed to improving some aspect of the world. Indeed, normative judgements often go hand in hand with scientific projects, which are then implemented through social and political institutions. The eradication of diseases, which cause massive human suffering, through a fruitful combination of scientific research and international political action is a prime example, as case study 1.1 shows.

Another important question in normative theory concerns the sources of human subjectivity and therefore of values, norms and moral sensibilities. One answer that may seem obvious is 'culture'. We tend to learn or absorb our norms and values from our immediate social environment. Initially, this means the family, but families are embedded in wider social groups – communities. And communities are frequently defined in terms of cultural factors – language, religion, socio-political organization, artistic expression and material culture. At a national level, states are often assumed to possess something called 'political culture' – a term used in comparative politics to denote the normative orientation of citizens to their political system. In IR theory, the idea of culture has played an important role, at least since the end of the Cold War, and has generated much debate over whether norms and values – especially those concerning democracy and human rights – can ever be

Case Study 1.1 Normative Theory and the Eradication of Smallpox

The smallpox virus is thought to have emerged up to 10,000 years ago, possibly in northeastern Africa, and spread as far as China by about 1100 BC. It arrived in Europe much later, but by the eighteenth century it was killing around 400,000 a year. It devastated indigenous populations in the Americas when introduced by Spanish, Portuguese and other intruders. Depending on the variant, death rates were around 30 per cent in adults and much higher in infants. Disfigurement and blindness was common among survivors. Various methods were used in attempts to control the disease, including early forms of inoculation practised in ancient China as well as in the Ottoman Empire and parts of Africa.

The best-known pioneer of smallpox vaccination, Edward Jenner (1749–1823), found that infectious material from cowpox provided immunity to the disease, a discovery that was to lead to widespread vaccination practices. Further research produced safer vaccines and, eventually, freeze-dried vaccines that remained effective when transported and stored, including in tropical areas (see, generally, Williams, 2011).

Despite continuing advances, around 300 million people, mainly from poorer countries, are thought to have died from smallpox in the twentieth century. This compares to an estimate of around 190 million deaths from warfare, both civil and interstate. If death from political violence is considered a major moral problem for international politics, what about death from disease, even though it is a 'natural' cause?

The United Nations was founded in 1945 in the immediate aftermath of the Second World War and with a mission to promote peace and better standards of life on a global scale. And so, in addition to eliminating the scourge of war, it aimed to eliminate other sources of human suffering and deprivation. As part of this effort, the World Health Organization (WHO) was established in 1948. In 1966 WHO initiated a worldwide smallpox eradication programme and the following year commenced a major vaccination campaign. This campaign saw the very last death from the disease in a natural setting occur in 1978 (WHO, 2001).

The smallpox eradication campaign was motivated by a normative political concern with the reduction of human suffering brought about by a naturally occurring scourge; it was made possible by the achievements of medical science and implemented at a practical level through an agency of the world's major organ of global governance. In other words, a normative position on human suffering led to practical political action on an international scale and delivered a successful result.

truly universal, or whether they are irredeemably products of particular cultures, and therefore always *relative* to that culture.

A further very prominent theme in various modes of theorizing in IR is the idea of 'nature' or the 'natural'. This is evident first and foremost in realist theories, where the 'state of nature' and 'human nature' are seen in rather negative terms, while liberal theories tend to see these in a more positive light. Then there are normative perspectives that take whatever appears to be 'natural' to determine what is right or good. For example, social hierarchies based on class, race or gender have often been portrayed as natural *and therefore right*. This approach has, at various times and in various places, justified the subordination of masses to elites, of black (or brown) to white and of women to men. Opponents of these practices have very often taken the position that the hierarchies are not natural at all but have been artificially contrived. In the contemporary world, and in light of serious environmental concerns, 'nature' has taken on a fresh normative symbolism. Nature itself is to be protected from the ravages of humankind. This still leaves open the question of whether there is any morality *in* nature, or whether nature provides a guide to what is right and good. As we see in the following chapters, issues relating to the idea of nature are embedded in a variety of theoretical perspectives.

Epistemology and Ontology

Debates about theory and method are closely related to the question of what constitutes 'knowledge', how can we acquire it, how much we can really 'know' about anything, how we can justify claims to knowledge, and whether the quest for objective knowledge, or absolute Truth, is viable. In short, what are the constraints on, and limits to, knowledge? Donald Rumsfeld, former US Secretary of Defense under George W. Bush, when asked about a report which indicated that Iraq had *not* supplied terrorists with weapons of mass destruction, replied with an interesting observation on the problem of 'knowing'.

Key Quote: The Epistemology of Donald Rumsfeld

Reports that say that something hasn't happened are always interesting to me because, as we know, there are known knowns; there are things we know we know. We also know there are known unknowns; that is to say we know there are some things we do not know. But there are also unknown unknowns – the ones we don't know we don't know. (Rumsfeld, quoted in BBC, 2003b)

The point was that we don't necessarily know *what* we don't know when it comes to the possible existence of a threat. Rumsfeld was ridiculed by any number of commentators for this particular statement. But it actually highlights issues that are central to the branch of philosophy known as epistemology, which means, literally, the study of knowledge.

Leaving aside Rumsfeld's epistemological musings, let us consider again the issue of positivism. Those subscribing to a *positivist epistemology* will claim that objective, value-free, positive knowledge is possible in both the natural and social sciences. But this follows if, and only if, a proper scientific method is pursued. Others may claim that only the natural sciences can produce such knowledge, and that a 'unity of method' is neither possible nor desirable. Still others may insist that objective knowledge is simply unattainable in any sphere. Those adopting the latter positions are often called 'postpositivists', although this label covers a range of positions, from fairly mild critical approaches to quite radical takes on epistemology. To various degrees, theorists working within feminism and gender studies, critical theory, postmodernism/poststructuralism and postcolonialism tend to adopt postpositivist approaches, as we see in due course.

Another concept requiring explanation is 'ontology', a branch of metaphysics concerned with the nature of existence or being. It may seem logical that we can only have knowledge of something that actually *exists*; that constitutes a reality in some material sense of the term. But reality itself is a slippery concept. Realities exist not simply as sets of objects or things that have a material form and can therefore be seen or touched. Numbers, for example, do not exist as material objects. They are completely abstract. You cannot see, touch or taste the number 8. You may see it represented in writing on a page – just as it appears on this page as an Indian-Arabic numeral, or as the Roman numeral VIII, or the Chinese numeral 八 – but these are representations, not an actual 'thing'. You may also see 8 cows in a field. But what you are seeing is a group of cows. If you have counted them to 8, you have simply quantified them mentally. You are still not seeing the number 8 itself. Does the number 8, then, really exist? If so, then 'reality' in this instance must be seen as having an *ideational* rather than a material existence.

Moving to a different level, we can say that the political world does not exist in a material sense. We can certainly see material manifestations of political systems, such as parliamentary buildings, border posts, embassies, ballot boxes, and the like. We can also see particular humans, such as presidents and prime ministers, and we 'know' they hold positions of political leadership. But the political world exists as a set of relations within a socially created system which runs according to ideas that proceed from the minds of people (agents), who act on those ideas to produce institutions and practices. We see how these questions of epistemology and ontology play out in the following chapters.

We should also consider the relationship between theory and ideology. 'Theory' has something of a neutral tone, especially when associated with the quest for objective knowledge. 'Ideology', on the other hand, denotes a specific set of ideas which in turn commend a particular world view. Interestingly, the originator of the term, Antoine Destutt de Tracy (1754–1836), saw ideology as a *science* of ideas which was meant to be as objective as the natural sciences. However, ideology was soon associated with various normative projects and acquired other connotations, some very negative. Karl Marx, for example, used the term 'ideology' to denote the distortion of the true state of politics, economics and society – a 'false consciousness' purveyed by the ruling classes to maintain their own positions of privilege (Garner, Ferdinand and Lawson, 2012, p.110). This was later developed as a theory of hegemony by Antonio Gramsci (1891–1937) and incorporated into a version of critical theory now influential in IR.

'Ideology' in contemporary usage continues to have certain negative connotations, and an 'ideologue' is seen as someone with a dogmatic mentality promoting a rigid world view based on a particular political orientation (Garner, Ferdinand and Lawson, 2012, p.110). Ideology, however, does not necessarily equate to a dogmatic world view. It is best regarded simply as a system of ideas incorporating a view of the world as it is, of how it ought to be from a particular normative standpoint, and promoting a plan of political action to achieve the desired state of affairs. It is therefore a normative belief system oriented to political action. Most of us with an interest in politics do have a normative view of the world based on a certain political orientation, so in this sense we are all 'ideologues'.

Traditional ideologies include conservatism, socialism, liberalism, nationalism and anarchism, all of which had developed in Western political thought by the nineteenth century. The first decade of the twentieth century witnessed the rise of fascism, while more recently we have seen the emergence of diverse ideological thinking associated with feminism, multiculturalism, ecologism and fundamentalism (see Hoffman and Graham, 2006). There are also many variations and combinations associated with these – for example, democratic socialism, liberal feminism, classical as distinct from neo-liberalism, strong and mild forms of multiculturalism, and different forms of fundamentalism depending on the religion underpinning it – Christian, Jewish, Islamic and Hindu being the main ones. There are numerous other 'isms' associated with ideological thought in different areas, and students of politics will routinely encounter terms such as militarism, authoritarianism, libertarianism, mercantilism, capitalism, communitarianism, cosmopolitanism, imperialism, and so on.

Some of the principal political ideologies mentioned above also bear exactly the same moniker as political theories – liberalism being a prime example. Marxism is often seen as an ideology associated with socialism, but we also talk about Marxist theory. Similarly, ecologism is associated with green theory, feminism with gender theory, and so on. All this raises the question of whether political theories are simply ideologies dressed up to resemble something more respectable. This is something to keep in mind as we examine each of the main fields of theory in later chapters.

Power and Interests

Issues of power and interests are obviously central to the study of politics in any sphere. One approach to international politics sees it as being *all about power*, with issues of morality and justice having little role to play. Power in this sense is usually conceived in terms of domination and control. Others would argue that this is a crude formulation, not only of the world of international politics but of power itself, and that we need to take a much more nuanced view of the subject. We may, for example, consider the extent to which power is deployed not only for the purpose of dominating and controlling others in the interest of state security but for bringing about positive goods in other ways. Another approach concerns the distinction between material and ideational power, sometimes conceived as 'hard' and 'soft' power respectively.

Power and interests also intrude on policy issues. One well-known example which links scientific with political and economic issues concerns the harmful effects of tobacco products on human health. Tobacco companies actually sponsored 'scientific' research in the late 1980s and early 1990s in an attempt to prove that passive smoking posed no real dangers and used such research in an effort to undermine regulatory policies instituted by government (see Muggli, Forster, Hurt and Repace, 2001). This is 'bad science'. And it illustrates how the power and interests of large corporations impact on public debates and policy processes.

More generally, it seems that, wherever power and interests are concerned, we will find politics at work. This occurs not just at the level of domestic and international politics but within and among the smallest of human groups. For feminist theorists, the sphere of intimate or personal relations has a form of politics that is as much subject to the dynamics of power as any other. Some may debate whether relations at this level belong properly to the sphere of 'the political' at all, preferring to confine discussion of the political as concerned specifically with the state (Swift, 2011, p. 5). Others argue that the institution of 'patriarchy', which starts within the family but embraces the whole pattern of male dominance in politics, economics and society – and is projected on to the international stage – has had, and continues to have, a very real impact on political practice. The field has broadened in recent years, and concerns with gender, including the study of masculinities, are now to be found on the 'gender agenda'. These are just some of the issues arising from a broad consideration of how power and interests operate in different spheres and impact on the world of international politics and its theorization.

The Purpose and Scope of International Relations

At the very broadest level, the discipline of international relations (hereafter IR) takes as its subject matter the interactions of actors in the global or international sphere, with an emphasis on the *political* nature of those interactions over both the short and the long term, and their implications for the security of people, generally understood. This scarcely precludes attention to economic, social, cultural and philosophical matters or to the consequences of scientific, technical or industrial developments. Indeed, all these are vital concerns to scholars of IR and provide the basis for many of the specializations within the discipline, such as international political economy, international history, global environmental politics, international organizations, global social movements, and so on.

The nature of these specializations also indicates that IR draws from and interacts with other academic disciplines: economics, history, philosophy, environmental sciences, geography, law and sociology, among others, all of which are underpinned by particular bodies of theory. Thus IR is a multifaceted enterprise, incorporating insights from various intellectual streams while focusing always on the political aspects of the issues it addresses. For this reason, IR theories, while drawing on diverse sources and addressing many different issues, are inherently theories of *politics*.

It follows that IR may also be understood as a branch of the broader field of political studies. It should be noted that the conventional distinction between IR and other branches of political studies rests on the broad differentiation between the study of politics within the state (the internal or domestic sphere) and the study of politics between states (the external or international sphere). By 'state' here is meant the modern sovereign state rather than states comprising a federal system such as the United *States* of America, or the states that make up Australia, Canada, India, Russia, Germany, Nigeria, the United Arab Emirates, Brazil, Micronesia, and so on.

In addition, there is the field of comparative politics, which is in the business of comparing similarities and differences in the institutions and conduct of politics within different states – for example, comparisons of constitutions, legislatures, electoral systems, political parties, interest groups, media and more diffuse matters such as political culture. Another specialization is political economy, which focuses on the relationship between states and markets. This was a well-defined field of study within politics well before *international* political economy developed as a distinctive branch of IR from about the 1970s.

Political theory underpins all of these sub-fields, and indeed it has been said that politics cannot be studied at all without theory: 'All our statements about parties, movements, states and relationships between them presuppose theoretical views, so that political theory is an integral part of the study of politics' (Hoffman, 2007). Note that the domain of political theory described here includes relations between states, the traditional subject matter of IR as it was articulated at an early stage in the development of the discipline, and so it follows that, just as IR is encompassed within the broader field of politics, so IR theory comes under the more general rubric of political theory.

Even so, a distinction between political theory, as concerned with issues within the state, and IR theory, as concerned with the external sphere, is often maintained. This was the position taken by Martin Wight in a well-known essay first published in the 1960s entitled 'Why Is There No International Theory?' His starting point was that political theory, understood as speculation about the state, was essentially concerned with the possibility of attaining 'the good life' within the state. The abundance of theorizing on this subject contrasted not only with a paucity of IR theory, which Wight maintained still barely existed as a distinctive field at the time, but with the sad fact that IR theory dealt with nothing more noble than issues of survival in a sphere where conflictual relations are the norm.

> **Key Quote: Martin Wight on International Theory**
>
> Political theory and law . . . are the theory of the good life. International theory is the theory of survival. What for political theory is the extreme case (as revolution, or civil war) is for international theory the regular case. (Wight, 2000, p. 39)

The idea that IR consists largely of the study of relations between states, separate from the study of politics within states as well as comparisons between domestic spheres, reflects the origins of the discipline in the immediate aftermath of the First World War, when the major concern was very much focused on the causes of war between states and the conditions for peace in an international system of states. This concern was clear enough in the trust deed formalizing the first professorship at Aberystwyth, the Woodrow Wilson Chair of International Politics. The deed defined the field as 'political science in its application to international relations, with special reference to the best means of promoting peace between nations' (quoted in Reynolds, 1975, p. 1). This definition placed IR squarely within the purview of political studies as well as stating a clear normative purpose for it. Reynolds goes on to note that this formulation was to be expected of those who had lived through the First World War, an experience that also spurred enthusiastic support for the League of Nations, in which high hopes for achieving long-term peace were invested (ibid., p. 2).

The Woodrow Wilson chair was endowed by a Welsh philanthropist, David Davies, who hoped that a better understanding of international politics would contribute to the quest for peace, and it was named after the US president for his contributions to that quest. The belief that peaceful relations between states could be achieved through the establishment of robust international institutions within a framework of international law is known generally as liberal institutionalism, and, as we see later, this remains a key element in liberal theory. Wilson was also a firm believer in the proposition that the spread of democracy goes hand in hand with the spread of peaceful relations. In the contemporary period this is known as the 'democratic peace thesis', and this, too, is central to liberal theory. In fact, much of the early development of the discipline as it emerged in the UK was based squarely on liberal principles, which also have a distinctive normative dimension when it comes to questions of war and peace.

It does not require much of an intellectual effort to see that a desire to identify the causes of war and the conditions for peace is driven by profound normative concerns about the impact of war. It kills and maims people, it devastates the environment, and it diverts resources from other important projects, leading indirectly to further human distress and suffering. These are indisputable facts about warfare, and it is therefore difficult to escape the conclusion that it is *wrong* from a normative standpoint, and that it is *right* to try and prevent it. As noted above, this was the original purpose of the discipline and it remains central to its concerns today, although it has expanded into many other areas as well. It also suggests that IR is, at a fundamental level, a profoundly normative discipline.

While both the concern with warfare and the relations between states remain a focus for IR, many take the view that the discipline's subject matter cannot be defined in such narrow terms and that the interactions between the domestic and international spheres are such that it is impossible to separate them. One very obvious example in the field of international political economy relates to financial crises. What happens in one major 'domestic' economy – the US in particular – has repercussions all around the world; this has been clear since at least the time of the Great Depression and was illustrated most recently by the global financial crisis of 2008. Another very obvious issue area in the present period, where the domestic/international distinction seems to make even less sense, is climate change. When it comes to more conventional issues of war and peace, the very porous nature of the domestic/international divide is well illustrated by case study 1.2, the international consequences of the conflict in Syria.

The Emergence of IR Theory

For a decade after the First World War, the goal of establishing a peaceful world order seemed at least possible, although the League suffered a number of difficulties. In 1929 the Great Depression struck, shattering economies and people's livelihoods around the globe. Then, as now, adverse economic conditions became a factor in the rise of extremist politics, especially of the far-right nationalist kind. Fascism and Nazism emerged in the heart of Europe, with Germany once again at the epicentre, while in the Pacific Japanese militarism, driven by an equally virulent form of nationalism, ensured that the second great conflagration was more truly a *world* war. All this dealt a blow to the optimistic expectations that had prevailed throughout much of the 1920s.

A conventional view of developments in IR theory sees the 'idealism' or 'utopianism' of that earlier period, including the hopes and expectations invested in the League of Nations by liberal institutionalists, repudiated by another, very different approach which promised to describe and analyse the sphere of international relations as it *really* is, rather than how it *ought* to be from some ideal point of view. Thus realism as a theory of international politics gained significant ground, initially in the form of 'classical realism', followed not long after by what is now the dominant form – neorealism or structural realism. Realism in its classic form operates on certain assumptions about human nature and the drive to power. Structural realists, however, argue that it is the *structure* of the international system itself which mediates the dynamics of power. The prime characteristic of that system, and the principal dynamic determining its structure, is *anarchy* – a condition characterized by an absence of government through which laws or rules are enforced. Here it is important to distinguish between world government and world governance.

Some may think that the United Nations and the entire system of international law that has emerged over the past couple of centuries constitutes a type of world government. The term commonly used to denote the agglomeration of rules and institutions that now pertain to the international sphere, however, is global *governance*. While this clearly implies the act of governing, it is not necessarily associated with government of or by a sovereign entity. Corporate governance, for example, refers to the way in which the affairs of a corporation are organized and managed, but corporations are not sovereign in a political sense. Govern*ment* as such does not exist in the international sphere because the UN is not constituted as a sovereign power capable of enforcing rules in the same way that governments within states may do, through police, courts of law, and so on. The international sphere certainly has courts of law and other decision-making bodies, such as the UN Security Council, but these do not sit under a supreme sovereign authority, and their decisions are often unenforceable if a state chooses not to obey. The UN is therefore a club of sovereign states, of which membership is optional, and is not itself a sovereign authority. Rather, sovereignty remains the exclusive property of states.

'Anarchy' is a term normally associated with chaos and disorder, and 'anarchists' in the popular imagination today consist primarily of radical groups prone to violence against both property and authority figures. They are often found swarming around summit meetings of various international bodies, especially those with an economic agenda, and protesting against 'globalization'. The concept of anarchy, however, cannot be reduced to an association with these kinds of groups and their activities. The word itself comes to us from ancient Greek and refers simply to the 'absence of government'. While chaos and disorder may follow, it does not follow as a matter of course. Indeed, anarchism as a political theory, separate from speculation about anarchy in the international sphere, emerged in the late nineteenth century. It holds that harmony, order and justice are eminently achievable without the coercive apparatus of the state. Rather than using threats of punishment to achieve order, anarchism places great trust in the ability of humans to act cooperatively and altruistically in devising social rules that people will follow voluntarily. This, incidentally, requires a certain view of 'human nature', a concept that plays an important role in political theory more generally (Lawson, 2012, pp. 23–7).

Case Study 1.2   The International Consequences of the Syrian Civil War

In March 2011, protests against the authoritarian regime of President Bashar al-Assad in Syria took place against a wider backdrop of political unrest in the Middle East and North Africa which included a civil war in Libya. The latter had erupted earlier in the same year, leading to intervention by NATO and the eventual overthrow of the regime of Colonel Muammar Gaddafi. In Syria, as in Libya, protests were met with violent suppression, serving only to exacerbate popular unrest and turn it into a full-scale rebellion. Within a few months, a loose coalition of groups drawn from different sectors of Syrian society collected under the banner of the Free Syrian Army.

The original rebels did not appear to take a fundamentalist religious line against the al-Assad regime. The latter's religious affiliations embrace a moderate minority Shia sect, called Alawis or Alawites, comprising little more than 10 per cent of the population. The majority of Syrians are Sunni, but the al-Assad regime had adopted a largely secular approach which allowed religious if not political freedom. Under the conditions of civil war, Alawites have been associated with the regime and have become targets for revenge attacks. They are also targeted by both local and foreign jihadi fighters, who have added another dimension to the war.

Many of those identifying as jihadists have become aligned with a group that emerged in 2013 calling itself first the Islamic State of Iraq and Syria (ISIS) and subsequently simply the Islamic State (IS), which is an offshoot of al-Qaeda. It draws much of its support from Sunnis in Iraq who have been marginalized since the overthrow of Saddam Hussein in the Iraq War. IS has attracted recruits from as far as Russia, the UK and other parts of Europe, North America and Australia willing to fight in the cause of 'global jihad'. IS has purported to establish a caliphate to bring all Muslims in the region, and beyond, under its authority in a 'pure' Islamic state. It appears willing to wipe out Shia Muslims, as well as Christians, to achieve this aim.

Jihadists and IS represent just one aspect of the internationalization of the war in Syria. Another is the involvement of the Lebanese Hezbollah organization in support of the al-Assad regime, initially on a clandestine basis from 2011 to 2013 and then more openly and robustly. Hezbollah, which has long directed much of its energies against Israel, has also been backed by Iran. Iraqi Shia have been involved more recently. Taken together, these forces comprise an 'Axis of Resistance' aligned primarily against Israel and the West – also the ultimate enemies of the Sunni-aligned jihadists. Such are the complexities of politics in the region.

The UN Security Council has been unable to present a united front in response to the conflict, partly because of Russian support for the al-Assad regime. But China has also shown marked reluctance to endorse a humanitarian role for the Security Council, especially if it involves interference in the internal or domestic affairs of a state. When the Security Council did endorse a no-fly zone in the Libyan conflict, NATO overstepped the mark by bringing down the Gaddafi regime.

One of the main consequences of the Syrian conflict for the international community has been the flow of refugees. As of August 2014, there were almost 3 million refugees from Syria, the largest number of persons displaced by violence in two decades and carrying with them concerns for broader issues of peace and security in the region. This is in addition to the almost 7 million displaced within Syria. Most of the refugees outside Syria are in Lebanon, Iraq, Turkey, Egypt and Jordan, all countries with limited resources of their own. Funding from the wider international community has been inadequate, and, in addition to the 150,000 or so who have died within Syria, both disease born of squalor and deprivation and lack of medical facilities in refugee camps add to the death toll.

In looking at the Syrian conflict overall, we can see how what initially seemed to be a strictly domestic conflict between the ruling regime and a section of its own population quickly became internationalized across a number of dimensions, from the involvement of foreign combatants and the destabilization of the region more generally to the massive outflow of refugees seeking protection. A more general point is that the occurrence of widespread political violence against civilian populations within the borders of any country is, from a normative point of view, regarded as an egregious violation of their fundamental human rights and as a matter with which the international community is rightly concerned.

Anarchist thought raises some interesting questions for political theory. Can humans really get by without the state in some form or another? The short answer is yes, but possibly only in circumstances that are unlikely to occur under conditions of modernity and mass society. Stateless societies certainly existed in the past. Indigenous Australians, for example, lived in small, hunter-gatherer groups without a state for more than 40,000 years. In fact, all early human groups did. Whether they achieved the degree of social harmony and order envisaged by anarchists, without violence, coercion or threats of punishment, is another matter. This brings us next to the historical development of states and the rise of the phenomenon we call modernity.

The Rise of States

States as settled political communities with distinctive structures of authority have been around for only about 6,000 years, having emerged in various places around the globe as humans acquired the capacity to domesticate plants and animals. This also depended on the environment, since the most basic requirement for the development of agriculture and animal husbandry is the availability of plants and animals susceptible to domestication. These were completely absent on the Australian continent, which explains why the hunter-gatherer lifestyle, and the technologies and social practices appropriate to it, persisted to the time of European settlement. Elsewhere, hunter-gatherer societies gradually gave way to more settled communities, which initially took the form of villages. On the larger continental land masses, towns and cities emerged in due course. Smaller-scale states tended to be confined to networks of villages, at least partly on account of environmental factors. Pacific island societies, for example, were largely restricted by land mass, and their oceanic location also made travel and communications more difficult. But settlement, of whatever size, meant that certain populations acquired a fixed relationship with a particular territory, a relationship that is a prerequisite of state formation.

As states developed, social organization became more complex, requiring new ideas and practices to maintain order and regulate property, possessions and dealings between people. Hierarchies of power, divisions of labour, production and trade, and military institutions emerged, all attended by the development of systems of government, and thus politics as we know it. In this process, anarchy is effectively dispelled by the authoritative structures of the state, for these embody rules and institutions which people are obliged to obey under threat of punishment if they do not. Hierarchies of power developed not only within these early states but between them as well. One particularly noteworthy development from quite early times in the history of human settlement was the emergence of empires. The most ancient for which we have evidence is the Mesopotamian Empire of Sargon the Great, dating back to about 2350 BC and located around the region of contemporary Iraq. Empires tended to be controlled by one powerful state capable of subordinating others, usually by military force, and maintaining authority over them.

Empires thus formed international systems with their own distinctive structure of hierarchical authority, so there is a strong case for arguing that they also tended to dispel anarchy in the international sphere. Empires emerged on all continents with the exception of Australia. In fact, it is evident that empire has been the most common form of international system since states first emerged, occurring in different times and different places across Africa, the Middle East, most of Asia and the Americas, and sometimes thriving for centuries (Lawson, 2012, pp. 20–3). Both states and empires are therefore common throughout the history of human settlement. They are not, however, universal phenomena, nor have they taken just one particular form.

If modern humans have been around for about 200,000 years, it means that states, defined as settled communities occupying a particular geographic space and with a recognizable structure of political authority, have existed for only a tiny fraction of that time. As for the modern sovereign/national state, that is even more recent, dating back only to the seventeenth century. Because it is this kind of state that provides the basis for the contemporary international system, and therefore for much of the theorization of international politics, some background is provided here together with a brief account of modernity.

Modernity and the Sovereign/National State

It is generally accepted that the phenomenon of modernity first arose in Europe around the sixteenth century. Modernity itself is a complex phenomenon involving a range of different factors. At a practical level it is linked to technological and scientific developments entailing, in turn, industrialization and the attempted mastery or control of nature. With respect to social organization, modernity is associated with the separation of religious institutions, beliefs and practices from the sphere of politics. This is essential to secularism, which is equated not with atheism, as many wrongly assume, but with the idea that the state should not be aligned with any particular religion. Secularism may actually protect freedom of religious beliefs and practices, which is linked in turn to the development of ideas about personal freedom and rights in which the state may not interfere. The rise of capitalism is another integral part of modernity's development in Europe, linked with industrialization, property, trade and finance. More general social changes associated with modernity include extended systems of communication and education and improvements in the status of women. These are commonly seen as positive changes, but many would argue that modernity has a 'dark side' as well, an issue to be considered later.

The rise of modernity in Europe followed a period of significant social change prompted by the Renaissance, a cultural movement that had begun around the mid-fourteenth century in Italy and whose influence spread throughout Europe. The revival of classical learning – which is what gave the Renaissance (literally 'rebirth') its name – was made possible by the rediscovery of ancient Greek and Roman sources, many of which had been preserved in the Arab intellectual world, while others had been hidden away in Christian monasteries. At the same time, new technologies began to play a key role. These included the magnetic compass and gunpowder, both from China, and later the printing press, an early form of which had also been invented in China. The compass expanded the possibilities for navigation and was to have enormous implications for European exploration, followed by trade and imperialism; gunpowder changed the nature of warfare, while the development of print technology marked a revolution in communication (Gombrich, 2001, pp. 28–9).

The expansion of knowledge through the reception of Arab learning in mathematics, medicine and science, as well as travel and trade, challenged the rather static world view of the medieval period in Europe, as did the extension of schooling, the development of humanism and changing attitudes to established religion. The Renaissance period witnessed the first glimmerings of the conceptual separation of church and state, while notions of popular sovereignty and individualism began to appear as well. In addition, the emergence of banking provided an important basis for subsequent capitalist development in Europe (Watson, 2005, pp. 530–3). Thus the seeds of modernity were well and truly planted in this period.

The Protestant Reformation, beginning in the early sixteenth century, provided a further major stimulus for political and social change, adding another dimension to modernity as it put an end to the religious unity of Europe and created space not only for the toleration of religious difference but also for secularism, understood as the separation of church and state. The Reformation was partly a revolt against the dominance of Italy, with implications for who could rightly claim authority with respect to political and theological matters. But it was hardly restricted to the level of intellectual cut and thrust between Protestants and Catholics. Rather, it was a key ingredient in the very literal cut and thrust of large-scale warfare, which, in the end, saw the consolidation of certain ideas about sovereignty and the state and in turn laid the foundations of the modern state and state system.

The event which is conventionally taken to mark the foundation of the sovereign state is the Peace of Westphalia, a treaty signed in 1648 between rival Catholic and Protestant parties which put an end to the Thirty Years' War and in which it was confirmed, among other things, that rulers within states possessed sovereign authority over a range of matters. We examine this moment in international political history in more detail in later chapters, but here we must note that the containment of sovereignty within states meant that the 'systemic chaos of the early seventeenth century was thus transformed into a new anarchic order' (Arrighi, 1994, p. 44). These developments were to mark a sea change in Europe's international system, not least with respect to the dynamics of power relations involved in the decline of the Catholic Habsburg Empire and in the strengthening of the secular realm of political authority (see Gutmann, 1988).

In this formulation it may appear that it was the ruler who was sovereign rather than the state as such, let alone the people within it. But, given that the identity of the state effectively merged with that of the ruler, the idea that the state itself possessed sovereignty and was entitled to non-interference in its internal affairs was a logical outcome. These ideas did not emerge as completely new ones in 1648 but, rather, were part of an evolution in political thought that had been ongoing for some centuries, and which is still ongoing. States today are sovereign entities in international law, and the principle of non-intervention remains a powerful one. In practice, however, it has been transgressed time and again, as the history of warfare among sovereign states in Europe and elsewhere in the modern period attests. Today, principles of sovereignty and non-intervention have also been attenuated by concerns about gross human rights abuses and a nascent doctrine concerning the 'responsibility to protect' – matters to be discussed later in the context of liberal theory.

In its early formulations, however, sovereignty was conceived as absolute, which meant that the authority of the ruler was absolute within his – or occasionally her – realm. Such ideas were implicit in the work of Niccolò Machiavelli of Florence (1469–1527) and developed more fully by Jean Bodin (1530–1596) in France and Thomas Hobbes (1588–1679) in England. Each lived through periods of political turmoil, the latter two experiencing civil war. Hobbes also had the lessons of the Thirty Years' War to contemplate. All were concerned with the conditions for establishing order and stability, and Bodin and Hobbes in particular saw in sovereignty the remedy for disorder and strife; in the process they turned it into an 'ideology of order' through which the authority of the state and its ruler could be justified (see King, 1999). As we see later, these ideas are especially important to realist theory.

Other key developments associated with modernity are the intellectual movement known as the Enlightenment, the further development of science and technology, the rise of democracy as a form of government embodying popular sovereignty, and nationalism as an ideology, which came to underpin the identity of sovereign states, giving us the concept of the national state or nation-state. One student of the Enlightenment finds its most interesting aspect in 'the encounter of ideas with reality', noting that the searing criticism of politics and society typical of much Enlightenment thought cleared the ground for new, constructive ideas while the possibilities of power could be explored afresh (Gay, 1977, p.xi). Existing political and social institutions were examined closely and often found wanting, as was the basis for their legitimacy. It was only in this sort of intellectual environment that the very idea of improvement in the human condition – of *progress* – could flourish. This was one of the most important ideas to challenge conservative ideology and underpins both liberalism and socialism, each of which has been concerned, albeit in different ways, with the notion that social life can be progressively improved given the right political, social and economic systems.

In France, these ideas contributed to the French Revolution of 1789, in which we find expressed the basic principles of democracy as well as nationality. The revolution in France saw sovereignty vested in the people rather than in a monarch, and so the people became citizens of a state rather than subjects of a monarch – an important shift in ideas and essential to principles of modern democracy. But the question now arose, who are 'the people'? The answer was found in the concept of a French nation. This may seem unremarkable from the vantage point of the twenty-first century, but it was a novel idea at the time. This was especially so since the 'French people' were remarkably diverse, speaking different languages, varying in a range of cultural practices, and identifying strongly with their region rather than the more abstract entity of France or the French state.

The unification of these diverse groups into a 'nation-state' was a long-term project, as it was elsewhere in Europe, where Germany and Italy emerged as unified 'national' states as late as 1871. If the Westphalian moment had seen the identity of the sovereign merge with that of the state, events from the late eighteenth century onwards saw the identity of the state firmly connected to 'the nation'. This was not, however, necessarily a democratic connection. Although the original impulse of the French Revolution had strong democratic elements, the subsequent history of Europe, and elsewhere for that matter, was to see 'the nation' appropriated by the most authoritarian of regimes. Nationalism as an ideology fusing nation and state was to become one of the most powerful and destructive forces of the twentieth century and a major ingredient in two world wars.

Interwoven with the ideas and events discussed above has been the extraordinary development of science and technology from the early modern period, which many take to be the key defining feature of modernity itself (Russell, 1979, p. 512). One important result of the emergence of scientific thinking and an expansion of knowledge about the natural world, along with the acquisition and development of new technologies, was the Industrial Revolution. If it has an actual birthplace, it is to be found in England, between Birmingham in the Midlands and Preston in Lancashire to the north, with the first recognizable factory established in Derby in 1721 (Watson, 2005, p. 746). Industrial technology and production was to play a key role in the rise of the West, along with the expansion of trade, the increasing sophistication of military methods, the rise of capitalism, and imperialism, all of which have contributed to the phenomenon we call globalization. As we see later, issues arising from science, technology and industrialization are especially important for green theory, while modern European imperialism and colonialism provide the point of departure for postcolonial theory.

A further aspect of modern imperialism is that European colonization – and decolonization – saw the European state system based on the formal principles of sovereignty, juridical equality and nationality exported around the world, thus introducing political organizational uniformity on a global scale; this is now crowned by a system of global governance founded on that uniformity. European colonialism has therefore been among the most powerful *structural* forces in the modern period, creating a political world in the image of the European state system. This world, for the time being at least, remains dominated by 'the West', an entity which emerged through the historical processes described above and whose most powerful constituent member is now the US, itself a product of European settler colonialism in the early modern period.

Conclusion

This introductory chapter has provided an overview of important debates about theory and methodology in both the natural and social sciences, introduced the general field of IR as a discipline and its major concerns, and provided a broad historic overview of major developments in the emergence of states along with the phenomenon of modernity. We have also examined some key concepts, including anarchy, sovereignty and the state. Taken together, these sections provide an outline of the essential background against which theories of IR may be understood. It is also obvious that the events and issues discussed above are primarily Europe-based. This is because IR as a discipline, as with many other fields of learning, has so far developed largely within the framework of European intellectual history – a history that extends to North America and other outposts of 'Western civilization', including Australia and New Zealand. IR theory, to date at least, is therefore part of a largely Western intellectual tradition, albeit one that has absorbed ideas from elsewhere over a long period of time. This trend is likely to continue as alternative centres of intellectual innovation across the globe contribute to the ongoing project of theorizing international relations.

This chapter has also identified an important theme that runs throughout the book, and that is the profoundly normative orientation of IR theory. Virtually every theory explored in this book, including the various versions of realism, not only seeks to describe the world of international politics as it actually *is* but also says something about how that world *ought* to be from some moral standpoint. At the same time, each theory makes a claim about 'reality', either implicitly or explicitly, which relates in turn to issues of subjectivity and objectivity. Another theme which underlies much theorizing, and which is linked closely to the normative aspects of the latter, is that of 'nature'. We shall see that different ideas about 'human nature', the 'state of nature', the 'naturalization of power', the 'natural' versus the 'artificial', the 'natural' dispositions of the sexes, 'nature' as a source of ultimate value, and so on, recur throughout the book.

A further feature of the discussion is the location of the various theoretical approaches in historical context. Some brief attention to the historical backdrop of modernity and events in Europe, in particular, has already been given in this introduction and this will be extended as each of the main bodies of theory is discussed and analysed. Ideas and theories can indeed be analysed at a purely abstract level, a tendency evident in political philosophy as distinct from political theory (see Swift, 2011, p.5), but some knowledge of the historical circumstances under which particular theories arose and developed leads to a much better understanding not just of the individual theories but of the role of theorizing vis-à-vis the practical world of politics more broadly. By examining the development of IR theory through a historical lens, we can also see how it emerges from and interacts with more general bodies of theory in the social sciences while always remaining inherently *political*. This reflects the fact that IR is a species of political studies and does not stand apart from it. Furthermore, theorizing in IR can be credited with extending the traditional concerns of political theory beyond the state in order to grapple more effectively with the complex problems and issues confronting the world in the twenty-first century.

QUESTIONS FOR REVISION

1 To what extent can theories of politics be considered 'scientific'?
2 What do you understand by the term 'positivism'?
3 How do we distinguish between material and ideational realities?
4 What is the difference, if any, between a theory and an ideology?
5 In what sense is IR a normative discipline?
6 How central are the concepts of anarchy and sovereignty to IR theory?
7 What are the key features of modernity?
8 What impact has European colonialism had on both practical and theoretical developments in IR?

FURTHER READING

Diez, Thomas, Ingvild Bode and Aleksandra Fernandes da Costa (eds) (2011) *Key Concepts in International Relations*. London: Sage.

Elman, Colin, and Miriam Fendius Elman (eds) (2003) *Progress in International Relations Theory: Appraising the Field*. Cambridge, MA: MIT Press.

Foot, Rosemary, John Gaddis and Andrew Hurrell (eds) (2003) *Order and Justice in International Relations*. Oxford: Oxford University Press.

Griffiths, Martin (ed.) (2005) *Encyclopedia of International Relations and Global Politics*. Abingdon: Routledge.

Puchala, Donald James (2003) *Theory and History in International Relations*. New York: Routledge.

USEFUL WEBSITES

www.irtheory.com (IR theory online resources)

http://polisciprof.blogspot.com.au/2006/03/what-should-we-expect-ir-theory-to-do.html (political science resource blog)

www.theory-talks.org/p/about.html (interactive forum on IR theory)

www.e-ir.info (general IR website, with articles, features, blogs, etc.)

www.aber.ac.uk/en/interpol/news-and-events/videocasts/title-145299-en.html (video proceedings of conference on IR theory; see esp. Panel III)

2

Classical Realism

The first version of realist thought in IR that emerged in the twentieth century is commonly referred to as classical realism because it drew insights from a range of classic authors or philosophers in the history of ideas. Some have argued that this 'classical tradition' is something of an artificial construct, since those whose works have been selected to constitute the tradition did not regard themselves as belonging to a particular line of thinkers presenting a unified view on the human condition (see Forde, 1992, p.62). As this chapter shows, however, they do share certain distinctive perspectives on the 'realities' of politics and power and the implications for morality. This includes a pessimistic and indeed despairing assessment of the human condition and more specifically of human nature, and it is this that determines, for classical realists at least, the tragic aspects of human existence in the struggle for survival.

Another commentator remarks that there has been a tendency among critics of realism to line up an 'identity parade' of historical figures with some connection to the tradition and to draw together a selective composite of fragments of their ideas in order to construct a 'grand narrative' which can then be attacked, and that this tends to undermine our ability to consider the realist tradition in any meaningful way (Murray, 1997, p.3). The approach taken in this chapter is one that introduces, in more or less chronological order, the principal figures associated with classical realism from the time of the ancient Greeks through to the twentieth century. This may be an 'identity parade', but it is not one devised simply to pick out a few aspects of their thought for condemnation – or praise, for that matter. Rather, it is designed to highlight those aspects of their thought which best illustrate their realist credentials and which have therefore led them to be placed in the classical tradition. This must form the basis of any meaningful analysis.

Thucydides and Machiavelli

The earliest figure claimed for the classical tradition is the ancient Greek historian Thucydides (*c.*460–395 BC), who articulates views on power politics, the tendency to violence and the implications for morality that underscore the central tenets of realism in virtually all its forms. But he also emphasizes the role of human nature, and it is this that makes the classical tradition distinctive. In introducing his *History of the Peloponnesian War*, which details a prolonged period of warfare between Athens and Sparta commencing in 431 BC, Thucydides expresses the hope that his words will be 'judged useful by those who want to understand clearly the events which happened in the past and which (human nature being what it is) will, at some time or other and in much the same ways, be repeated in the future' (Thucydides, I, p. 48).

Thucydides goes on to provide one of the most frequently cited case studies of realist ideas in action. He describes one particular episode of the war in which the Athenians show their utter determination to subjugate the island of Melos, which had hitherto been neutral, but which the Athenians believed must be brought under their control. It is this passage that has led Thucydides to be cast in the role of an amoral realist by IR theorists. But if we extend our study of Thucydides to include his account of and commentary on another episode in the war, sparked by the outbreak of civil war in Corcyra (present day Corfu) between a democratic faction supporting Athens and an oligarchic faction supporting Sparta, we find a rather different approach. Case study 2.1 therefore compares the two episodes to give a fuller account of Thucydides' thought.

The next most prominent figure in the classical tradition is Niccolò Machiavelli (1469–1527) of Florence, who lived through a time of incessant political instability and whose political thought was directed largely to the establishment of order. His realism is evident in his pragmatic advice to 'the Prince' (by which he means any given ruler) that, when faced with a choice between acting morally and acting to preserve the vital interests of the state, the latter must always prevail. This doctrine of necessity by no means endorses gratuitous cruelty, and the Prince is advised to tread a cautious path, 'in a temperate manner ... with prudence and humility' (Machiavelli, 2010, p. 68). Sheer cruelty leads to hatred and contempt which may place the Prince in a dangerous position.

But on the question of whether it is better to be loved or feared,

Case Study 2.1   Thucydides, The Melian Dialogue and the Civil War in Corcyra

The Melian Dialogue consists of an exchange between the generals of the powerful Athenian forces, sent to negotiate a peaceful surrender under which Melos would survive intact but become subject to the Athenian Empire, and the spokesmen for the citizens of the island, who were determined to remain independent. The Athenians clearly possessed a preponderance of force, but the Melians insisted that justice was on their side.

Athenians: [Y]ou know as well as we do that, when these matters are discussed by practical people, the standard of justice depends on the equality of power to compel and that in fact the strong do what they have the power to do and the weak accept what they have to accept. . . . This is no fair fight, with honour on one side and shame on the other. It is rather a question of saving your lives and not resisting those who are far too strong for you. . . .

Melians: It is difficult . . . for us to oppose your power and fortune . . . Nevertheless we trust that the gods will give fortune as good as yours, because we are standing for what is right against what is wrong. . . .

Athenians: Our opinion of the gods and our knowledge of men lead us to conclude that it is a general and necessary law of nature to rule whatever one can. This is not a law that we made ourselves, nor were we the first to act on it when it was made. We found it already in existence . . . [and] are merely acting in accordance with it, and we know that you or anybody else with the same power as ours would be acting in precisely the same way.

Melians: We are not prepared to give up in a short moment the liberty our city has enjoyed from its foundation . . .

Athenians: [Y]ou seem to us quite unique in your ability to consider the future as something more certain than what is before your eyes, and to see uncertainties as realities, simply because you would like them to be so. (Thucydides, V, 84–116)

Thucydides further records that the Melians refused to submit, following which the Athenians laid siege to the city and eventually forced surrender. All males of military age were put to death and the women and children enslaved.

The passage is generally taken to illustrate certain fundamental principles of political realism: first, that, in the final analysis, power trumps morality in terms of right and wrong and will always be used to the advantage of those who hold it; second, that pragmatism in the calculation of interests should prevail over perceptions of honour and justice which may lead to pointless sacrifice; and, third, what one wishes for in terms of outcomes should not be confused with the reality of what one is likely to get in any given set of circumstances. Above all, the position articulated by the Athenians rests on an assumption that this is simply the way the world is and always will be, reflecting a universal law of nature embedded in the human condition and, by implication, not subject to historical or cultural particularities.

An equally compelling passage appears in Thucydides' account of revolution and civil war sparked by the Athenian–Spartan conflict, which spread throughout much of the region. Here, however, the interpretation is Thucydides' own rather than a record of another's speech. And here we see a lament for the loss of humanity, reasonableness and all other virtue as the breakdown of law and order descends into political violence. Human nature is depicted in unremittingly grim terms as the driving force behind the mindless cruelty and violence, but Thucydides shows himself to be a thoroughgoing moralist, valuing justice and humanity as superior virtues.

> Love of power, operating through greed and through personal ambition, was the cause of all these evils. To this must be added the violent fanaticism which came into play once the struggle had broken out. . . . terrible indeed were the actions to which they committed themselves, and in taking revenge they went farther still. Here they were deterred neither by the claims of justice nor by the interests of the state . . . the savage and pitiless actions into which men were carried [were] not so much for the sake of gain as because they were swept away into an internecine struggle by their ungovernable passions. Then, with the ordinary conventions of civilized life thrown into confusion, human nature, always ready to offend even where laws persist, showed itself . . . as something incapable of controlling passion, insubordinate to the idea of justice . . . in these acts of revenge on others men take it upon themselves to begin the process of repealing those general laws of humanity that are there to give a hope of salvation to all who are in distress, instead of leaving those laws in existence, remembering that there may come a time when they, too, will be in danger and need their protection. (Thucydides, III, 82–4).

Most scholars of international relations cite only the Melian Dialogue as an illustration of Thucydides the realist, but the quotation above shows Thucydides is much more the moralist than the amoral realist, for, even as he highlights the wickedness of unrestrained human nature under conditions of anarchy produced by civil war, he refers at the same time to the 'ordinary laws of civilized life' and the 'general laws of humanity' as setting the standards for right action. Looking at both passages, it is the Athenian generals rather than Thucydides himself who stand out as the archetypal realists.

Machiavelli says that, if either must be dispensed with, it is safer to maintain fear. Machiavelli's reasoning on this point is based on his general assessment of the very nature of humankind.

> [T]hey are ungrateful, fickle, false, cowardly, covetous, and as long as you succeed they are yours entirely; they will offer you their blood, property, life and children . . . when the need is far distant; but when it approaches they turn against you. . . . and men have less scruple in offending one who is beloved than one who is feared, for love is preserved by the link of obligation which, owing to the baseness of men, is broken at every opportunity for their advantage; but fear preserves you by a dread of punishment which never fails. (Machiavelli, 2010, p. 68)

Machiavelli further suggests that, if his advice is to be at all useful, it is far preferable to take heed of the realities of politics than the imagination of them.

> ### Key Quote   Machiavelli on Reality versus Imagination
>
> . . . for many have pictured republics and principalities which in fact have never been known or seen, because how one lives is so far distant from how one ought to live, that he who neglects what is done for what ought to be done, sooner effects his ruin than his preservation; for a man who wishes to act entirely up to his professions of virtue soon meets with what destroys him among so much that is evil.
>
>   Hence it is necessary for a prince wishing to hold his own to know how to do wrong, and to make use of it or not according to necessity (Machiavelli, 2010, pp. 61–2).

Machiavelli also adopted an approach to the study of politics whereby the lessons of history, focusing in particular on the ways in which humans actually behave in politics – rather than on how they ought to behave in terms of Christian morality – become key to understanding human nature. Machiavelli held a deeply pessimistic view of the latter, emphasizing the propensity for great cruelty among people. This drives him to a hard-headed pragmatism, urging recognition of the realities of politics among very imperfect humans. This will achieve, not an impossible ideal, but a workable and secure state.

Does Machiavelli have an ethic at all? Certainly, the preservation of an orderly state is seen as a prime good and the foremost duty of the ruler. Machiavelli himself never used the exact term *raison d'état* (reason of state), but this is the paramount consideration for Machiavelli's Prince – and one that remains at the heart of modern conceptions of political realism, where it is more commonly expressed as 'national interest'. Machiavelli is also a strong supporter of what we might now call 'good governance', in the sense that he disapproved very deeply of corruption in government while supporting rule of law principles, both of which are necessary to a durable, resilient state. What Machiavelli does not consider, however, are the ends for which the state exists – to secure justice, freedom, good order, and so on. The purpose of power is to preserve the state, an end that justifies whatever means are taken to preserve it. Thus Machiavelli's amorality asserts 'not the denial of moral values in all situations, but the affirmation that . . . the rules of power have priority over those of ethics and morality' (Ebenstein and Ebenstein, 1991, p. 318).

Religious Thought and the State of Nature

It is clear in both Thucydides and Machiavelli that themes of human nature underscore their political realism. By Machiavelli's time this had been reinforced by Christianity, although Machiavelli himself had little time for Christian virtues, believing they produced a servile character, especially in contrast with the more 'virile' religions of antiquity (Sabine, 1948, p.292). Basic Christian ideas about the essential wickedness of human nature are explained through the biblical account of the 'fall from grace' into a condition of 'original sin', occasioned by Eve plucking the fruit from the tree of knowledge of good and evil and tempting Adam to share it. Before that, they lived completely blameless lives in the tranquil surroundings of the Garden of Eden, a condition called the 'state of grace'. But, with the commission of the original sin, human character was changed forever, although a subsequent story tells of God having one more go at eliminating evil by sending the great flood, preserving only the virtuous Noah and his immediate family. Following the flood, however, human wickedness continued to flourish, and so God apparently acknowledged failure and pledged: 'I will not again curse the ground for man's sake, for the imagination of man's heart is evil from his youth' (Genesis, 8:21).

The best God could do from that point onwards was to issue a set of commandments designed to guide human behaviour along a righteous path and to make clear that dire punishments awaited transgressors, in the next life if not in this one. The greatest sin of all, however, is not to believe in God at all. For this there is no forgiveness, while all other sins can in principle be absolved. This is a major theme in the Koran, too, and, as with Christianity and Judaism, is a key element reinforcing the authority of religion through fear of dreadful, unremitting punishment in the next life. Beyond that, the idea of the sinful condition of humankind was to become an essential precondition for the immense power of the medieval Church in Europe.

The notion of original sin also provided an explanation for the recurrence of conflict, the most violent form of which is warfare, either within or between states (Knutsen, 1997, p.23). It is further implicated in the notion of the 'state of nature' in Western political theory, although in principle this construct needs no religious basis as it is derived just as readily from secular ideas. The state of nature usually refers to a time in the far distant human past when there was presumed to be no civil state, no set of laws, no government. This is implicit in 'social contract' theory, a later development in the history of ideas, which posits a hypothetical original condition of humankind and then proceeds to speculate on the conditions under which people come together, contracting among themselves to form political communities within which legitimate authority prevails.

The 'state of nature' first appeared in the work of St Thomas Aquinas (1225–1274), who, working with Christian precepts, held that 'the normal state of nature is bereft of grace through the corruption of original sin' (Fairweather, 2006, p. 116). Interestingly, Aquinas believed that government possessed of coercive authority would exist even in the state of grace for the purpose of promoting the common good. This was contrary to the earlier thought of St Augustine (354–430), who maintained that the state became necessary only with the fall from grace, when the human propensity for wickedness required the constraints of authoritative sanctions provided by government. Humans in the state of grace, in contrast, possessed no propensity for evil and therefore no need for authoritative political institutions. Whatever the case before the fall from grace, Augustinian thought generally supported the notion that humans needed to be kept in check. Indeed, some authors see a distinct 'Christian realism' emanating from Augustine which was to have a significant influence on a number of later figures in the classical tradition (Murray, 1997, p. 47–8).

Hobbes, Spinoza and Rousseau

The state of nature became a dominant theme in the work of Thomas Hobbes (1588–1679), whose *Leviathan* stands as the foremost of the classic texts on power – how to control it to prevent evil, particularly warfare, and how to channel it to produce good, which is based on peace. For Hobbes, the state of nature is anarchic, and the single law governing humans in this 'natural condition' is founded on self-preservation. This is based in turn on reason, for it is eminently rational for humans to look first and foremost to this goal and to use whatever power one possesses to secure it.

Hobbes proposes that people in the state of nature are in constant fear of each other as they compete for the resources necessary to secure their own survival. So when two people want the same thing, and can't both have it, they become enemies, each trying to subdue or destroy the other. Ego is an additional factor, since humans (unlike animals) also seek honour and glory. But security from threats can only be obtained by the pursuit of power 'till he see no other power great enough to endanger him' (Hobbes, 1985, p.184). As for social life, it is virtually non-existent, because whatever pleasure people may have in the company of others is cancelled out by the fear and uncertainty generated by the dangers of anarchy, where no higher power stands above individuals to preserve them from each other.

Key Quote   The Hobbesian State of Nature

[W]ithout a common Power to keep them all in awe, they are in that condition which is called Warre; and such a warre, as is of every man, against every man. . . . In such conditions there is no place for Industry; because the fruit thereof is uncertain: and consequently no Culture of the Earth . . . no Arts; no Letters; no Society; and which is worst of all, continuall feare, and danger of violent death; And the life of man, solitary, poore, nasty, brutish, and short. (1985 pp. 185–6)

The remedy for Hobbes's state of nature is to be found in the concept of sovereignty, embodied in a supreme 'common power' charged with responsibility to make and enforce general laws not only enabling the cessation of war among those coming under this authority but also providing unity against foreign enemies. This assumes a distinction between fellow countrymen and alien populations, and thus a distinction between the national and international spheres, although these are not clearly delineated. Nor does Hobbes go on to theorize about relations between states. Rather, his concerns remain focused primarily on the problem of violence among those living in close proximity.

The key to the sovereign's authority is a compact among individuals to give up the freedom and equality they possess in the state of nature, because it is precisely these that make them all so vulnerable to violence, constraining enjoyment of a secure life and everything that goes with it, including the development of industry, arts, letters, and so on, which, in the end, constitute civilization.

Hobbes was not the first to theorize sovereignty in the early modern period. A near contemporary, the French philosopher Jean Bodin (1530–1596), had also developed a theory of sovereignty as a means of securing order. By Bodin's time, the Protestant Reformation had become a major factor in politics throughout Europe, and Bodin himself lived through a period of civil and religious turmoil in France marked by episodes of gross violence. Civil war in England also provided the essential backdrop to Hobbes's theorization of sovereignty as the ultimate guarantor of order. The focus is therefore on establishing a civil state whereby the perilous state of nature is banished and social life can flourish. To the extent that the interactions of individuals are peaceful, this is the artificial achievement of the social contract. Peace therefore does not come naturally but is, rather, an aberration, albeit a positive one (King, 1999, p.197). Outside of the civil state, however, the state of nature still prevails.

By Hobbes's time, this 'outside' sphere was still barely conceptualized. Indeed, the word 'international' was not coined until 1780, when the English legal theorist Jeremy Bentham (1748–1832) first used it in application to law operating between states rather than just within them (Suganami, 1978). The Dutch philosopher Baruch Spinoza (1632–1677), however, recognized it as a space in which 'the state of nature' continued to prevail. Indeed, the creation of separate sovereign entities effectively reproduces the state of nature in the interactions of states, each of which 'stand[s] towards each other in the same relations as ... men in the state of nature' (Spinoza, quoted in Knutsen, 1997, p.98). Thus Spinoza observes the necessity for states to be preserved against subjugation by other states, with the concentration of absolute power ensuring both the security of the state itself and the lives of those within it (see Balibar, 1998, p.56; Piirimäe, 2002, p.368). This is an important early step in theorizing the state in its relations with other states.

The founding figure of structural realism, Kenneth Waltz, draws directly on some of Spinoza's ideas, noting that Spinoza sees peace as the purpose for which the state exists for its citizens, but that states are nonetheless natural enemies of each other. For Spinoza, this inherent enmity arises from the fact that human passions often obscure the more rational interests that people have in cooperating, not only within states but between them (Waltz, 2001, p.25). As we see in chapter 3, Waltz rejects the argument concerning the relevance of passions emanating from human nature, and looks instead to the structure of the international system as creating the conditions for enmity.

The Swiss-French philosopher Jean-Jacques Rousseau (1712–1778) is a particularly interesting figure in the classical realist tradition, for, although he too regards human nature as a key factor, he believes that it is essentially good. But it becomes corrupted by society, only then appearing more in the image of the Hobbesian version of 'natural man', and so requiring the remedies provided by the state and sovereign power which encapsulates the general will of all those within its bounds. Although this positive view of an essential human nature appears to set Rousseau at odds with other realist thinkers, his depiction of the sorry state of humankind has seen him firmly located in the tradition. In addition, Rousseau's theorization of the social contract makes it 'a hard headed political work directed primarily against the dangers of moral doctrine' (Melzer, 1983, p. 650). Rousseau's parable of the stag hunt, used subsequently by Kenneth Waltz in laying the foundations for his neo-realist account of international politics, has also ensured his inclusion in the realist canon. In the briefest of narratives, Rousseau hypothesizes about a group of men initially engaged in a plan to hunt down a stag, for which cooperation is essential. The plan soon falls apart as a result of the opportunism inspired by individual self-interest.

Key Quote   Rousseau's Parable of the Stag Hunt

[E]veryone was quite aware that he must faithfully keep to his post in order to achieve this purpose; but if a hare happened to pass within reach of one of them, no doubt he would have pursued it without giving a second thought, and that, having obtained his prey, he cared very little about causing his companions to miss theirs. (Rousseau, 1992, p. 47)

Clausewitz and Weber

The Prussian military theorist Carl von Clausewitz (1780–1831) was among the first to theorize war in a systematic way, and in a manner deploying both historical and logical analysis as well as military strategy and tactics (Paret, 1985, p. 8). The general background against which Clausewitz wrote included a period of political violence in Europe unleashed by the French Revolution and leading to the Napoleonic wars, a time also characterized by increasing modernization and rising nationalism. His general aim was to devise a universally valid theory of warfare capable of explaining fundamental principles, on the one hand, and the processes and practices of war, on the other, from which general patterns of behaviour might be deduced (Lebow, 2003, p. 44). Much of Clausewitz's work focuses on state power and *raison d'état*. War is a means of achieving political purposes – an instrument of policy. The reasoning behind this once again draws on familiar realist themes. 'There is [an] incompatibility between war and every other human interest, individual and social – a difference that derives from human nature, and that therefore no philosophy can resolve.' These contradictory elements are unified in real life through politics and the recognition that war is simply another branch of political activity and does not stand apart from it. In other words, 'war is simply a continuation of political intercourse, with addition of other means' (Clausewitz, 1989, p.605). Politics, however, can have a moderating effect on war, restraining its worst excesses and passions. Even so, there is nothing in Clausewitz that hints of the possibility of progress with respect to the elimination of war as a political strategy.

The thought of the German sociologist Max Weber (1864–1920) brings us to the twentieth century, but at a time when the study of international politics, let alone a fully developed theory of political realism applicable to the international sphere, had barely emerged. Weber observes that all states are based on force and that, if violence was unknown, the concept of the state would disappear. Anarchy in its literal sense would prevail, there being no need for coercive state power. The modern state, however, emerges as a means of managing violence and in fact becomes 'an institutional form of rule that has successfully fought to create a monopoly of legitimate force as a means of government within a particular territory' (Weber, 2005, p.1216). It is Weber's analysis of the tensions between ethics and politics, however, that constitutes a more specific contribution to the realist canon.

Weber proposes two different standards of morality: one for an ideal world – the way the world ought to be – and another for the real world of politics – the way it actually is. This reflects in turn a distinction between ethics and politics, although the two are related. Weber's message for politicians who live in the real world is that they must be prepared to get their hands dirty. 'Politics is no place for those who wish to remain pure' (quoted in Rosenthal, 1991, p.45). This led Weber to propose two different ethics: an ethic of ultimate ends, whereby an act is judged by the good intentions behind it, and an ethic of responsibility, which takes account of the means employed to achieve one's goals and the consequences of one's actions. The latter recognizes that violent means may have to be used to achieve a desired outcome. It follows that good may come out of evil. But it is also possible for evil to come out of good. After all, the proverbial road to hell is paved with good intentions.

Carr and Aron

E. H. Carr (1892–1982) was among the first of the twentieth-century scholars to start delineating the field of international relations as an enterprise separate from history and law as well as distinct from the study of politics within states. The immediate post-First World War period saw, among other things, the emergence of the League of Nations, in which great hopes had been invested for a more secure and peaceful world order. As events in Europe unfolded in the 1930s, however, Carr, a former British diplomat turned academic, became a leading critic of what he branded the utopianism of the liberal optimists. Along with the remaining authors discussed in this chapter, and while remaining largely within a classical tradition grounded in assumptions concerning human nature, Carr was to make a significant contribution to the development of a more systematic account of realism as a theory of international politics in the twentieth century.

Carr emphasizes the role of power politics and the complete neglect of this factor by those who, in the wake of the First World War, believed that its dangers could be eliminated through acts of political will manifest in concepts such as collective security and embodied in international institutions. This he regarded as an act of utopian wishful thinking requiring, in response, a thoroughgoing realist critique. Carr, however, presents a more balanced conceptual critique of the contrasting positions than one might at first assume. The utopian, he says, believes in the possibility of rejecting reality and substituting will, while the realist analyses a predetermined course of action which cannot be changed; the utopian gazes at the future with a creative eye, while the realist is rooted in the past, gazing only at causality; by rejecting the causal sequence, the 'complete utopian' fails to understand reality and therefore the processes by which it can be changed, while the 'complete realist', who accepts unconditionally the causal sequence of events, cannot grasp even the possibility of change: 'the characteristic of the utopian is naivety; of the realist, sterility' (Carr, 2001, p. 12).

The apparent antithesis of utopia and reality also corresponds to the apparent antithesis of theory and practice. 'The utopian makes political theory a norm to which political practice ought to conform. The realist regards political theory as a sort of codification of political practice' (Carr, 2001, p. 13). Both approaches, Carr says, distort the relationship between theory and practice. Politics as a science actually requires 'recognition of the interdependence of theory and practice, which can be attained only through a combination of utopia and reality' (ibid., p. 14).

Some of the most important insights offered by Carr concern the relationship between power and morality. In addition to the notion that only an effective authority can produce morality, which is consistent with Machiavelli, Hobbes and others, Carr explores the extent to which high-minded moral ideas are put to profoundly instrumental use in the rhetoric of international politics, in turn justifying aggressive, self-serving action. Actual or potential enemies are discredited through purveying stories of their inherent moral depravity, while one's own policies appear in the most favourable of moral lights. Ethics are therefore extracted from one's preferred policies and are not formulated prior to them (Carr, 2001, p. 69). The general lessons for Carr are clear. Theories of social morality are the products of dominant groups which identify themselves with the community as a whole; theories of international morality are the products of dominant nations (ibid., p. 74).

Carr's critique included an attack on liberal economics, paying particular attention to the doctrine of the 'harmony of interests' popularized by Adam Smith in which the pursuit of individual interest turns out to be compatible with that of the community in general. Carr remarks that this is 'the natural assumption of a prosperous and privileged class, whose members have a dominant voice in the community and are therefore naturally prone to identify its interests with their own' (2001, p. 75). This doctrine, he suggests, is then projected to the international sphere where nation-states, pursuing their own interests, somehow produce a harmony of interests in the form of internationalism, where the mistaken assumptions are simply magnified (ibid., pp. 42–61). Thus the realist critique of internationalism exposes it as 'an absolute standard independent of the interests and policies of those who promulgate it' (ibid., p. 78).

But what of human nature, the virtual bedrock of classical realism? Carr observes that humans have always lived in groups, larger than single families, with codes of conduct regulating relations between them and which in turn constitute politics. It follows that 'All attempts to deduce the nature of society from the supposed behaviour of man in isolation are purely theoretical, since there is no reason to assume that such a man ever existed.' This sets Carr somewhat at odds with Hobbes. Carr further suggests that two types of behaviour are evident in the human being – 'egoism, or the will to assert himself at the expense of others ... [and] sociability, or the desire to cooperate, to enter into relations of good will and friendship' (2001, p. 91). The state is therefore built on two conflicting aspects of human nature, and both must always be recognized (ibid., p. 92). It follows that power politics is not an aberration but part of normal political life, as are actions inspired by moral considerations, and that it is fatal to ignore either. For Carr the lesson is illustrated by the unhappy fate of China in the nineteenth century, a country that was 'content to believe in the moral superiority of its own civilization and to despise the ways of power' (ibid.). It therefore became subject to the power of others.

The limitations of realism, however, are also important. Although its logic is persuasive, realism turns out to be just as ideological as utopianism. Realism also lacks the means for moral judgement and a ground for meaningful action. Carr therefore concludes that sound political thought must incorporate elements of both utopia and reality.

Key Quote   E. H. Carr on Utopianism and Realism

Where utopianism has become a hollow and intolerable sham, which serves merely as a disguise for the interests of the privileged, the realist performs an indispensable service in unmasking it. But pure realism can offer nothing but a naked struggle for power which makes any kind of international society impossible. . . . The human will [continues] to seek an escape from the logical consequences of realism in the vision of an international order which, as soon as it crystallizes itself into concrete political form, becomes tainted with self-interest and hypocrisy, and must once more be attacked with the instruments of realism.

Here, then, is the complexity, the fascination and the tragedy of all political life. (2001, p.87)

A more systematic account of a realist theory of international politics was to emerge in the work of the French theorist Raymond Aron (1905–1983). Aron has been credited with 'almost single-handedly creating an autonomous discipline of international relations' in France aimed at making intelligible the specific form of social action engaged in by the main actors in international politics (Hoffman, 1985, p.13). These actors are symbolized by the diplomat and the soldier, both agents of the state in whose name they act and on behalf of which it becomes legitimate for the soldier to kill (Aron, 2003, p.5). International relations presents one particular feature which distinguishes it from all other types of social relations – it takes place 'within the shadow of war' – and Aron quotes Clausewitz on the categorization of war as intrinsic to social life (ibid., p.6). He further suggests that the emergent discipline of IR must recognize the multiple links between national and international contexts, for, as long as humanity is unable to achieve unification in a universal state, an essential difference will be maintained between the domestic and the foreign spheres. In the former, violence is reserved to those wielding legitimate authority, while the latter is characterized by a plurality of centres of armed force. Thus mutual relations among states have not emerged from the state of nature. 'There would be no further theory of international relations if they had' (ibid., pp. 6–7).

Aron's treatment of morality owes something to Weber's ethic of responsibility, although Aron calls it a 'morality of prudence' or a 'morality of wisdom'. He contrasts his prudential account with both the 'morality of struggle', which the cruder followers of Machiavelli tend to invoke and which is little more than the law of the jungle, and the 'morality of law' favoured by liberals, which is its antithesis, but which rests on an abstract universalism that does not take account of concrete circumstances. Aron's morality of prudence, while taking account of elements of both of these opposing moralities, recognizes that people retain a certain humanity under conditions of anarchy even as they pursue a pragmatic path of action, but which is both reasonable and moderate. For some, this has led to an assessment of Aron's work as one of 'humane liberalism' rather than as an exposition of the inevitability of power politics (Mahoney, 1992, p. 99). For others, it remains firmly in the classical realist tradition for its focus on the dynamics of power under conditions of anarchy. But it is distinctive in its defence of moral values, its refusal to dwell only on the negative aspects of human nature and its rejection of the notion that politics is defined exclusively by the struggle for power (Cozette, 2008, pp. 3, 10). Even so, Aron's approach does not provide a defence of moral*ism* in international politics, which Aron finds as objectionably self-serving as any other realist critic of the phenomenon.

Niebuhr, Morgenthau and Herz

From the late 1940s onwards, developments in realist thought were dominated by intellectuals located primarily in the US, although many had close European associations. Of the three figures considered here, two were born in Germany and one, Reinhold Niebuhr (1892–1971), was a first-generation German American. Niebuhr was also a theologian and is often credited with formulating a modern doctrine of Christian realism which rejects pacifism as unsustainable in a world so evidently filled with evil (see Lovin, 1995). The propensity for evil, moreover, was much more dangerous at the group level than that of the individual, for, while individuals 'are endowed by nature with a measure of sympathy and consideration for their own kind', and are capable of acting morally *as* individuals, it is much more difficult, if not impossible, for groups to do so (Niebuhr, 1947, p. xi). Niebuhr also directed his arguments against those moralists, whether religious or secular, who believe that individual egoism is 'being progressively checked by the development of rationality or the growth of a religiously inspired goodwill', and who fail to recognize 'those elements in man's collective behaviour which belong to the order of nature and can never be brought completely under the dominion of reason or conscience' (ibid., p. xii).

Niebuhr regards modern nation-states as the most cohesive human groups, largely on account of the presence of an undisputed central authority. He further proposes not only that their selfishness is legendary but that their most significant moral characteristic is hypocrisy. Furthermore, nationalist and patriotic sentiments will always dominate, while idealists of both rationalist and religious varieties espousing universalist principles remain a minority (1947, pp. 83–95). And, like Carr, Niebuhr understood the tendency for self-serving nationalist practices to disguise themselves in the rhetoric of universal morality. Although some among the more educated will recognize this, for most, 'the force of reason operates only to give the hysterias of war and the imbecilities of national politics more plausible excuses' (ibid., p. 97). Here we are reminded of Dr Johnson's well-known aphorism that 'patriotism is the last refuge of a scoundrel', in the sense that it too often serves as a cloak of self-interest rather than as a genuine love of one's homeland (cited in Primoratz and Pavković, 2007, pp. 18–19).

Niebuhr is not entirely without hope for a better future for humankind, but he has little doubt that the brutal elements of collective human life will persist along with the spiritual, and that this is simply in the nature of things. 'The perennial tragedy of human history is that those who cultivate the spiritual elements usually do so by divorcing themselves from or misunderstanding the problems of collective man, where the brutal elements are most obvious. . . . The history of human life will always be the projection of the world of nature' (1947, p. 256).

Hans Morgenthau (1904–1980) has been described as 'a refugee from a suicidal Europe, with a missionary impulse to teach the new world power all the lessons it had been able to ignore until then but could no longer afford to reject' (Hoffman, 1977, p. 44). His *Politics among Nations: The Struggle for Power and Peace* (1978), first published in 1948, proposes that modern political thought has tended to divide into two opposing camps. On the one hand, there is a belief that a rational, moral political order resting on abstract universal principles can be achieved – a belief associated with the notion that human nature is essentially good as well as malleable. The failure of the social order to live up to these expectations to date is because of a lack of knowledge and understanding, inadequate institutions, and the behaviour of certain depraved individuals and/or groups. Education, reform and the occasional use of force is the remedy. On the other hand, there is a belief that the unfortunate state of the 'real' world is due to problems inherent in human nature, reflected in the tendency to competition and conflict, and which mean that moral principles can never be fully realized. Theory resting on these assumptions aims to achieve less evil rather than absolute good, so it is at once less optimistic but much more realistic (Morgenthau, 1978, pp. 3–4). Morgenthau goes on to set out 'Six Principles of Political Realism', summarized as follows.

First, politics, as with social processes generally, is determined by objective laws rooted in human nature. Because these are objective, it is possible to develop a rational theory of politics which distinguishes between truth and opinion, the former supported by evidence and illuminated by reason. The latter is merely subjective judgement divorced from facts and informed by prejudice and wishful thinking.

Second, political realism deploys the concept of interest defined in terms of power, just as economic theory defines interest in terms of wealth. This concept also supplies the necessary link between the reasoning processes deployed in understanding international politics and the relevant facts to be understood. Political realism, as a social theory, also has a normative element. This is manifest in the requirement that rational foreign policy must be good policy, minimizing risks and maximizing benefits and therefore remaining attuned to its own practical and moral purposes.

Third, the key concept of interest defined as power is to be understood as an objective category with universal validity, although the concept of interest itself is not fixed with a specific meaning, for this depends on the cultural and political context in any given case. Similarly, power relates to all social relationships that serve to establish the control of one person or group over another. It may be disciplined by moral considerations, as in Western democracies, but it is also manifest in barbaric force that finds its justification in its own aggrandisement.

Fourth, political realism acknowledges the moral significance of political action while remaining aware of the inevitable tension between morality and successful politics. Realism also holds that universal moral principles cannot be applied in abstract form to all situations but can only be filtered through the concrete circumstances of time and place. Furthermore, abstract ethics conforming to moral laws cannot be used to judge the ethics of political action, for this can only be judged according to its actual consequences.

Fifth, political realism refuses to equate the moral aspirations of any particular nation-state with universal moral laws; no one state has a monopoly on universal moral truths, although most are tempted, from time to time, to conceal their own ambitions behind such a façade. Even more pernicious is the claim that God is on one's side. It is the concept of interest defined in terms of power that prevents both moral excess and political folly.

Sixth, it follows from the first five points that the distinction between political realism and other schools of thought is profound in that it maintains the autonomy of the political sphere, just as economics, law and morality should be maintained within their own spheres. These spheres have relevance but are subordinate to the requirements of successful politics (Morgenthau, 1978, pp. 4–12).

Morgenthau further explains the twin concepts underpinning his approach – power and peace – noting the circumstances of the latter part of the twentieth century, in which 'an unprecedented accumulation of destructive power' gives the problem of peace a particular urgency. Two devices are available for maintaining peace – a balance of power in the international system and the normative limitations placed on the struggle for power by international law and morality as well as world public opinion (1978, pp. 24–5). On power itself, Morgenthau sees this as the defining element of politics in any sphere in which actors, in striving to achieve their goals, are engaged in a constant struggle for power (ibid., p. 29).

Although power is clearly taken as central to politics, Morgenthau goes on to illustrate, through historical examples, the extent to which it remains a crude and unreliable instrument. If we focus only on the struggle for power and the mechanisms through which it operates, he says, the international sphere would certainly appear as the state of nature described by Hobbes and governed by the political expediency commended by Machiavelli. The weak would be at the mercy of the strong, and might would indeed constitute right (1978, p. 231). The strong, however, could not depend simply on maintaining power in such a crude form. Here, again, is where normative systems have a role to play.

Key Quote   Hans J. Morgenthau and the Revolt against Power

[T]he very threat of a world where power reigns not only supreme, but without rival, engenders that revolt against power which is as universal as the aspiration for power itself. To stave off this revolt, to pacify the resentment and opposition that arise when the drive for power is recognized for what it is, those who seek power employ, as we have seen, ideologies for the concealment of their aims. What is actually aspiration for power, then, appears to be something different, something that is in harmony with the demands of reason, morality, and justice. (1978, p. 231)

Morgenthau's remarks in the above quotation echo Carr's critique of power masquerading as morality. It has been equally central to the views of other figures associated with US policy in the postwar period such as George Kennan and Henry Kissinger. Kennan clearly viewed as futile any US attempt which might set out 'to correct and improve the political habits of large parts of the world's populations' (quoted in Donnelly, 1992, p. 102). But Morgenthau does not dismiss morality as nothing more than a mask for self-interest. He says that the analysis of morality in international politics must guard against two extremes: either of overrating the influence of ethics on international affairs or of underestimating it by denying that political actors are motivated by anything but material power (1978, p. 236).

As for sovereignty, Morgenthau argues that it remains the possession of states regardless of the growth of international law and institutions. But has the development of the modern sovereign state and state system mitigated the prospects of war? The short answer is no. In fact, Morgenthau argues that state sovereignty is the main obstacle to restraining the struggle for power in international politics (1978, pp. 332–4). This brings into question the prospects for international order under the UN system, which Morgenthau says is built on erroneous political assumptions, namely, that a unified approach on the part of the great powers, and their combined wisdom and strength, would deal effectively with all threats to peace and security; and, further, that threats would not emanate from the great powers themselves. These assumptions had not stood the test of experience with a clear divide between the interests of the Soviet Union and those of the US ensuring a veto on important decisions (ibid., pp. 474–5).

Even so, Morgenthau does not dismiss the UN entirely, noting that, although it had not been able to prevent wars, there had been some success in shortening their duration. He further suggests that, as long as the US and the USSR coexist within an international organization, prospects for peace remain alive. But he has much greater faith in traditional diplomacy, providing it is divested of the moralizing and crusading tendencies apparent in the postwar system. '[It] will have a chance to preserve the peace only when it is not used as the instrument of a political religion aiming at universal domination' (1978, p. 551). The mitigation of conflict through the revival of diplomacy is also the key to the establishment of a world community – a prerequisite for any attempt to build a world state, which, in the final analysis, offers the only hope of eliminating international conflict (ibid., p. 560).

Morgenthau's work, like Carr's, often appears as one of contradictions. While he sets out a strong case for political realism and is scathing of the moralizing tendencies of alternative approaches, Morgenthau cannot maintain a consistent line of argument when it comes to international institutions. So, while his realist critique of idealism 'is at its most devastating when it comes to existing plans and hopes for the construction of world government', he also argues that the advent of nuclear weapons has rendered the nation-state obsolete and world government essential for human survival, and thus '[t]he sentiment he most ruthlessly dismisses becomes the sentiment required to prevent species extinction' (Craig, 2007, p. 195).

In the world of practical foreign policy, Morgenthau is also renowned for his strident opposition to the Vietnam War (case study 2.2). Such opposition comes as a surprise to those who assume that realism is a doctrine supporting mindless aggression and gross immoralism.

Although Morgenthau remains the giant of American postwar realism in a classical mode, another refugee from Hitler's Europe also made a lasting contribution through his articulation of the 'security dilemma'. John H. Herz (1908–2005) begins by noting the tragic conditions of a Cold War world in which nuclear-armed superpowers confront each other in a dangerous bipolar configuration, a situation representing the extreme manifestation of a dilemma arising from a fundamental condition which has always faced human societies, 'where groups live alongside each other without being organized into a higher unity' (Herz, 1950, p. 157). Any given group, fearful of attack by others, shores up its own security by acquiring more power. But this makes other groups feel less secure, and so they too are compelled to acquire more power: 'Since none can ever feel entirely secure in such a world of competing units, power competition ensues, and the vicious circle of security and power accumulation is on' (ibid.).

Case Study 2.2   Hans Morgenthau and the Vietnam War

The Vietnam War – known in Vietnam as the American War – had its origins in the early Cold War period when the US decided to support the French colonial regime in opposing communist pro-independence forces, led by Ho Chi Minh, based in the north. This accorded with the US policy of containing communism and the notion, expressed in the 'domino theory', that, if Vietnam was permitted to fall to communism, then the rest of Southeast Asia would almost certainly follow.

The French eventually pulled out in 1954, at which time a border, meant to be temporary, was drawn between north and south. The US continued to back anti-communist forces in the south, led initially by Ngo Dinh Diem, although in 1963 the administration of President John F. Kennedy supported a coup against him. Diem's corrupt, repressive leadership had simply fuelled opposition within the south, but his overthrow solved nothing, except to commit the US even more deeply.

In the meantime, the US had already provided several hundred military advisors to the south to help train their forces, but this number was to increase rapidly in the next few years. All this occurred in the broader context of Cold War developments. In 1961 US prestige had suffered a serious blow in relation to the botched operation against Cuba known as the 'Bay of Pigs' and the building of the Berlin Wall had commenced. Kennedy reportedly stated: 'Now we have a problem in making our power credible, and Vietnam is the place' (quoted in Gelb and Betts, 1979, p.70). By the time of his assassination in November 1963, Kennedy had overseen a rapid increase in US forces to over 16,000, still officially in an 'advisory' capacity. Although advisors initially thought the military campaign was eminently winnable within a relatively short time-frame, developments over the next few years proved otherwise. By the time the US finally pulled out, in 1973, around 9 million American military personnel and allied forces from South Korea, Australia and the Philippines had served and over 58,000 US and allied military personnel had been killed. Possibly more than a million Vietnamese, both military and civilian, died in the conflict (see Tucker, 2011, p.175).

There were both liberal and conservative supporters, as well as both liberal and conservative opponents, of the war within the US. Morgenthau, however, saw Vietnam as exemplifying the folly of crusading liberal interventionism to which true realists should be strongly opposed. He was adamant that there was no American national interest to be served by the war and that arguments about the containment of communism in Southeast Asia were entirely specious from a strategic viewpoint. There was also a strong moral edge to Morgenthau's denunciation of the war, emphasizing the tragedy of the enormous loss of life both of young Americans and among the Vietnamese. In 1969 he highlighted the consequences for the Vietnamese of US intervention, leaving no doubt as to his moral position.

> Here is the champion of the 'free world' which protects the people of South Vietnam from Communism by the method of destroying them. Here is the last best hope of the downtrodden and enslaved, to which men of good will

> throughout the world have looked as a shining example, relieving its frustration in blind ideological fury and aimless destructiveness upon a helpless people. (Zimmer, 2011, p. xviii)
>
> By 1975, Morgenthau's assessment of US failure highlighted the flaws of the idealistic 'crusader' approach to Vietnam with the realities on the ground and again stressed the moral consequences.
>
> > We failed in Vietnam because our conception of foreign policy as a noble crusade on behalf of some transcendent purpose clashed with the reality of things that not only refused to be transformed by our good intentions but in turn corrupted our purpose. The purpose, far from ennobling our actions, instead became itself the source of unspeakable evil. (Quoted ibid., p. xvi)

In contemporary international relations, the security dilemma is seen in terms of the perception of the intentions of states, on the one hand, and an assessment of their material military capabilities, on the other. Thus when one state enhances its military capacity, and hence its overall security, another state (or states) will feel less secure. Although the first state's intentions may be purely defensive, other states may not perceive it in this way and, being fearful of the possible security consequences, may respond by further enhancing their own military capability. The first state may react, in turn, by acquiring even more military capability, again provoking further responses by other states. 'Since none can ever feel entirely secure in such a world of competing units, power competition ensues, and the vicious circle of security and power accumulation is on' (Herz, 1950, p. 157).

Whether humans are naturally peaceful and cooperative or domineering and aggressive is not the issue here. For Herz, social cooperation is another fundamental fact of human life, but even cooperation and solidarity become elements in conflict situations when they function to consolidate certain groups in their competition with other groups, and here there is a hint of Niebuhr's warning of the dangers of 'groupism'. Herz goes on to make a case for his 'liberal realism', which he asserts will prove 'more lastingly rewarding than utopian idealism or crude power-realism' (1950, p. 179). It is not clear, however, exactly how this would resolve the security dilemma. As with other realist approaches, as long as there is no world state the fundamental problem of anarchy remains.

Conclusion

Each of the figures introduced here responded to the circumstances of their time – from widespread political instability to outright civil war or interstate warfare, with the threat of nuclear annihilation adding a further dimension to the problem of intergroup violence in the twentieth century. Their analysis of the causes underpinning these events include a negative assessment of human nature, the primacy of power in political relations, and an imperative for moral considerations to be subordinated to those of necessity. These factors are generally complemented by the assertion that harsh political realties must be recognized for what they are and not wished away by the imagination of an ideal world in which good will towards all of humanity is in fact enacted by all of humanity.

Does this make the classical realists discussed here essentially immoral? Certainly, Machiavelli appears to subscribe to the latter when it comes to preserving the state. However, none of the classical realists, including Machiavelli, commend immorality as such. Thucydides clearly laments the breakdown of moral sensibilities under conditions of civil war, tantamount to the breakdown of civilization itself. Similar conditions confronted Hobbes, for whom the conditions of civil war were equivalent to a 'state of nature', the only solution to which is the establishment of sovereign authority. Morality is a product of this order, which dispels the amorality of anarchy. In the works of Carr, Aron and Morgenthau, we see no objection to morality as such but, rather, to the hypocrisy of *moralizing* politicians and others who seek to cloak their interests in the language of morality. Thus realism is best understood as challenging moral*ism*, not morality, although realists themselves often fail to make the distinction clear (Bell, 2010, p. 99).

Historically, the more general problem of religious warfare in early modern Europe gave rise to a state system in which each ruler was to be regarded as possessing sovereign rights in their respective states. Sovereignty thus acquired two dimensions – one internal, and concerned with the maintenance of domestic order, the other external, concerned with maintaining independence from other states. With authority confined to the domestic sphere, however, anarchy, along with the moral vacuum it creates, is simply displaced to the sphere of relations between states. In this sphere there may well be a 'right' of non-interference, but for the political realist this becomes more or less irrelevant in the face of power politics. This provides the starting point for the next generation of realists, who turn from classical conceptions of the problem of violence being grounded in human nature to the location of the problem in the anarchic structure of the international sphere itself, albeit one that remains akin to the state of nature.

QUESTIONS FOR REVISION

1 Which fundamental principles of realism are said to be illustrated by the Melian Dialogue?
2 What does Machiavelli's 'doctrine of necessity' entail?
3 How important is religious thought in the development of political realism?
4 What 'single law' governs Hobbes's state of nature?
5 What lessons are to be drawn from Rousseau's parable of the stag hunt?
6 How does Carr explain the relationship between power and morality?
7 What devices does Morgenthau identify for maintaining international peace?
8 On what basis do realists distinguish between morality and moralism?

FURTHER READING

Crawford, Robert M. A. (2013) *Idealism and Realism in International Relations*. Abingdon: Routledge.
Donnelly, Jack (2000) *Realism and International Relations*. Cambridge: Cambridge University Press.
Frankel, Benjamin (ed.) (1996) *Realism: Restatements and Renewal*. London: Frank Cass.
Spegele, Roger D. (1996) *Political Realism in International Theory*. Cambridge: Cambridge University Press.
Williams, Michael C. (2005) *The Realist Tradition and the Limits of International Relations*. Cambridge: Cambridge University Press.

USEFUL WEBSITES

www.youtube.com/watch?v=UnKEFSVAiNQ (Theory in Action: on the role of power in realist thought)
www.stratfor.com/video/conversation-realism#axzz37y9ghrEh (a conversation on realism)

www.youtube.com/channel/UCoIC97YHklHy2oYFTmkubBA   (Reorienting
   Realism)

http://plato.stanford.edu/entries/realism-intl-relations/ (Stanford Encyclopedia of Philosophy, 'Political Realism in International Relations').

3

Other Realisms and the Scientific Turn

Political realism provided an image of the international sphere that scholars of the postwar period, especially in the US, found compelling (Vasquez, 1998, p. 42). This period followed a second horrendous world war, an emergent bipolar international order, and the possibility of nuclear warfare capable of destroying humankind along with just about every other creature on the planet. The centre of Western power had also shifted from a devastated Europe to the US which, by the end of the Second World War, had assumed economic dominance as well as superpower status. It is in this context that IR as an 'American social science' was born, although it did so on the intellectual foundations laid earlier by E. H. Carr and carried forward in the US by Hans Morgenthau in particular (Hoffman, 1977). Foreign policy discussions in the US were now expressed largely in the realist language of power and interests, and, when policy-makers wished to appeal to some kind of ethic, it was now firmly aligned with the concept of 'national interest' (Keohane, 1986, p. 9).

Although realism remained dominant, the particular form it took changed considerably. There was a decisive shift from the 'inside-out' approach of classical realists, who saw behaviour in the international sphere as determined at the individual (human nature) and domestic (state) levels. A new approach – neorealism – held that state behaviour is ultimately determined by the anarchical structure of the international sphere itself, which has little or nothing to do with human nature, individual actors, regime type (democratic, authoritarian, theocratic, etc.) or other domestic matters, which constitute separate levels of analysis. In the ungoverned realm of competitive interaction, neorealism holds that each state is driven to act according to a self-help principle, striving to ensure its own security and survival vis-à-vis other states. This, moreover, is an entirely rational way to behave under conditions of anarchy. The essential structure of this system can change only in the event of world government, possessing sovereign authority over the entire planet, somehow emerging. This remains highly unlikely.

While neorealists might agree on these basics, they do not speak with one voice on many other matters. One significant division within the neorealist camp concerns whether states pursue power only to the extent that ensures their own survival under conditions of anarchy, or whether states want to maximize their power relative to other states. The former position, known as 'defensive realism', is best represented by Kenneth Waltz. The most prominent exponent of the latter, 'offensive realism', is John Mearsheimer. The first two sections of this chapter therefore focus on these contrasting approaches. This is followed by a discussion of 'neoclassical realism', which attempts to broaden the scope of neorealism to include foreign policy issues relating to domestic politics. We then consider certain questions relating to methodology, focusing in particular on the extent to which positivism has impacted on the discipline of IR, especially in the US. Although positivism is not to be conflated with realism, and has been just as readily deployed in some neoliberal approaches, it is highly pertinent to the discussion of theories which purport to explain the realities of international politics from an objective, scientific standpoint. The final section looks at the more recent field of critical realism, which emerges largely from the philosophy of science and which has some interesting implications for concepts of reality in IR.

Kenneth Waltz and the Foundations of Neorealism

Kenneth Waltz's earliest substantial work, *Man, the State and War*, first published in 1959, notes the propensity of previous thinkers concerned with war and peace, both secular and religious, to locate the essential causes of conflict in human nature. But for Waltz the problem is to be found elsewhere. States in the international system have no assurance that other states will behave peacefully and so may be tempted to undertake a 'preventive war', striking while in a position of relative strength rather than waiting until the balance of power shifts. This problem is related neither to the level of the individual nor to the internal structure of states, but solely to the anarchic structure of the international system (Waltz, 2001, pp. 6–7).

This leads Waltz to propose three 'images' of politics which equate more or less to three spheres of human existence: the individual, the domestic sphere of the state, and the international system (2001, p. 12). The notion that war occurs because humans are wicked (the classical realist view), as well as the optimistic view that humans can be changed for the better (shared by liberals and socialists), relates to the first image. The character of the state – authoritarian or democratic, socialist or capitalist – belongs to the second image. Individuals are, for all practical purposes, contained within the domestic sphere of the state. Further, the character of states makes no real difference to their behaviour internationally. It is therefore in the anarchic structure of the international system itself that the problem of war lies. With the distractions of the first two images removed, and a firm dividing line between the domestic and internal sphere established, the scholar of IR can focus squarely on the third image.

This approach was much more compatible with positivism, which had adapted and refined quantitative methods suitable for deployment in IR. But although Waltz was influenced by economics, he was not mesmerized by numbers, nor did he consider the notion of 'reality' entirely straightforward. His most influential work, *Theory of International Politics* (1979), begins by noting a popular, but mistaken, view of theory creation which holds that it can be built inductively by producing correlations. 'It is then easy to believe that a real causal connection has been identified and measured ... and to forget that something has been said only about dots on a piece of paper and the regression line drawn between them' (1979, pp. 2–3). Numbers can provide useful descriptions of what goes on in some part of the world, he says, but they do not explain anything.

Despite its deficiencies, Waltz notes that students of politics nonetheless display a strong commitment to the inductive method, hoping that connections and patterns will emerge and thereby establish a 'reality that is out there' (1979, p. 3). 'Reality', he says, is congruent neither with a theory nor with a model depicting a simplified version of it (ibid., pp. 7–8). This begs the question: if theory is not a reproduction of reality then what is it? Waltz suggests that a theory is a mentally formed picture of a particular domain of activity, of its organization and the connections between its parts, and that that domain must be isolated from others to deal with it intellectually (ibid., pp. 8–9).

With respect to the subject matter of IR, Waltz says that traditionalists such as Morgenthau had been prone to analysing the field in terms of inside-outside patterns of behaviour – that is, by looking at how domestic politics affects international politics and vice versa. But, given the marked variability of states through both space and time, what accounts for the continuities observed over millennia? To illustrate, Waltz argues for the ongoing relevance of Hobbesian insights even in a period of nuclear-armed superpower rivalry. Thus 'the texture of international politics remains highly constant, patterns recur, and events repeat themselves endlessly.' And it is the enduring condition of anarchy that accounts for the essential sameness of international politics throughout history (1979, p. 66).

Waltz also elaborates the concepts of balance of power and self-help in an anarchic system, noting first that, because some states may at some stage use force, all states must be prepared to do so or remain at the mercy of more militant neighbours, for, among states, as among individuals in the absence of government, 'the state of nature is a state of war' (1979, p. 102). Elaborating on the difference between the use of force in the domestic and international spheres, Waltz notes Weber's point that, because states have a monopoly on the legitimate use of force within their boundaries, governments will organize agents of the state to deal with violence as and when it occurs. An effective national system in which citizens have no need to organize their own defences is therefore not a self-help system. But the international system is (ibid., p. 4). In a self-help situation, states are concerned about survival, which in turn conditions their behaviour. They worry about their strength relative to other states rather than about any absolute advantage. This limits their cooperation with other states, especially if it means they may become dependent on them. Small, poorly resourced states will be unable to resist dependence. But stronger ones will avoid this, even if it means devoting considerable resources to military expenditure (ibid., p. 107).

Anarchy may seem to be alleviated by the growth of international institutions and the fragments of government they provide, along with some sentiments of community and certain orderly and coordinated procedures across a range of international activities, but this notion, says Waltz, confuses process with structure. In the absence of a world state, the essential structural conditions imposed by anarchy remain. Even when peace breaks out over an extended period, warfare will inevitably return at some stage. In short, war will continue to occur with law-like regularity. The critique of international institutions, and the liberal hopes invested in them, is illustrated by Waltz's analysis of NATO in the post-Cold War period and its implications for Russian foreign policy choices, the subject of case study 3.1.

What structural realists seek to emphasize is that, while the domestic sphere remains one of authority and law, competition and force are the

Case Study 3.1   Kenneth Waltz's Critique of NATO and the Implications for Russia

NATO – the North Atlantic Treaty Organization – was established in April 1949 as a collective security organization in which an attack on one member by an external party was to be regarded as an attack on all, thereby requiring a collective response in defence of the state under attack. NATO was very much a creature of the Cold War given that the main threat to the US and Western Europe was perceived to be the Soviet Union, which initiated the Warsaw Pact (more formally the Warsaw Treaty Organization or WTO) in 1955. This was partly as a response to the integration of West Germany into NATO when it became its fifteenth member in May of that year, although it also aimed to consolidate Soviet control over Eastern and Central Europe. NATO has transformed its mission since 1989 and now projects an image of an organization dedicated to the pursuit of peace through cooperation both among its members and with others, including Russia. It currently has twenty-eight member countries, having expanded to take in most of the former Eastern bloc.

Kenneth Waltz, writing in 2000, argued that the fact that NATO had outlived its original purpose by taking on a new one does not support the case of liberals, who interpret this as evidence for the strength and vitality of international institutions. It actually supports the assumptions of structural realism. NATO, he says, remains both a treaty made by states and, while a deeply entrenched bureaucratic organization does indeed sustain and animate it, a creature of state interests. More than that, it is a means by which the US can maintain a grip on the foreign and military policies of European states.

The survival and expansion of NATO tell us much about American power and influence and little about institutions as multilateral entities. The ability of the United States to extend the life of a moribund institution illustrates nicely how international institutions are created and maintained by stronger states to serve their perceived or misperceived interests (Waltz, 2000, p. 20).

Waltz went on to suggest that NATO's continuation, and its expansion eastwards in the post-Cold War world, was actually dangerous, for it could only lead to the alienation and isolation of Russia. Thus justification for expansion was weak, while justification for opposing it was strong.

> It draws new lines of division in Europe, alienates those left out, and can find no logical stopping place west of Russia. It weakens those Russians most inclined toward liberal democracy and a market economy. It strengthens Russians of the opposite inclination. . . . Throughout modern history, Russia has been rebuffed by the West, isolated and at times surrounded. . . . With good reason, Russians fear that NATO will not only admit additional old members of the WTO but also former republics of the Soviet Union. (2000, p. 22)

There is no doubt that Waltz would see the Ukraine–Russia conflict as emanating precisely from the expansion of both NATO and the EU into Russia's former sphere of influence. John Mearsheimer certainly takes this view, arguing that the US – through NATO – has played a key role in precipitating the conflict and that Putin's behaviour has been motivated by exactly the same geostrategic considerations that influence all great powers, including the US. 'The taproot of the current crisis is NATO expansion and Washington's commitment to move Ukraine out of Moscow's orbit and integrate it into the West' (Mearsheimer, 2014).

key dynamics of the international system. This may be analysed in terms of *realpolitik*, the essential elements of which are:

1 self-interest (on the part of states or rulers) provides the spring of action;
2 the necessities of policy emanate from the unregulated competition of states; and
3 calculations based on these necessities produce policies that best serve state interests.

Success – the ultimate test of policy – is defined as preserving and strengthening the state. 'Ever since Machiavelli, interest and necessity – and raison d'état, the phrase that comprehends them – have remained the key concepts of Realpolitik' (Waltz, 1979, p. 117).

This brings Waltz to balance of power theory and its key assumptions about states: they are unitary actors which, at minimum, seek their own preservation; at maximum, they aim for universal domination (1979, p. 118). The means employed involve internal efforts (such as increasing economic capabilities and military strength) and external strategies (such as maintaining and strengthening one's alliances and weakening those of actual or potential enemies). The theory is built on the assumed motivations and actions of states; it identifies constraints imposed on state action by the system and it indicates the expected outcome in terms of the formation of balances of power.

Waltz further indicates the source of this model: 'Balance-of-power theory is microtheory precisely in the economist's sense. The system, like a market in economics, is made by the actions and interactions of its units, and the theory is based on assumptions about their behaviour' (1979, p. 118). Furthermore, a self-help system means that those who fail to help themselves expose themselves to dangers. 'Fear of such unwanted consequences stimulates states to behave in ways that tend toward the creation of balances of power' (ibid). One commentator has pointed out that Waltz is careful to state that the primary goal of states is to achieve or maximize security rather than maximize power itself, and so power is a means to an end rather than an end in itself. This further suggests that states seek power only relative to other states, which again does not indicate power maximization to some kind of absolute measure but, rather, corresponds to a balancing strategy (Guzzini, 1998, pp. 135–6).

More generally, the principal features of Waltz's structural realism have been summarized succinctly as explaining (and not merely describing) the international system by reference to the dominant structure imposed by anarchy, defined by the interplay between component units (in terms of states seeking survival), and characterized by the particular distributions of power reflecting the capabilities of the units. It is causality within this system that counts rather than factors such as differing political cultures that may shape foreign policy practice and other forms of interactions between the units. This 'systemic' approach is therefore parsimonious, not seeking to explain everything in the world of politics (Booth, 2011, p. 5).

Waltz's ideas have had an enormous impact on IR scholarship and its theoretical development in particular. For just as realism was a reaction in many ways to idealism, so many subsequent theoretical debates are a reaction to realism in general and neorealism in particular. Not all of these reactions have been in opposition to Waltz's basic ideas. Indeed, many have been supportive but have sought to refine or extend Waltz's insights in one way or another. One result has been a burgeoning of books and articles running into the thousands – a veritable academic industry that has produced a literature now so vast that it is difficult to sift through and summarize all the variations. We next consider an influential approach that builds on the neorealist edifice created by Waltz but which shifts the emphasis to the offensive dynamics generated by the anarchic structure of the international sphere.

John Mearsheimer and Offensive Realism

John Mearsheimer is a leading proponent of another form of neorealism (although he prefers the term 'structural realism'), which takes a distinctive approach to the question of how much power states actually want. He has been described as one of the more pessimistic of contemporary structural realists for his emphasis on the tragic nature of the inescapable realities of politics under conditions of anarchy in the international sphere and from which there is no escape for the foreseeable future (Toft, 2005, p. 381). This suggests that, although he might like to see a better, safer world – as most surely would – he takes the long-standing realist line that we must face the facts as they are, unpleasant though they may be. And Mearsheimer sees an even more unpleasant world than most.

Mearsheimer offers his 'offensive realism' as a formulation of structural realism superior to what he describes as the 'defensive realism' of Waltz. The latter, he proposes, embraces a certain optimism that is simply not warranted. Mearsheimer in fact believes that his approach is more realistic. Whereas Waltz sees anarchy as encouraging only defensive behaviour which maintains the balance of power, and thus preserves the status quo, Mearsheimer's central argument is that the system provides incentives to act offensively (2001, pp. 19–20).

Mearsheimer also contrasts his approach with the 'human nature realism' of the classical tradition, where the causes of state aggression are located in the human 'will to power' and anarchy is relegated to a second-order cause (2001, p. 19). Where offensive realism and human nature realism meet in agreement is in their portrayal of great powers as relentlessly seeking power. Where they differ is that offensive realism rejects the claim arising from Morgenthau's analysis that 'states are naturally endowed with Type A personalities'. For Mearsheimer, however, great powers behave aggressively not because of an innate drive to dominate derived from human nature, but because they want to survive (ibid., p. 21). One could argue here that the drive to dominate perceived by human nature theorists is due precisely to the imperative to survive, and that the desire of states to survive is simply the projection of that need onto the state itself. States, after all, are entities created by humans to ensure their survival vis-à-vis each other and, although they may take on a life of their own in the international sphere, are not entirely autonomous entities. But this is not Mearsheimer's line.

The basic contours of Mearsheimer's offensive realism are set against the background of the early post-Cold War period, when liberal hopes for a more peaceful world order were high and envisaged a situation in which 'great powers no longer view each other as potential military powers, but instead as members of a family of nations . . . of what is sometimes called the "international community"' (2001, p. 1). However, even a brief consideration of security issues in Europe and Northeast Asia – both crucial arenas for great power politics in the twenty-first century – must give pause for more sober assessments.

Key Quote   Mearsheimer on Power Politics

The sad fact is that international politics has always been a ruthless and dangerous business, and it is likely to remain that way. Although the intensity of their
competition waxes and wanes, great powers fear each other and always compete with each other for power. The overriding goal of each state is to maximize
its share of world power, which means gaining power at the expense of other
states. . . . the desire for more power never goes away, unless a state achieves
the ultimate goal of hegemony. Since no state is likely to achieve hegemony,
however, the world is condemned to perpetual great-power competition.
(2001, p. 2)

The pursuit of power in the circumstances described by Mearsheimer
is unrelenting, and, because they are always seeking opportunities to tilt
the distribution of power in their favour, great powers are primed for
offence and not merely defence. Three specific features of the international system combine to produce this effect. First, no central authority
able to enforce a protective mechanism exists; second, states will always
have some offensive capability; and, third, states can never be certain
about the intentions of other states. This situation is genuinely tragic
because great powers that have no real reason to fight each other, being
concerned simply with their own survival. They are nonetheless compelled to seek domination over other states in the system. Mearsheimer
quotes the 'brutally frank' comments made by the Prussian leader Otto
von Bismarck in the 1860s in the context of the possible restoration
of Poland's sovereignty and its implications for regional order. Such a
move, said Bismarck, would be 'tantamount to creating an ally for any
enemy that chooses to attack us', and so he advocated that the Poles be
smashed until, 'losing all hope, they lie down and die'. He continued,
'I have every sympathy for their situation, but if we wish to survive we
have no choice but to wipe them out' (quoted in Mearsheimer, 2001, p. 3).
Bismarck's words bear comparison with those of the Athenian generals
in the Melian Dialogue, although the Athenians evinced less sympathy
for those they were about to annihilate, perhaps because the Melians
had at least been offered a way to survive.

Mearsheimer summarizes his account of offensive realism through a
set of arguments about the behaviour of great powers – defined as such
on the basis of their military capabilities and held to be responsible
for the deadliest wars – and the identification of conditions that make
conflict more or less likely. A key argument holds that multipolar systems are more war-prone and therefore more dangerous than bipolar

ones, especially those containing powerful, potential hegemons. For Mearsheimer this is more than just an assertion; it has a causal logic.

A further task Mearsheimer sets himself is to show how the theory stands up to the test of real-world cases by reference to a detailed historical study of great power relations in Europe from the last decade of the eighteenth century through to the end of the twentieth century, together with a substantial discussion of Northeast Asia, focusing on Japan and China, as well as the US. A third task is to make some cautious predictions about great power politics in the twenty-first century, while acknowledging the inherent difficulties that social science theories have with highly complex political phenomena (2001, pp. 4–8).

A particular focus is on the rise of China, its prospects for achieving regional hegemony in Northeast Asia, and the likely strategies of the US in response. The most sensible response, according to Mearsheimer, is not to engage China so much as to contain it. A strategy of engagement reflects the liberal belief that, if China could be made both democratic and prosperous, it would simply become a status quo power and therefore not inclined to engage in security competition. This view is mistaken, he says, because an economically and militarily strong China will be driven, as a matter of logic, to maximize its prospects for survival by becoming a regional hegemon. This has nothing to do with China having wicked intentions; it is simply in its own security interests to pursue regional hegemony, just as it is in the interests of the US to contain China's growth to forestall such a development (Mearsheimer, 2001, p. 402).

The case of Northeast Asia also illustrates Mearsheimer's analysis of 'offshore balancing', an explanation of which starts from the fact that, although great powers would wish to achieve global hegemony as a matter of security logic, in practical terms this is not feasible, largely because of the problem of projecting effective military power over large bodies of water, such as the Pacific or Atlantic oceans. Because hegemony is confined to a regional level, the US is therefore only truly hegemonic in its own hemisphere. But even if great powers can only dominate their own regions, they are still concerned about the potential of hegemons to emerge in other regions and pose a threat. It is therefore preferable that another significant region, such as Northeast Asia, has two or three great powers in competition with each other because that would make it much more difficult for any of them to threaten a distant hegemon, namely the US. If one of these does start to look like a regional hegemon – and China is the obvious candidate here – the US's first preference would be to allow the other powers in that region to check the threat. This is a form of buck-passing rather than balancing as such. If that fails, then is the time for the US to move in with more explicit balancing actions. In effect, then, 'regional hegemons act as offshore balancers in other areas of the world, although they prefer to be the balancer of last resort' (Mearsheimer, 2001, pp. 140–1).

Mearsheimer also considers US attitudes to international affairs generally, suggesting that the message of realism, with its emphasis on the pursuit of power for self-interested reasons, lacks broad appeal, and the rhetoric of presidents throughout the twentieth century is actually littered with examples of 'realist bashing'. Further, the hostility to realism resonates with a deep-seated optimism combined with a pervasive moralism, values which are essentially liberal in orientation.

Key Quote   Mearsheimer on Moralism

Most people like to think of fights between their own state and rival states as clashes between good and evil, where they are on the side of the angels and their opponents are aligned with the devil. Thus leaders tend to portray war as a moral crusade or an ideological contest, rather than as a struggle for power. Realism is a hard sell . . . [and] Americans appear to have an especially intense antipathy towards balance-of-power thinking. (2001, p. 23)

Almost a decade later, Mearsheimer says that, although realism was pronounced virtually dead in the decade that followed the end of the Cold War, the events of 11 September 2001 and its aftermath have seen optimism about the prospects for a peaceful world order in serious decline while realism has made a 'stunning comeback'. He argues that this is at least partly because almost every realist opposed the war in Iraq, a war that turned into a strategic disaster for both the US and the UK. This position is directly comparable to that of Morgenthau in relation to the Vietnam War. In addition, Mearsheimer suggests that there is no good reason to suppose that globalization and international institutions have undermined the state. Rather, the state continues to have a 'bright future' if only because the ideology of nationalism, with its glorification of the state, remains such a powerful ideology (Mearsheimer, 2010, p. 92).

As is the case with every major author, Mearsheimer has both critics and supporters. Some have taken issue with his general structural approach, which, they say, reduces causality simply to the conditions of anarchy in the international sphere. They argue that domestic factors, leadership ideology, and institutional, technological, economic and systemic factors all influence state behaviour, and they provide numerous examples to support this argument (see May, Rosecrance and Steiner, 2010, pp. 4–5; also Kaplan, 2012). Interestingly, these authors go over much of the very same historical ground that Mearsheimer ploughs but reach very different theoretical conclusions. This illustrates, among other things, that the same set of facts may elicit very different interpretations and explanations according to the theoretical standpoint of the theorist, a point made earlier by Waltz. Few could disagree with this.

Neoclassical Realism

Neoclassical realism is not a reassertion of the primacy of human nature as a causal factor in explaining the aggression of states over and above the structural account of the conditions of anarchy. Rather, it attempts to synthesize elements of classical realism and neorealism by combining structure under conditions of anarchy with relevant factors arising from the internal dynamics of states, including ideology, personalities, perceptions, misperceptions and other factors which feed into foreign policy. It is, in effect, the joining of foreign policy analysis, which, by definition, accounts for domestic factors, with structural realism. In reviewing a collection of works described as neoclassical, Gideon Rose explains that they incorporate both external and internal variables, thereby updating and systematizing certain insights drawn from classical realist thought.

Key Quote   Gideon Rose on Neoclassical Realism

[Neoclassical realists] argue that the scope and ambition of a country's foreign policy is driven first and foremost by its place in the international system and specifically by its relative material power capabilities. This is why they are realist. They argue further, however, that the impact of such power capabilities on foreign policy is indirect and complex, because systemic pressures must be translated through intervening variables at the unit level. This is why they are neoclassical. (Rose, 1998, p. 146)

Rose further proposes that neoclassical approaches are distinctive in attempting to develop a generalizable theory of foreign policy as well as a common mode of argumentation. 'Their central concern is to build on and advance the work of previous students of relative power by elaborating the role of domestic-level intervening variables, systematizing the approach, and testing it against contemporary competitors' (Rose, 1998,

p. 153). Neoclassical realism is therefore not so much a new departure as a reformulation of elements of structural realism but now attuned to the domestic dynamics implicated in foreign policy formulation. If it is less parsimonious than structural realism because of this, its proponents would argue that it at least has the virtue of potentially explaining more. Defenders of structural realism as a limited theory, however, reject this broadening of its purview, seeing 'lean and mean' as key to its success (Legro and Moravcsik, 1999, p. 50).

But what kinds of issues, exactly, does neoclassical realism bring to light? A more recent study by Randall Schweller adopts an explicit neo-classical realist approach in investigating the phenomenon of 'underbal-ancing' in the international system, an issue clearly related to balance of power analysis. Domestic politics, he argues, provides the most plausible explanation of the phenomenon. Put simply, states generally attempt to balance against other states but, for various reasons, don't necessar-ily get it right. The opposite phenomenon is overbalancing. This is a form of overkill behaviour, perhaps driven by a paranoid assumption that 'they're out to get us', and in which misperception enlarges the actual threat (somewhat like those rear-vision mirrors that make objects behind you appear much bigger than they really are). Schweller notes that there is no word in the English language for a psychosis of the con-trasting type which may induce one to believe that 'everyone loves you, when, in fact, they don't even like you' (Schweller, 2006, p. 3). Perhaps narcissism comes close to describing this condition.

The framework for this theory, which is based on elite calculations of costs and risks, does not take statecraft as consisting simply as a response to the 'particular geostrategic risks and opportunities presented by a given systemic environment'. It is also a consequence of four prime factors. First, elite preferences and perceptions of the external envi-ronment; second, which preferences and perceptions actually matter in policy-making; third, the domestic risks associated with particular foreign policy choices; and, fourth, the variable risk-taking propensities of national elites. 'Once these "unit-level" factors have been established, they can then be treated as inputs (state strategies and preferences) at the structural-systemic level in order to explain how unit- and structural-level causes interact to produce systemic outcomes' (Schweller, 2006, p. 46). This whole approach is contrary to the core structural realist assumption that states are coherent, rational unity actors which act in predictable ways to maintain an acceptable balance of power to ensure survival.

Another take on neoclassical realism assesses it as a logical development, rather than a rejection, of Waltzian structural realism. Brian Rathbun (2008) argues that structural realists have never claimed that domestic politics and ideas have no part to play in international politics, and what the neoclassical realists are doing is simply filling out Waltz's rather sparse understanding of power 'through reference to nationalism or state-society relations' (2008, p. 296). What neoclassical realism actually demonstrates is that, when domestic politics and ideas do interfere significantly in foreign policy decision-making, 'the system punishes states'. Put another way, if elites wander too far into the bog of liberal and constructivist ideas, where state interests are readily subordinated not only to parochial interests but to subjective ideas that distract from a firm grip on objective reality, there will be consequences, and unpleasant ones at that. Following this line, neoclassical realists have joined more conventional neorealists in strongly opposing the Iraq War. Case study 3.2 shows how both have provided a critique of the Iraq War which they claim was inspired by an ideology of neoconservatism, which held sway under the administration of George W. Bush and which appeared to have incorporated elements of liberal interventionism.

Positivism and 'Scientific' IR

The shift from classical realism to neorealism occurred at much the same time as a more general methodological trend in political studies, the latter reflecting a growing intellectual conviction in the US that all problems, including social and political ones, are capable of resolution through the application of a scientific method leading to practical application and genuine progress (Hoffman, 1977, p. 45). This resulted in a heavy emphasis on quantitative (statistical) analysis and, through this, the testing of hypotheses in accordance with the positivist approach discussed in chapter 1. As the new methodology aspired to compile objective, value-free data concerning human behaviour, the direct observation and measurement of which was the only reliable source of knowledge, it is commonly referred to as behaviouralism (Heywood, 2004 p. 9). Given that one of neorealism's claims to superiority over its classical predecessor was its parsimony, the narrowing of analytical scope to what can be directly observed and measured became a virtue rather than a vice. Further, the most appropriate tools were those already deployed in economic analysis. As Hoffman (1977, p. 46) argues: 'Like economics, political science deals with a universal yet specialized realm of human

Case Study 3.2   Realism, Neoconservatism and the Iraq War

The Iraq War commenced in March 2003 when forces led by the US invaded the country, alleging that Iraq possessed weapons of mass destruction and that its leader, Saddam Hussein, was planning to use them against certain Western countries and its allies. No weapons of mass destruction, or even materials capable of producing them, were ever found to justify a pre-emptive strike.

The Iraq War followed a similar attack on Afghanistan, which had indeed harboured the Islamic terrorist organization, al-Qaeda and its leader Osama bin Laden, responsible for the attacks on the twin towers of World Trade Center and the Pentagon on 11 September 2001 ('9/11'). Afghanistan's governing Taliban organization was not involved in the 9/11 attacks, and evidence suggests they may have preferred to cooperate with the US and NATO allies to turn bin Laden and other al-Qaeda operatives over rather than risk military action against them. The US under the George W. Bush administration, however, pushed for immediate action, and less than a month after 9/11 commenced military operations against Afghanistan.

The war on Afghanistan was dubbed the 'War on Terror', and when the Bush administration decided to invade Iraq it was brought under this rubric as well, even though Iraq had nothing to do with Afghanistan, the Taliban, al-Qaeda or the 9/11 attacks. But it was the rhetoric of the 'War on Terror' that was essential to 'sell' the war on Iraq. This rhetoric was used to considerable effect both in the US and among some of its NATO allies, especially the UK, where Prime Minister Tony Blair was equally determined to depict Iraq as a terrorist state, armed with weapons of mass destruction, and therefore representing a clear and present danger to Western security interests.

Both Bush and Blair also appear to have believed that Iraq could be turned into a model democracy and an inspiration for the rest of the Arab world and the Middle East more generally. Indeed, Bush used some quite explicit arguments based on the liberal idea that the spread of democracy would enhance the prospects for a future of peace. More generally, their language was infused with a very strong moralism concerning the justification of war both in removing an evil dictator in the form of Saddam Hussein and in the prospects for bringing peace, security and prosperity to the region.

After a decade in Iraq, leading to half a million dead Iraqis and the loss of almost 5,000 US military personnel, along with smaller numbers of British and other allied forces comprising the 'coalition of the willing', the US finally withdrew in November 2011. Iraq remains in a state of widespread civil disorder as a result of a continuing insurgency against the new regime and the threat of all-out civil war, primarily between Sunni and Shia factions. Whereas al-Qaeda and its affiliates or offshoots were virtually non-existent in Iraq before 2001, the country faces an ongoing battle with Islamic extremists backing the mainly Sunni insurgency. There is no end in sight.

The ideology that drove the Bush administration is grounded in neither liberal nor realist premises but is, rather, 'neoconservative'. Neoconservatism has a history in American social and political thought as an amalgam of certain conservative ideas that makes selective use of elements of liberal thought and that has serious implications for international politics. In the hands of the Republican administration of George W. Bush, and in the context of the 'War on Terror' precipitated by the events of 9/11, it operated as something of an ad hoc doctrine driven by a heroic vision of America's role in the contemporary world. One former supporter of the doctrine, now turned critic, writes that neoconservatism emanates from a particular set of individuals 'who believe in American values and American power – a dangerous combination' (Cooper, 2011, p. xi). The emphasis on values chimes with liberalism and the focus on power appears to resonate with realism.

John Mearsheimer, among others, has associated neoconservatism with liberalism, describing it as 'Wilsonianism with teeth' and placing it very far from the main tenets of realism (quoted in Caverley, 2010, p. 594). But Jonathan Caverley (ibid., p. 613) argues that neoconservatism, although incorporating one element of liberalism associated with democratization, is better understood as a species of neoclassical realism. Neoconservatism pushes aggressively for the democratization of other countries, not on any principled moral grounds, but on the grounds that regime type matters for America's own security interests.

Neoconservatism thus embodies the realist primacy of self-interest even as it appears to push a liberal agenda. The notion that regime type matters, however, is embedded in neoclassical realism, and indeed that is what makes it neoclassical rather than simply structural. Caverley goes on to argue that, although realists can justifiably claim that they opposed the Iraq War, their arguments were empirical and strategic rather than realist as such. Further, although neoclassical realists have not argued specifically for the spread of democracy to enhance America's security interests, the logic of the theory strongly supports it (Caverley, 2010, p. 613).

Rathbun (2008, p. 320) claims that neoclassical realism helps to illuminate some of the most important foreign policy events in recent times. He notes the vigorous campaign led by Mearsheimer against the US-led war on Iraq, a campaign grounded in the conviction that it would distract the US from more important strategic issues. The diagnosis of America's mistake is provided by neoclassical realism, for US government policy 'was dictated not objectively by considerations of power and material interests but by ideological myths promulgated by neoconservatives' (ibid.).

activity . . . on the creative and coercive role of a certain kind of power, and on its interplay with social conflict.' This draws it closer to 'that other science of scarcity, competition, and power' – economics.

The origins of the behavioural turn in political science in the US has been traced to the 1930s, when a conscious shift from normative to positive approaches featured in the work of several prominent scholars at the University of Chicago (Friedan and Lake, 2005, p. 137). The nascent discipline of IR, however, was initially less receptive to its promises.

Morgenthau himself was strongly opposed to this approach, noting that the tools of economic analysis on which it depended were simply inappropriate to international politics: 'In such a theoretical scheme, nations confront each other not as living historic entities with all their complexities, but as rational abstractions, after the model of "economic man", playing games of military and diplomatic chess according to a rational calculus that exists nowhere but in the theoretician's mind' (Morgenthau, 1970, p. 244).

Although Morgenthau and other classical realists may have found the positivist turn in politics and IR objectionable, and not just because of its close association with the 'dismal science' of economics, there are nonetheless elements of its methodology that resonate with certain basic tenets of political realism. As noted in chapter 1, the idea of an objective body of science requires that normative considerations be set aside, for objective science is defined in terms of the study of what is, not what ought to be. Here we may recall that the 'first great debate' in the discipline of IR between realism and idealism was directed, by realists, to the defence of a conception of objective reality against the deeply normative orientation of the idealists. The 'second great debate' centred on the methodological divide over whether the new positivist/behaviouralist approach, with its claims to objectivity and rigour, was superior, or inferior, to the traditional historical and philosophic approaches favoured by Morgenthau and others at that time. This became a 'battle of the literates versus the numerates', the latter claiming the mantle of science while excluding all those who believed that the study of politics cannot be reduced to numbers (Hoffman, 1977, p. 54).

The terms 'positivism' and 'science' became more or less interchangeable throughout the remainder of the twentieth century (Wight, 2002, p. 25), while genuine social science in the US has been similarly equated with positivism ever since (Smith, 2000, p. 398). In their assessment of IR as a social science, half a century on from positivism's rise to dominance in the US, Frieden and Lake (2005) argue that the discipline needs to become even more 'scientific' in its approach to ensure its theoretical rigour and policy relevance – 'rigour' being a term reserved for theory associated with positivist methodologies. IR, they say, 'is most useful *not* when its practitioners use their detailed empirical knowledge to offer opinions, however intelligent and well-informed, but when they can identify with some confidence the causal forces that drive foreign policy and international interactions' (ibid., p. 137; emphasis added).

It is important to note here that behaviouralism was to find favour not only with a new generation of realist scholars in the American academy but also with those of a new generation of liberal scholars. The latter were, after all, very much concerned with the idea of progress – a notion foundational to liberal theory – and not at all averse to employing methods providing a semblance of scientific objectivity to their own enterprise. Moreover, the more scientifically attuned approaches were more likely to attract research funding and all the prestige associated with large grants of money. Writing towards the end of the twentieth century, one commentator noted that both neorealism and neoliberalism had converged around a set of core assumptions in which moral considerations rarely rated a mention, and with both sides now assuming that 'states behave like egoistic value maximizers' (Baldwin, quoted in Smith, 2000, p.381).

Although positivism has its practitioners throughout the global academic community, in the UK and elsewhere in the English-speaking world, as well as in Europe, methodological and epistemological approaches have been much more diverse, finding 'rigour and relevance' in very different conceptualizations of how best to pursue enquiry in international politics. As we see next, critical realism offers one alternative while remaining 'scientific'.

Critical Realism

The topic of critical realism, grounded as it is in the philosophy of science, may seem to move us away from the 'real world' of international politics, but it has implications for how we understand 'science', the nature of reality, and the methods used to pursue understanding and explanation. Moreover, it offers alternatives for those wishing to pursue a social scientific form of study, but not along positivist lines. Critical realism is a variant of scientific realism and, although the terms are sometimes used synonymously, there are some distinctions (see Chernoff, 2002, p.399). For present purposes it must suffice to say that scientific realism, like any form of realism, is founded on a notion that reality exists independently of the perceptions of any observer, although this does not mean that reality confronts us in obvious ways.

Critical realism, as a variant of scientific realism, thus accepts 'the real'. But what sets critical realism apart from the varieties of political realism discussed above is a concern with human emancipation. It therefore has a distinctly normative edge. This is also a primary concern of those who align themselves with post-Marxist critical theory, which we explore later. But, although critical realism may have this edge, it is nonetheless a theory of scientific realism, or rather a metatheory, because it transcends particular theories within disciplines such as IR while lending itself to adaptation by any of them.

The form of critical realism most frequently discussed by IR scholars emerges from the work of Roy Bhaskar, who is widely acclaimed for breaking new ground in moving the concept of science decisively away from positivism, which had 'usurped the title of science' (Bhaskar, 2008, p. xxix). The starting point of Bhaskar's critique of positivism is that it is essentially a theory of causal laws which fails because a constant conjunction of events is neither a sufficient nor even a necessary condition for a scientific law (ibid., p. 1). Looking to the nature of experimental activity, which is the focus of positivism, Bhaskar notes that the experimenter is actually the causal agent of a sequence of events. This suggests an ontological distinction between scientific laws, on the one hand, and patterns of events, on the other.

The problem thus created for a theory of science can be resolved if we accept that at the core of theory is a picture of natural mechanisms at work. These, in turn, denote the objective existence of natural necessities. Such mechanisms must be viewed as independent of the events they generate. Then, and only then, can we be justified in assuming that the mechanisms themselves endure in their normal, natural way 'outside the experimentally closed conditions that enable us empirically to identify them'. This underpins the notion of an independent reality in which events occur independently of our experiences (Bhaskar, 2008, pp. 1–2). This is complex stuff for anyone not familiar with basic philosophical language and style, and only the barest of expositions can be given here. But let us briefly consider some of the implications for the study of politics generally.

Ruth Lane (1996), writing broadly on scientific realism rather than on critical realism in particular, notes the strong tendency among those studying politics to assume that positivism equals science and, further, that those who criticize positivism actually support an anti-science position (1996, p. 361). Scientific realism comes to the rescue of those who reject positivism without necessarily wanting to reject science. It does not follow that positivism is 'wrong', but rather that it is just one part of a broader scientific enterprise (ibid., p. 364). Furthermore, 'practices that were thought to be unquestionably scientific, such as massive data collection and highly sophisticated statistical methods of analysis, are less central to scientific realism than they were to positivistic behaviouralism; practices that were thought to be dubiously scientific, such as the emphasis on the meaning of political actions to the subjects themselves, are given greater legitimacy' (ibid., p.365).

Lane also notes that at least part of the relevance of scientific realism for the study of politics is that it emphasizes the role of theory much more than does positivism, because, while the latter is concerned mainly to define correlational regularities, 'theory is intended to describe complex real-world processes' (1996, p.365). More specific applications of critical realism have been evident in the theorization of IR. Although it has yet to make a major impact, it obviously has an appeal for those who believe that reality does indeed exist 'out there', but who find persuasive neither the versions of political realism discussed here nor the positivist approach to correlation and causation.

On issues of causation, Milja Kurki (2007) argues that causality itself has acquired an undeservedly negative image at the hands of scholars who, in opposing positivism, have simply lumped causal theory in with it, and then dismissed both. To rescue causality, Kurki proposes that we rethink it through from the way it is conceived to how it is deployed in analysis. She starts from a core assumption of a realist philosophy of science that causes exist as ontologically real forces in the world around us, which accords with the equally realist proposition that 'nothing comes of nothing'. Many causes are unobservable and often exist in complex contexts in which multiple causes interact. In the social and political world, moreover, 'causes' can range from reasons and norms to discourses and social structures. Interpretation rather than simple measurement is therefore key (2007, p.364).

The causal analysis of positivists, on the other hand, is entirely dependent on the empirical observation of regular patterns and facts. Critical realism, however, 'emphasizes that causes always exist in open systems where multiple causal forces interact and counteract in complex ways and where individual causes cannot be isolated as in a laboratory.' Critical realism is also capable of recognizing that 'ontologically social causes' vary significantly from those causal powers studied in the natural sciences (Kurki, 2007, pp.365–6). This still leaves open the question of whether the realities of the social world are as 'real' as those of the natural world. Scientific (and critical) realism certainly answers in the affirmative.

Critical realism is not a theory of IR and does not claim to be, although at least one aim of Bhaskar's work, according to Chris Brown (2007, p.414), is to breathe new life into a materialist approach to social theory that was undermined by the radical idealism of the 1960s and which has yet to recover. The main aim of critical realism as discussed here, however, has been to rescue science from a simple equation with positivism and perhaps also, given its optimistic project of the 'emancipation of humanity', to rescue reality itself from the pessimism of the political realism dealt with in these last two chapters.

Conclusion

The shift from classical realism to structural realism marked a major shift not only in the conception of political realism as applied to the international sphere but in the discipline itself, particularly in the US, where IR flourished in the postwar period and became an 'American social science'. In Waltz's neorealist conception, the structure of the international system became everything, despite the difficulty of defining what either a system or a structure is except in the vaguest of terms (James, 1993, p. 124). In the course of conceptualizing this system, Waltz drew heavily on microeconomic theory in positing states as rational utility maximizers with pay-offs counted in relative power. This abstract mode of theorizing attracted numerous followers, making neorealism perhaps the most influential IR theory of the twentieth century. This is despite a period of decline after the Cold War when liberalism seemed to be in the ascendant and the phenomenon of globalization dominated so many intellectual debates. If we are to believe Mearsheimer's claim about realism's 'stunning comeback' in the wake of the fiasco of the war in Iraq, however, it may have a great deal of mileage left yet. Whether this will be at least partly because of a growth in the popularity of neoclassical realism, with its more expansive conception of relevant factors impacting on the international system, remains to be seen.

Neorealism also provided an attractive model for those who, in their droves, took the positivist turn in the postwar period and sought to align their research agendas with what was considered to be – and still is for many – a genuinely scientific approach to the study of international politics. Neorealism, however, is not the only mode of IR theory to adopt a positivist or behaviouralist approach. As noted earlier, neoliberalism, as well as some versions of constructivism, has found it equally attractive. Nor is positivism the only way in which a scientific mode of research can be pursued. We have seen that scientific/critical realism offers an alternative, but again it remains to be seen just how attractive it turns out to be. Positivism, at least in the US, is well entrenched, and the rewards in terms of publishing and research grants are likely to remain a major factor in shaping the trajectory of methodological approaches there for some time to come.

The study of IR outside the US is another matter. Neorealism and positivism have had far less impact, and in the latter half of the twentieth century IR gained a very different and diverse profile in the UK and elsewhere in the English-speaking world, as well as in key intellectual centres in Europe (see Wæver, 1998). Here it is also worth noting that another aspect of IR theory that has remained largely unchanged to date is the dominance of the 'West' in the production of theoretical work of any kind, as discussed in chapter 9.

The final word on political realism generally goes to the issue of ethics. Duncan Bell highlights a tendency to regard political realism as 'the antithesis of ethical speculation, not a species of it' (Bell, 2010, p. 2). Most of the figures associated with classical realism, however, deplored the amorality of the state of anarchy, regarding the violence it generates as a deeply tragic aspect of the human condition. Hobbes's work clearly sought to dispel anarchy so that people would be spared the nasty, brutish conditions inherent in the state of nature and enjoy the kind of social life that is only possible in a civil state with an essential moral framework enforced by a sovereign authority. But what seems to disappear with the advent of neorealism, along with a role for human nature, is a concern for ethics. This is not simply a result of the serious antipathy to moralizing in international politics that developed among realists in the twentieth century. Carr and Morgenthau were among the most vociferous critics of such moralizing, although there can be no doubting their commitment to morality as such. With neorealism, however, there is a distinct detachment from moral issues. Bell points out that Waltz actually celebrated the transition from 'realist thought', with its normative concerns, to 'realist theory', which was supposedly stripped of them (ibid.). As we have seen, this was complemented by the rise of positivist behaviouralism and its explicit orientation to a model of scientific objectivity that eschewed normative concerns. It is at this conjuncture that the discontinuities between the classical and structural variants of political realism in IR are most evident. But they remain united in their pessimistic and indeed tragic perspective on the consequences of anarchy.

QUESTIONS FOR REVISION

1 What are the key differences between classical and structural realism?
2 Is the firm dividing line between domestic and international politics drawn by structural realists tenable?
3 What lessons do structural realists draw from the behaviour of Russia under Putin vis-à-vis NATO?
4 On what grounds have structural realists opposed the Iraq War and the ideology that supported it?
5 Does the objection to moralizing on the part of realists generally mean that they repudiate ethics altogether?
6 How is neoclassical realism to be distinguished from both classical and structural realism?
7 What methodological issues were involved in the 'second great debate' in IR?
8 What sets critical realism apart from conventional political realism?

FURTHER READING

Brown, Michael Edward, Sean M. Lynne-Jones and Steven E. Miller (eds) (1995) *The Perils of Anarchy: Contemporary Realism and International Security*. Cambridge, MA: MIT Press.
Dyson, Tom (2010) *Neoclassical Realism and Defence Reform in Post-Cold War Europe*. Basingstoke: Palgrave Macmillan.
Hanami, Andrew K. (ed.) (2003) *Perspectives on Structural Realism*. Basingstoke: Palgrave Macmillan.
Joseph, Jonathan, and Colin Wight (2010) *Scientific Realism and International Relations*. Basingstoke: Palgrave Macmillan.
Resende-Santos, João (2007) *Neorealism, States and the Modern Mass Army*. New York: Cambridge University Press.

USEFUL WEBSITES

www.theory-talks.org/2011/06/theory-talk-40.html (interview with Kenneth Waltz)
www.youtube.com/watch?v=djV0n_k8pCs (public lecture by John Mearsheimer on structural realism on why China cannot rise peacefully)
http://plato.stanford.edu/entries/structural-realism/ (Stanford Encyclopaedia of Philosophy entry on 'Structural Realism')

http://criticalrealismblog.blogspot.com.au (website of the International Association of Critical Realism)

www.e-ir.info/2013/02/13/is-there-anything-new-in-neoclassical-realism/ (e-international relations article on 'Neoclassical Realism')

4

The Foundations of Liberal Thought

Liberal approaches to international relations acknowledge the tendency to conflict in human affairs but focus much more on the human capacity to cooperate – to create effective laws and institutions and to promote norms which moderate the behaviour of states in the sphere of international anarchy. It was noted earlier that 'liberalism' names one of a number of political ideologies, and that ideologies may be regarded as sets of ideas which both incorporate a view of the world as it is and how it ought to be from a particular normative standpoint and promote a plan of political action designed to bring about the desired state of affairs. In short, an ideology is a normative belief system oriented to political action. Liberalism is usually regarded as *progressive*, with progress defined in terms of certain key social and political goods. Individual human liberty, along with a notion of the essential equality of individuals, takes pride of place. It was also noted earlier that liberalism, as a distinctive body of thought concerning conflict and cooperation in the international sphere, rose to prominence in the aftermath of the First World War. Like realism, it did so on the basis of a longer tradition of thought. But, unlike realism, at least in its classical form, liberalism is associated closely with the phenomenon of modernity. This is linked in turn with a set of ideas which, in addition to the notion of progress, included distinctive approaches to the universality of the human condition and the inherent rationality of individual humans.

Liberal political thought is also deeply implicated in economic thought, but again there are significant variations on the theme of liberal political economy, ranging from moderate, left-of-centre social liberalism to quite extreme versions of economic neoliberalism on the political right. Here is where the terminology can get quite confusing, for 'neoliberalism' names both a body of liberal thought in IR which underwent a period of conscious renewal in the postwar period to meet the challenges of neorealism and the contemporary body of economic thought associated with radical free market ideas in the context of globalization. These will be discussed in chapter 5. The present chapter deals first with the rise of liberalism, examining key concepts ranging from ideas of natural law, freedom, tolerance, individualism, rule of law, and democracy, and their implications for the international sphere, to important elements of political economy, all of which have shaped the world as we know it. Once again, we focus on various influential figures whose ideas have provided the basis for contemporary liberal theory in its diverse forms.

The Origins of Liberal Thought

Of the modern, major political ideologies, which include conservatism, socialism, fascism, nationalism and, more recently, feminism, postcolonialism and ecologism, liberalism is said to be the earliest, originating in the seventeenth century following the collapse of feudalism and the emergence of capitalism in Western Europe. Liberal ideas were initially articulated by Protestants who challenged both secular and religious authorities in the name of individual rights, claiming that 'ordinary people were competent to judge the affairs of government as well as to choose their own path to salvation' (Eccleshall, 2003, p. 18). Against a background of Enlightenment thought and the challenges posed by the development of scientific thinking for traditional explanations of the world around us, as well as revolutions in France and America, liberal ideas made significant advances.

The British philosopher John Locke (1632–1704) is regarded as the founding figure of classical liberalism, although his ideas drew from earlier philosophers, including Hobbes. This may seem odd, given that Hobbes is portrayed in IR theory as the archetypal realist logically opposed to the essential principles of liberalism in international theory. Hobbes's political realism, however, did not preclude elements that are considered central to liberal thought. His emphasis on the inherent equality of individuals, as well as the idea of a social contract in which the consent of the governed to government itself is implicit, is very much part of the liberal tradition. Like Hobbes, Locke endorsed the idea of the social contract as a logical step towards creating a more ordered social and political life. But his view of the state of nature was largely benign, bearing little resemblance to the brutish state depicted by Hobbes.

Locke proposed that *natural* law gives rise to *natural* rights. These are antecedent to the laws established by a civil order under a sovereign authority, providing a framework for living together in peace even in the absence of a civil state. Locke's state of nature further depicts humans as enjoying equal entitlements to life, liberty and property: 'The state of nature has a law of nature to govern it, which obliges every one: and reason, which is that law, teaches all mankind . . . that being all equal and independent, no one ought to harm another in his life, health, liberty, or possessions' (Locke, 2008, p. 4). These rights are not lost with the advent of the civil state but, rather, should be protected. With respect to the exercise of political authority, Locke proposes that no legitimate government can violate these rights or exercise any form of absolute, arbitrary power, for this is tantamount to slavery (ibid.). Because these rights are given by nature to each and every individual human, they are also held to be inalienable and universal, holding good for all times and in all places. It is not difficult to see how this would translate into a theory of universal human rights in which civil and political rights hold pride of place.

As with philosophy generally, however, Locke's work was a response to the conditions of his time – hereditary privilege, the despotism of monarchy, religious intolerance and the example of revolutions against tyranny in America and France. Indeed, the American Declaration of Independence is deeply influenced by his ideas. These ideas are also infused with Locke's own Protestant Christianity. Interestingly, although he supported tolerance between different expressions of faith, his deep religiosity precluded acceptance of atheism and any secular foundation for political philosophical principles.

Not all early liberal thinkers held such views. David Hume (1711–1776), a key figure of the Scottish Enlightenment, offered a scathing critique of religious dogma of all kinds, dismissing miracles as absurdities and rejecting the idea that the universe is a product of divine, let alone benevolent, design. But Hume shared with Locke, and a number of other leading liberal thinkers, a strong commitment to empiricism – a belief that knowledge can be gained only through direct sensory experience rather than through reason or intuition. This formed a basis for the idea of scientific method discussed in chapter 1. It also provided a starting point for Hume's theorization of human nature and the state of nature which, like Locke's, was far removed from the Hobbesian vision. If it existed at all, Hume believed, the savage condition of the state of nature described by Hobbes could only have been fleeting. This did not mean that Hume rushed to endorse an equally unrealistic romantic vision of a lost 'golden age' of peace and love. His own view was much more circumspect.

> **Key Quote　David Hume on the State of Nature**
>
> [W]e may conclude that it is utterly impossible for men to remain any considerable time in that savage condition that precedes society, but that his very first state and situation may justly be esteemed social. . . . philosphers may, if they please, extend their reasoning to the supposed *state of nature*; provided they allow it to be a mere philosophical fiction, which never had, and never could have, any reality . . . not unlike that of the *golden age* which poets have invented; only with this difference, that the former is described as full of war, violence, and injustice; whereas the latter is painted . . . as the most charming and most peaceable condition that can possibly be imagined. (Hume, 2007, p. 198; original emphasis).

The Rise of Liberal Political Economy

Both Locke and Hume also devoted considerable attention to economic issues, but it was the moral philosopher Adam Smith (1723–1790), another major figure of the Scottish Enlightenment, who is regarded as the founding figure of political economy. Smith's ideas were initially developed as a critique of the doctrine known as mercantilism which accompanied the rise of capitalism in the seventeenth century. This doctrine was based on the assumption that there was a limited amount of wealth in the world, and that wealth accumulation by one state – preferably one's own – necessarily comes at the expense of others, making the one stronger and the others relatively weaker.

The ultimate form of national wealth consisted in accumulated reserves of precious metals – mainly gold and silver – and European states of the time took extraordinary measures to build and maintain their hoards. Mercantilism is in fact a form of economic nationalism concerned with how best to accumulate *national* wealth rather than just individual or corporate wealth. The accumulation of economic wealth – achieved primarily through balance-of-trade strategies whereby imports are restrained while exports expand – is not an end in itself but is directed towards the ultimate end of building state power, conceived primarily as military capacity. Mercantilism has therefore been seen as the logical ally of realist IR.

Mercantilism was also a powerful ally of colonialism, where the latter appropriated the resources of colonial possessions for the purpose of building up national wealth. The British East India Company, originally founded by Royal Charter in 1600, was particularly notorious in this respect, as was the abuse of its monopoly rights. Smith roundly criticized this company not only for its grossly adverse impact on the lives of colonized people but also for the fact that ordinary people consuming its goods in Britain were paying both for its extraordinary profits and for the abuses and mismanagement perpetrated under its monopoly privileges, which were supported by mercantilism (Smith, 2009, p. 372).

In opposition to mercantilism's rigid protectionist policies, Smith formulated and advocated free trade principles, incorporating assumptions about supply and demand in a competitive market through which everyone could gain greater wealth. This approach assumed, contrary to mercantilist ideas, that resources are virtually unbounded and that one country's gain does not necessarily come at the expense of another. The still popular idea that the earth can somehow yield limitless resources to increase wealth for everyone, however, has consequences for the environment, as we see in chapter 10.

Smith coined the phrase 'the invisible hand' to illustrate the consequences of competitive, self-interested individual actions in the market which, while intended by the individuals that performed them to promote their own interests, have a fortuitous outcome for the wider society.

Key Quote   Adam Smith and the Invisible Hand

[B]y directing that industry in such a manner as its produce may be of greatest value, [the individual] intends only his own gain, and he is in this . . . led by an invisible hand to promote an end which was never part of his intention. . . . By pursuing his own interest he frequently promotes that of the society . . . (2009, p. 28)

The role of government in private business was to be strictly limited, for no government should presume to know better than individuals how they should conduct their own affairs. Smith and other liberal thinkers of the period also gave rise to the idea of a 'natural economy' operating in a rational world of self-interested individuals. The idea persists to this day, when, in the US especially, it has become 'an unconscious presupposition of both elite and ordinary life' (Rossides, 1998, p. 113). It is important, however, to read these and other aspects of Smith's liberal ideas in the context of his broader message. Smith was opposed neither to government as such nor to a robust public sphere. His support for public infrastructure projects and appropriate government regulation, as well as an overriding concern for wider social goods such as health and education, brings him much closer to the social end of the liberal spectrum than one might at first suspect. Smith's endorsement of firm rules for the banking industry to constrain irresponsible behaviour also resonates strongly with contemporary calls for more robust regulation in the wake of the 2008 global financial crisis. Although the principles of banking, Smith says, may appear rather perplexing, banking practices are perfectly capable of being brought under strict rule. 'To depart upon any occasion from those rules, in consequence of some flattering expectations of extraordinary gain, is almost always extremely dangerous and frequently fatal to the banking company which attempts it' (2009, p. 447).

The liberal tradition of political economy was further developed by many other figures, including David Ricardo (1772–1823), best known for his theory of comparative advantage; Thomas Malthus (1766–1834), one of the first to warn of the problem of unchecked population growth outstripping the resources available to feed increasing numbers; and John Stuart Mill (1806–1873), who, although a robust defender of economic and political liberty, was very much a social liberal in his promotion of public social goods. Mill was also an early supporter of women's rights, opening his famous essay on the subjection of women with the statement that 'the principle which regulates the existing social relations between the two sexes – the legal subordination of one sex to the other – is wrong in itself, and now one of the chief hindrances to human improvement, and . . . ought to be replaced by a principle of perfect equality, admitting no power or privilege on the one side, nor disability on the other' (Mill, 1869, p. 1).

We discuss feminism in chapter 8, but here we may note that debates about the rights of women took place in a more general era of social and political reform in the nineteenth century which saw the rise of social movements concerned with progress in one sphere or another, including the abolition of child labour and slavery. These movements therefore addressed practices which had thrived under modern capitalism and which were defended by some liberals, but which were antithetical to the morality of other forms of liberal thought.

Free trade, however, remained the centrepiece of liberal economic thinking and was carried forward by, among others, Richard Cobden (1804–1865), a major figure in repealing the Corn Laws, which had imposed such high tariffs on cereals from outside the UK that it was impossible to import products produced much more cheaply abroad, even in times of food scarcity. Cobden also applied free trade principles to the international political order, which he contended was hampered in the pursuit of peace by balance of power politics which simply fuelled militarism, violence and despotism (Claeys, 2005, p. 382).

By the beginning of the twentieth century, a group of prominent liberal economists proposed that the projected economic costs of major warfare in Europe were so high as to make it unthinkable to any rational mind. A major figure in this group, Jan Bloch, produced a six-volume study on *The Future of War*, first published in 1898, which predicted 'with chilling accuracy the protracted and brutal character of any forthcoming war', as well as the intolerable financial burdens that would be placed on domestic economies, the international system of food supply and distribution, and international finance generally (Claeys, 2005, p. 292).

Liberalism and Evolutionary Theory

In the meantime, liberal ideas about social and political progress had been encouraged by the growth of scientific knowledge and its increasing ability to explain the natural world. New findings in biology became a source of speculation about social life, and the emergent theory of evolution was particularly influential. The key figure here of course is Charles Darwin (1809–1892), whose work on *The Origin of Species: Or the Preservation of Favoured Species in the Struggle for Life* was first published in 1859, although he drew on existing ideas about how species change and evolve. Herbert Spencer (1820–1903), author of the phrase 'the survival of the fittest', had earlier suggested that human progress was the outcome of evolutionary dynamics; the French naturalist Jean-Baptiste Lamarck (1744–1829) had worked on acquired characteristics; Thomas Malthus had written on the struggle for existence in terms of population dynamics; and several others had produced ideas of natural selection and sketches of evolutionary theory. But Darwin's work outstripped all others in both scope and substance. While drawing on Malthus's notion of the geometric powers of the increase of populations and other recently formulated ideas, Darwin spelt out the implications of the struggle to survive for all biological life. These were based, first, on the observation that many more individuals of any given species are born than can possibly survive. A struggle for existence ensues in which any being that varies in even the slightest manner so as to give it an advantage will have a better chance of surviving, 'and thus be *naturally selected*' (Darwin, 1985, p. 68; original emphasis).

While Darwin's line of reasoning in explanation of his theory of biological evolution was both logically sound and backed up by a mass of data, it gave rise to competing interpretations which were used in turn to support very different agendas. Modern scientific racism, for example, was extrapolated from Darwin's work, presenting a superficially plausible justification for elevating Caucasians generally to a position of *natural* superiority on an evolutionary scale which was then used to justify colonialism and slavery (Watson, 2005, p. 914). Similar lines of argument were produced to justify the *natural* subordination of women under patriarchal social and political arrangements. The idea of 'nature' thereby became assimilated to a species of biological determinism which aligned in turn with a strong form of social determinism. The implications for both racial stereotyping and gender relations became manifest in various forms of political conservatism, which included opposition to the extension of legal and political rights for women.

In political theory, other aspects of Darwin's ideas were used to back two different lines of argument, one essentially realist in its emphasis on the natural human propensity for violence and conflict, and the other more liberal in highlighting the human capacity for cooperation as well as competition. With respect to the former line of argument, Darwin's ideas were 'vulgarized and distorted', and 'militarists frequently invoked his name to back up their contention that conflict was not only "natural", but also an agent of evolution' (Claeys, 2005, p. 290). Darwin, however, placed at least as much emphasis on human sociability and intelligence, as well as the capacity for education and culture, to moderate behaviour (ibid., p. 292).

Herbert Spencer was, interestingly, strongly opposed to militarism and despaired of the tendency, evident in Europe at the beginning of the twentieth century, to the glorification of war. His scathing condemnation of this tendency was expressed as 'a recrudescence of barbaric ambitions, ideas and sentiments and an unceasing culture of blood-lust' (Spencer, 1902, p. 188). In domestic politics, however, Spencer promoted a rather extreme form of individualism, advocating minimal government intervention in the social sphere, especially in the alleviation of poverty. The idea that evolution was designed to weed out the least adaptable people and leave only the fittest became known as 'social Darwinism' (Watson, 2005, p. 885). This particular biological evolutionary view of a 'law of nature', however, was very different from the idea of 'natural law' developed by philosophers and legal theorists, as we see next.

From Natural Law to International Law

It has been suggested that international law and international politics 'cohabit the same conceptual space' and together comprise 'the rules and the reality of the international system' (Slaughter, 1995, p. 503). The concept of natural law provided the foundation for the development of ideas about what became known as the 'law of nations' that gave way in the twentieth century to the more contemporary usage 'international law', the importance of which has become a hallmark of liberal international thought. Natural law is understood as an unwritten standard of right action applicable at all times in all places, and natural law theory assumes that humans, as rational creatures, are *naturally* capable of understanding right conduct and acting accordingly, no matter where and when they are situated. In addition, proponents of natural law theory assumed that positive law, which consists of particular laws developed by different societies according to their circumstances, also derives its basic principles from natural law. In other words, although positive law may differ in content according to place and time, it nonetheless follows the moral prescriptions of a universal natural law.

Elements of natural law appeared in ancient Greek and, especially, in Roman thought, and were propounded by influential Christian thinkers such as St Thomas Aquinas in the medieval period. But it was not until the sixteenth and seventeenth centuries in Europe that it was more fully developed as an underpinning for international law. The emergence of international law at this stage was a product of the rise of the sovereign state and the legacy of both the Renaissance and the Reformation. But while this modern form of state asserted autonomy and independence, and was sovereign by virtue of the fact that no legal or other authority stood above it, it was also enmeshed in a world which increasingly required the regulation of state-to-state relations, not least because of the expansion of commerce and trade precipitated by the settlement of the Americas and the spread of European imperialism.

Another major factor was the experience of prolonged, violent warfare among European states, demonstrating the extremes to which religious intolerance could be taken. Case study 4.1 examines the Thirty Years' War, which was to have a significant impact on liberal ideas and the desire to provide legal foundations for international order.

Grotius's conception of international law as a kind of social order was repudiated by Hobbes and Spinoza, who, as we have seen, emphasized very different aspects of human nature and constructed their versions

Case Study 4.1 The Thirty Years' War and the Emergence of International Law

The Thirty Years' War was a series of battles and sub-wars, fought largely between Catholic and Protestant forces in Europe, beginning in 1618, when the Catholic heir to the Hapsburg Empire, Archduke Ferdinand II of Austria, attempted to impose Catholicism on Protestants within his domain. Initially, this provoked a revolt in Protestant Bohemia which eventually spread across the continent. Although a definite religious character was evident in all phases and sectors of the war, other dynamics were involved, as illustrated by the fact that Catholic France supported Protestant forces against the Hapsburgs. Europe at the end of thirty years was devastated. Up to a third of the population, especially in the German regions, had died as a direct result of the violence, through starvation, or as a result of the spread of diseases such as typhus, dysentery and bubonic plague, which thrived in conditions of war.

Hostilities were finally brought to an end as much by exhaustion as by diplomacy. The formal end came after four years of negotiations marked by the Peace of Westphalia, which consisted of the treaties of Münster and Osnabrück. The treaty negotiations involved numerous diplomats with extensive entourages. Taken together, the diplomatic processes and negotiations culminating in the Peace of Westphalia are sometimes described as Europe's first peace conference. At the very least, the treaties established a set of principles and practices that reflected recognition of the need for a legal framework through which different realms of authority could operate *and* cooperate. Among these are the principles of state sovereignty and non-interference – principles that remain a foundation of international order today. Westphalia also opened the way to secularism, now seen as an essential characteristic of the modern liberal state as well as of the state system.

Given the experience of religious intolerance and prolonged warfare in Europe, the idea of natural law, theoretically capable of transcending the authority of individual states and imposing obligations on them in their relations with each other, began to acquire considerable appeal. Indeed, natural law ideas implied that 'it was not in the nature of things that those relations should be merely anarchical; on the contrary they must be controlled by a higher law, not the mere creation of the will of any sovereign, but part of the order of nature to which even sovereigns were subjected' (Clapham, 2012, p. 17). Early natural law theories had been based partly on religious ideas (where God was equated with 'nature'), but these became increasingly secularized after 1648.

An early work in the field, *De jure belli ac pacis* (*On the Law of War and Peace*), first published in 1625 during the war, was produced by Hugo Grotius (1583–1645). It provided a secular foundation for the development of international law at a time when there was an urgent practical need for regulating relations between states. It was the spectacle produced by religious rivalries, in particular, that had led Grotius to appeal to natural law as a way of transcending difference. For Grotius, God is the author of natural law, which must therefore apply universally. But, once in place, it cannot be altered even by God: 'For although the power of

God is infinite, yet there are some things, to which it does not extend. . . . Thus two and two must make four, nor is it possible to be otherwise' (Grotius, 2004, p. 6). This leads to the conclusion that natural law exists even in the absence of a God to enforce it.

For Grotius, natural law was the necessary consequence of the fact that humans live together in societies and know, at a rational level, that they need rules for living together – rules that transcend the will of any particular individual. And because natural law operates independently of human will, it embraces all humans and not just Europeans.

Grotius's natural law was therefore underpinned by universal reason or rationality, directed in turn to the intrinsic good of maintaining peaceful social order. While different people or groups may have different ways of doing this, the overriding principle, derived as it is from natural law, remains constant. This further assumes that humans are inherently sociable creatures, so, when extended to the international sphere, this sphere also becomes a space of sociability, thereby providing the foundations of the eminently liberal idea of 'international society'.

The Peace of Westphalia is taken to mark the birth of the modern sovereign, the territorial state and a framework of international law sustaining the state system – and, beyond that, a 'society of states'. These had been developing well before 1648, and there was still a long way to go before the system was consolidated and then exported beyond Europe through colonization and decolonization. The year 1648 is therefore taken more as a symbolic marker than as the precise moment at which the modern state and the body of law surrounding it was born.

of the state of nature accordingly. Furthermore, for these thinkers, this state of nature did not vanish with the advent of the sovereign state but simply shifted to the realm of relations between states, where enmity, not friendship, was the dominant theme.

The challenge to Grotian principles of international order presented by Hobbes and Spinoza was taken up by Samuel Pufendorf (1632–1694), author of *De jure naturae et gentium* (*The Law of Nature and Nations*). His particular genius is said to 'grant the premises of the state of nature theory and turn them to his advantage' by arguing that the inclination to social life among otherwise selfish, petulant and malicious humans actually arises out of the self-preservation instinct (Murphy, 1982, p. 487). 'For such an animal to enjoy the good things . . . it is necessary that he be sociable . . . to join himself with others like him, and conduct himself towards them in such a way that, far from having any cause to do him harm, they may feel that there is reason to preserve and increase his good fortune.' It follows that there is a fundamental law of nature which gives rise to a sociable attitude among humans 'by which each is understood to be bound to the other by kindness, peace, and love, and therefore by mutual obligation' (Pufendorf, quoted ibid.). Even so, the peaceful state of nature is not so robust that it is immune to evil, and Pufendorf recognizes that human nature has many aspects, ranging from avarice and greed to altruism and love. Thus the state emerges as a form of cooperation among humans driven both by the problems engendered by the less attractive aspects of human nature and by a desire for friendship.

A notable point of difference between Grotius and Pufendorf is that, whereas Grotius believed that God was not needed for the enforcement of natural law once it was in place, Pufendorf required the absolute certainty of God's existence as both the source of law and the punitive agent. The fear of God's wrath and the prospect of eternal punishment is the ultimate sanction for breaking the law (Monahan, 2007, p. 90). This meets the Hobbesian objection that natural law is not 'real' law because it is not enforced by a sovereign power. God is the effective sovereign power, even though punishment lies in the next life.

Pufendorf wrote in the aftermath of the Thirty Years' War, and much of his thinking, like that of Grotius, was therefore concerned with the problem of religious difference. He came up with the idea, radical for its time, of effectively depoliticizing religion by arguing that it is a strictly private matter that does not, or ought not, intrude on the public sphere. In formulating this idea, he was well aware of the unscrupulous uses to which religious difference could be put: '[I]t is not absolutely necessary to maintain the public tranquility that all the subjects in general should be of one religion . . . [for] are not the true causes of disturbances in a state but the heats and animosities, ambition and perverted zeal of some, who make these differences their tools, wherewith they often raise disturbances in the state' (Pufendorf, 1698, p. 132). In this, Pufendorf not only highlights the mischief that can be made out of any kind of difference but gives expression to what was to become a cornerstone of liberal thought – toleration of difference.

Other highly influential figures contributed to the development of ideas about international law in the course of which the position of the sovereign state itself came to be more clearly defined. Figures such as the German philosopher Christian Wolff (1679–1754) and the Swiss diplomat and philosopher Emmerich de Vattel (1714–1767) are credited with developing the doctrinal foundations for international law as it exists today. While Hobbes had advanced the idea of the self-preservation of states as an absolute right, Wolff and Vattel incorporated this right into their concept of a *law-governed* international society of states (Orakhelashvili, 2011, p. 94). Wolff and Vattel did not abandon the notion that natural law underpinned this law-governed society, but there was nonetheless a discernible shift, especially in Vattel's work, from a focus on natural law to one on positive law – of law as actually created and practised by states – although for Vattel it was still to be guided by natural law principles. One of his most important contributions was to promote the idea that the state had a separate legal personality, separate even from its sovereign ruler and its body of citizens (Portmann, 2010, p. 38). This remains a cornerstone of international law today.

The Quest for Perpetual Peace

In the second half of the eighteenth century, philosophical arguments supporting schemes to secure lasting peace converged with those of economists. This was inspired partly by the extraordinary costs of military campaigns in the earlier part of the century which had had devastating economic effects. In France, a school of thought led by François Quesnay (1694–1774) known as the physiocrats (physiocracy = rule of nature) had emerged, based on the notion that the only source of *renewable* wealth was agriculture. The physiocrats also promoted trade liberalization and are closely associated with laissez-faire ideas of minimal government regulation. Both the physiocrats in France and Adam Smith in Britain, through delving into the mechanisms of agriculture, manufacturing and trade, are credited with laying the foundations for a new theory of international relations which held that humankind, rather than being divided by competing demands, was in fact united by reciprocal needs. Both government intervention in markets *and* warfare disrupted the 'natural order'. Left to its own devices, the natural economy 'would generate greater wealth and bring the various peoples of the world ever closer together' (Claeys, 2005, p. 286).

The British liberal thinker Jeremy Bentham (1748–1832), credited with coining the term 'international' itself, also contributed to the liberal notion that humankind was bound by a set of laws that would, once properly comprehended, lead to the permanent cessation of war. His *Plan for a Universal and Perpetual Peace*, first published in 1789, promoted not only reduced military spending and free trade but also the relinquishing of colonies, the disentanglement from alliances, and the development of democracy as key factors in promoting pacific relations (Kant, 2007). Bentham certainly attributed the tendency to war to regime type rather than to any feature of the international system itself. This clearly differentiates liberal from realist thought, for, although Bentham believed that war was driven by 'passions, ambitions, insolence and a desire for power', these were all much more likely to be found in autocratic systems than in democratic ones (Holsti, 1987, p. 27).

Many of these themes were taken up by Immanuel Kant (1724–1804), whose moral philosophy has had a profound impact on liberal international thought, from his attempts to establish an ethical basis for the conduct of politics within and between states to his schemes for an international federation of states to secure peace on a permanent basis. Kant's whole approach is founded on a conception of a universal moral principle which accords with a standard of rationality called the Categorical Imperative (CI). The CI is 'categorical' because it is absolute and cannot therefore be qualified; it is 'imperative' because it is commanded. For example, the moral injunction 'do not commit murder' is a categorical imperative. This is contrasted with a hypothetical imperative such as 'do not commit murder, otherwise you may expose yourself to a revenge attack'. The latter imperative is joined to a consequence – the possibility of a revenge attack. The CI is not – the act of murder is simply wrong *in itself*.

In moral or ethical theory, to judge an action as wrong in itself because it contravenes a general guiding principle is called a deontological approach (from the Greek *deon*, meaning obligation or duty). This contrasts with a moral theory that judges the rightness or wrongness of an action in terms of its consequences, which is called a consequentialist or teleological approach (from the Greek *telos*, meaning end or purpose). Kant articulated an overriding CI from which all other imperatives can be derived, including the essential moral requirement that we treat all other persons as having value in themselves, and never simply as objects whose value is judged by their usefulness to others. In other words, an individual must never be treated as a means to an end.

Key Quote Kant's Prime Categorical Imperative

Act only according to that maxim whereby you can at the same time will that it should become a universal law. (Kant, 1994, p. 30)

Because the CI is universal, treating all humans as sharing a common rationality and therefore a common moral order independent of local cultural or other circumstances, Kant is thoroughly cosmopolitan.

Similar formulations to the CI can be found in the work of Hobbes and Locke, as well as in the more contemporary work of the liberal theorist John Rawls, also a social contract theorist, whose theory of justice starts from the assumption that moral principles are a product of rational thought (see Pogge and Kosch, 2007, p. 189).

Important elements of Kant's ethical thought were directed more explicitly to the practical world of relations between states. Since at least the time of the Thirty Years' War, various schemes had been proposed for some kind of league or union of European states, all of which assumed that the only reliable basis on which peace could be secured in Europe, and ultimately the world, was through some kind of federal (or confederal – a weaker form of federation) system. Of these, Kant's essay on *Perpetual Peace: A Philosophical Sketch*, originally published in 1795, is the best known. In format, it emulates the structure of a peace treaty, beginning with six preliminary articles dealing, first, with the correct basis for peace treaties; second, with the integrity of each state's independence; third, with the (eventual) abolition of standing armies; fourth, with a prohibition on the creation of national debts through external affairs; fifth, with a prohibition on violent interference by one state in another's constitutional affairs; and, finally, with a prohibition on tactics that would otherwise undermine mutual confidence in a prospective state of peace, such as the violation of any surrender agreement following a cessation of hostilities, the use of assassins, or the fomenting of treasonous activities (Kant, 2007, pp. 7–12).

Next are three 'definite articles of a perpetual peace between states', prefaced by an observation that could have come straight from Hobbes. 'A state of peace among men who live side by side is not the natural state . . . which is rather to be described as a state of war; that although there is not perhaps always open hostility, yet there is a constant threatening that an outbreak may occur. Thus the state of peace must be *established*' (2007, p. 9). The following articles provide a foundation for this, each accompanied by the reasoning behind them, summarized briefly below.

1 *The civil constitution of each state shall be republican.* This is the only form of constitution which can be derived legitimately from an original contract and which reflects the basic principle of human beings as free members of society. Furthermore, it has the best prospect of attaining perpetual peace because it requires the consent of those whose lives and property are put at risk in the prosecution of war. This contrasts with a despotic state, where subjects are not citizens

with voting rights and where the ruler effectively owns the state and can use it as he pleases.

2 *The law of nations shall be founded on a federation of free states.* Here nations, as states, are like individuals in the state of nature. They are uncontrolled by an external law and may therefore injure those in close proximity. For the sake of their security, each state should therefore submit to the conditions similar to those of a civil society where individual rights are guaranteed. This would give rise to a federation of nations, but not a composite state as such.

3 *The law of world citizenship shall be limited to conditions of universal hospitality.* Hospitality here refers to the rights of strangers not to be treated as enemies when visiting foreign lands, although it is not the right to be a permanent visitor. Originally, however, no one had more right than another to inhabit any particular part of the earth's surface. More generally, this law allows for the gradual movement towards a constitution establishing world citizenship. (Ibid., pp. 13–22)

In the further elaboration of his plan, Kant proposed a 'league of peace', potentially a world federation of states – but not a world government, which, he believed, carries the potential for despotism. The federation is to be distinguished from a peace treaty, which terminates only one particular war, whereas a league of peace seeks to end all wars permanently. This league would not 'tend to any dominion over the power of the state but only to the maintenance and security of the freedom of the state itself and other states in league with it' (2007, p. 19). Furthermore, if such states are republics (i.e., democracies), which by their nature are inclined to peace, 'this gives a fulcrum to the federation with other states so that they may adhere to it and thus secure freedom under the idea of the law of nations. By more and more such associations, the federation may be gradually extended' (ibid., pp. 19–20).

One can see very clearly here the foundations of the 'democratic peace thesis', which rests on two key assumptions: first, that democratic states are inherently more peaceful in their relations with each other; and, second, that the greater the number of democratic states, the wider a 'zone of peace' becomes. Thus if all states were democratic in their internal political governance, the entire world would enjoy peaceful relations on a more or less permanent basis. This is supplemented by the 'spirit of commerce' which people pursue to obtain the goods they desire, and which is incompatible with war (2007, p. 39).

For Kant, the attainment of peace through these means amounts to a case of practice following correct theory. Kant contrasts this with the rejection of what is correct in theory by those who seek a legal right to make war. This, he says, simply justifies the use of force by unilateral maxims, and so it 'serves men right who are so inclined that they should destroy each other and thus find perpetual peace in the vast grave that swallows both the atrocities and their perpetrators' (2007, p. 20).

Kant acknowledged that his sketch of the conditions for perpetual peace represents an ideal which, although correct in theory – and therefore correct morally – is very far from being achieved in practice. For Kant, however, the ideal ought to be pursued and the effort may well bring about significant progress, if not the ideal state of affairs itself. As for the universal thrust of Kant's arguments, this was also in accord with the liberal ideas of his time. But, as with many other European philosophers of the period, his ideas were prompted by the conditions of the world immediately around him – a war-prone Europe – rather than through any personal experience of other parts of the world. Kant's cosmopolitan vision was therefore necessarily limited and confined to broad principles. In addition, and despite his denunciation of colonialism as incompatible with cosmopolitan morality, he exhibited many of the prejudices against non-Europeans common in his time, and so regarded Europe as possessing a very superior level of civilization (see Kant, 2003). Even so, Kant's broader deontological moral vision, sparse as it is in the details of how it applies in a world of states, counsels against 'reducing the good of humankind to the prejudices of a single community, collective or nation', as well as using other people as a means to one's own end (Donaldson, 1992, pp. 154–5).

Another important principle traceable to Kant is self-determination. In accord with the principle of universal rationality, individuals are autonomous agents, capable of directing themselves to act in accord with the universal moral principle embedded in the CI. Beyond this, the principle of self-determination finds practical expression in the notion that both individuals and groups (for individuals, after all, have a group life) are entitled to autonomy. For groups – such as 'the nation' – this justifies the autonomy to determine their own political and legal status of 'giving the law to oneself' (Kant, quoted in Williams, Hadfield and Rofe, 2012, p. 185). After the First World War, Woodrow Wilson became just one among many who supported the notion that 'a group of people need only consider themselves to be a definable national unit to claim the right to exist within a defensible state entity' (ibid.). This has become one of the most powerful political ideas of the modern period.

Liberalism and International Politics in Nineteenth-Century Europe

Kant's thought clearly presages the rise of liberal institutionalism and liberal internationalism, the first denoting the development of international institutions in concert with the development of international law, the second the conduct of republican, or what we would now generally call democratic, states in international politics and their relations with each other. Kant did not live to see the end of the Napoleonic wars in 1815 or the Congress of Vienna of 1814–15 (the subject of case study 4.2) which marked the beginning of a new period of international cooperation in Europe, at least for a time.

The unification of Germany had created the largest state in Europe, one with considerable industrial and economic strength and ambitions to expand within Europe as well to extend its imperial activities elsewhere. Other significant developments in this period were the continuing decline of the Ottoman, Russian and Austro-Hungarian empires while, on the other side of the Eurasian continent, Japan had begun to transform itself into a modern, industrialized and militarily proficient state at the same time that the Chinese Empire was crumbling under a variety of pressures.

More generally, the modern state in Europe had continued to transform, consolidating a range of functions from control of military forces to more sophisticated systems of fiscal control and bureaucratization generally. European states were also sustained by industrialization and the fruits of imperialism, while at an ideational level the spirit of progress, allied with the notion that Europe enjoyed the highest standard of civilization, was pervasive. Since the French Revolution the doctrine of popular sovereignty had also spread, reinforcing the idea of 'the nation' as the bearer of state sovereignty. It has been argued that these dynamics, in particular, transformed the social bases of international order, providing a powerful legacy for contemporary international relations (Buzan and Lawson, 2013).

The Hague Peace Conferences of 1899 and 1907, supported both by politicians (albeit sometimes for their particular political purposes) and by what we now call civil society groups (including various societies for the promotion of peace), produced a Convention for the Pacific Settlement of International Disputes, a Permanent Court of Arbitration, and conventions for the conduct of war which introduced important humanitarian principles for the treatment of civilians and prisoners

Case Study 4.2   The Congress of Vienna and the Concert of Europe

Despite achieving a measure of agreement among leading states or 'great powers' over principles of international order at Westphalia, Europe had continued to suffer episodic warfare. The Napoleonic wars (1803–15) represented a continuation of the violent conflict precipitated by the French Revolution of 1789, enmeshing most of Europe and resulting in the death of as many as 5 million people from direct violence or disease. It also had consequences for the European empires, sparking revolutions in Latin America which saw almost all of Central and South America break free of Spanish and Portuguese rule. And, despite Napoleon's defeat, ideas of democracy and nationalism emanating from post-revolutionary France were to take hold throughout the continent.

The Congress of Vienna, beginning in 1814, and subsequent diplomatic meetings, which came to be known as the Concert of Europe, were initiated by the 'quadruple alliance', comprised of Russia, Prussia, Austria and Great Britain, which sought to stabilize borders and establish a balance of power. This represented the first serious attempt to establish international order throughout Europe. The Concert had some successes, and, compared to the period of the Napoleonic wars, the continent achieved a fair measure of stability in the first part of the nineteenth century. The ideology of nationalism, however, was also on the rise throughout Europe, and independence and national unification movements were gathering momentum.

The outbreak of hostilities in the Crimea in 1853 – a tussle over influence in the Ottoman Empire – was between Russia on the one side and mainly France and Britain on the other. It effectively ended the Concert period and, although this did not trigger major warfare, created a new diplomatic configuration, particularly with respect to the Balkans, which contributed to the descent into total war early in the next century. Other minor wars around the continent contributed to the breakdown of the Concert system, while the emergence of unified states in Germany and Italy in the early 1870s also saw a reconfiguration of power relations. However, warfare in the latter part of the nineteenth century remained small scale.

For much of the nineteenth century, then, international relations were relatively peaceful, at least within the continent. While ever more sophisticated methods of violent coercion were used to maintain and extend imperial rule around the globe, warfare in Europe in the period after 1815 was limited in scope and purpose, a situation which liberal theory suggests arose directly from practical attempts at international cooperation among the great powers.

of war. A third convention was planned for 1915 but was overtaken by events.

A commentator of the period noted in 1909 that European states had at last begun to prepare the way 'for a systematic statement of the rules of international law' (Higgins, 2010, p. xiv). From a more recent perspective, one commentator has said that what was especially striking was not just the idea of arbitration but its institutionalization 'in the foundations of an improved world order' (Best, 1999, p. 628). However, he also suggests that, whether one is talking about national or international society, law may consolidate a social order that already exists, but it cannot impose a self-sustaining order where the will for it does not exist (ibid., p. 634). The events of 1914–18 demonstrated only too clearly that such a will was sorely lacking.

Conclusion

Liberal thought is not merely a product of modernity but one of its distinguishing features. The rise of science, technology and industrialization, the challenges to autocratic religious and political authorities, and the development of capitalism all went hand in hand with a set of ideas promoting new ways of thinking about the world as it emerged from the medieval period. Born at least partly out of the turmoil of the Protestant Reformation, liberal ideas of individualism, liberty, equality, tolerance and progress had a profound influence on all aspects of social, economic and political thought in both Europe and North America and the entity that we have come to know as 'the West' more generally. Liberalism also challenged influential pessimistic views of the 'state of nature', offering a much more positive account of pre-civic human sociability, which provided in turn the basis for a liberal conception of the modern, sovereign, civic state and its relations with other such entities. At an international level, liberal political economy promoted the doctrine of free trade. The notion that free trade would bring positive economic benefits to all was linked to the idea of promoting peaceful political relations through mutually beneficial trade relations.

In the field of legal thought, early ideas about natural law produced a philosophical foundation not only for a notion of rights but of 'right action', which accorded with a universal moral standard accessible to all humans by virtue of their shared rationality. This also provided the basis for the positive law of nations – 'positive' here referring to actual rules and regulations enacted by appropriate authorities and, in the international sphere, often taking the form of treaties. In domestic politics, liberal thought underscored the growth of democracy, a form of government in which ultimate sovereignty became vested in 'the people'. In the language of self-determination, however, sovereignty became attached to '*a* people' – understood as a singular entity forming 'a nation' and which very often demanded a state of its own.

Schemes for 'perpetual peace' based squarely on liberal assumptions and principles emerged in the late eighteenth century, and that of Kant, in particular, deeply influenced later thinking about international institutions and the measures required to discourage the resort to armed force to settle disputes. Kant's scheme also embodied the notion that the internal character of states was decisive for the way in which external affairs were conducted, thereby laying the foundations for the 'democratic peace thesis'. The relationship between the domestic and the international, in this and other respects, remains a key feature of liberal thought today, in contrast to neorealist assumptions, which are firmly committed to the divide between the domestic and the international, with state regime type or economic interdependence playing no role in determining international dynamics. However, the circumstances of Europe in the late nineteenth century, the decline of the old empires, the dynamics of new state formation and the rise of nationalism were to overwhelm all efforts to establish a basis for ongoing peace in Europe, although the Hague peace conferences did succeed in establishing some key institutions. These not only survive to this day but have been built on in order to produce a complex system of global governance underpinned by a substantial body of international law, all of which bears the legacy of four centuries of liberal thought.

QUESTIONS FOR REVISION

1 What features of liberal thought make it distinctly modern?
2 How does John Locke's conception of the state of nature compare with that of Hobbes?
3 What did Adam Smith mean by a 'natural economy'?
4 In what ways were Charles Darwin's ideas about evolution used for different political purposes?
5 How did theories of natural law influence the development of international law?
6 Does the 'state of peace' in Kantian thought occur naturally?
7 To what extent is the idea of self-determination a product of liberal thought?
8 Which specific developments in nineteenth-century European diplomacy may be read as practical expressions of liberal ideas?

FURTHER READING

Dilley, Stephen C. (ed.) (2013) *Darwinian Evolution and Classical Liberalism: Theories in Tension*. Lanham, MD: Lexington Books.

Hochstrasser, T. J., and P. Schröder (eds) (2003) *Early Modern Natural Law Theories: Contexts and Strategies in Early Enlightenment*. Dordrecht: Kluwer Academic.

Jahn, Beate (2013) *Liberal Internationalism: Theory, History, Practice*. Basingstoke: Palgrave Macmillan.

Razeen, Sally (1998) *Classical Liberalism and International Economic Order: Studies in Theory and Intellectual History*. London: Routledge.

Van der Haar, Edwin (2009) *Classical Liberalism and International Relations Theory*. New York: Palgrave Macmillan.

USEFUL WEBSITES

www.oxfordbibliographies.com/view/document/obo-9780199743292/obo-9780199743292-0060.xml (bibliographic site on 'Liberalism', with an introductory essay)

www.historyguide.org/intellect/lecture26a.html (lecture notes on 'Charles Darwin and Evolutionary Theory' from *The History Guide*)

www.peacepalacelibrary.nl/research-guides/ (Peace Palace Library site with research guides on various topics in international law)

www.princeton.edu/~achaney/tmve/wiki100k/docs/Classical_liberalism.html (Princeton University site on classical liberal economics)

http://www.youtube.com/watch?v=NpigLtQdEC0 (lecture by Ralph Raicoon classical liberalism)

5

Liberal International Theory

Liberal international thought appeared to have made some significant practical gains by the early twentieth century with the Hague peace conventions. But the events of 1914–18 demonstrated the inadequacy of the rudimentary international institutions that existed then to prevent or even mitigate the unprecedented scope and violence of world war. For liberal thinkers, this simply demonstrated the desperate need for institutions that could play a more effective role in the future. This was the spirit in which the architects of the post-First World War international order approached the task of crafting a major international institution in the form of the League of Nations. These developments also provided the initial context for the formal establishment of the IR discipline, the first university chair for which was established at Aberystwyth, University of Wales, in 1919 for the purpose of pursuing the systematic study of international politics with an emphasis on the causes of war and conditions for peace (Long and Wilson, 1995, p. 59). The Royal Institute of International Affairs (otherwise known as Chatham House) was founded in London in the same year.

The failure of the League of Nations to prevent the Second World War, and the display of aggressive power politics that led to the cataclysmic events of 1939–45, occasioned much criticism of liberal 'idealism', as we have seen in earlier chapters. Even so, a major effort was made to build more robust international institutions for the management of international conflict. This led to the establishment of the United Nations and international economic institutions, as well as the strengthening of international law. In addition, much more attention was paid to the idea of universal human rights, as reflected in the UN Charter. All this occurred in a period of rapid decolonization which saw the liberal principle of self-determination in the form of sovereign statehood come into its own as a right for colonized peoples, although the dynamics of the Cold War, problems of underdevelopment and continuing dependence on former colonial powers and aid donors severely compromised the formal sovereignty of many former colonial states.

The early twentieth century saw major developments in liberal economic theory. John Maynard Keynes (1883–1946) founded one of the most influential schools of thought in economics to date. Keynesian economics promoted free trade and other liberal goods but was also concerned with the importance of strategic government action in stimulating the economy through public spending at times of economic recession. Other challenges for liberal thought in the mid- to late postwar period were presented by realist thought, especially in its influential neorealist manifestation, which came to dominate the study of IR in the US in particular. This in turn saw the rise of neoliberal IR theory, highlighting phenomena such as increasing transnationalism, interdependence, the development of international regimes and the role of non-state actors.

Another boost to liberal ideas brought about by the end of the Cold War was the 'end of history' thesis, which rests on the assumption that the failure of communism in its heartland signalled the final triumph of both capitalism and liberal democracy as the only really viable economic and political systems. These developments stimulated fresh liberal theorizing on the 'democratic peace', although this was to be more or less hijacked under the administration of George W. Bush as a part of the justification for a war that actually contravened liberal principles. This prompted in turn the further elaboration of another liberal idea, 'soft power', which may be understood as a form of public diplomacy suited to a complex world which simply cannot be managed effectively through coercion or economic manipulation. Continuing problems of violence and suffering within states in the post-Cold War world have also seen the principle of non-intervention come under greater scrutiny, with notions of humanitarian intervention and 'the responsibility to protect' challenging the principle of inviolable state sovereignty. In addressing these and other issues introduced above, we shall see more clearly the tensions between realist and liberal visions of world order as they developed from the early twentieth century onwards.

Liberalism and the Rise of International Institutions

It has been suggested that liberals writing after world wars have usually been on the defensive about human nature but have nevertheless persisted in 'resisting the dark conclusions of the realists' (Smith, 1992, p. 203). But such resistance, while requiring a certain optimism about the possibilities for progress, has rarely entailed a starry-eyed view of natural human goodness on the part of serious liberal writers. Two of the most prominent liberals of the early twentieth century, Leonard Woolf and Norman Angell, adopted a much more circumspect view (Sylvest, 2004, p. 424). Angell's book *Human Nature and the Peace Problem*, first published in 1925, opened with a critique of the kind of idealism that overlooks the worst aspects of human nature. 'Man, after all, is a fighting animal, emotional, passionate, illogical' (quoted ibid.) But Angell went on to argue that this is precisely why it is so important that international institutions be created.

Key Quote   Human Nature and the Necessity of International Institutions

If mankind were 'naturally' peaceful, if men had not this innate pugnacity, were instinctively disposed to see the opponent's case, always ready to grant others the claims that they made themselves, we should not need these devices; no League of Nations would be necessary, nor, for that matter, would courts of law, legislatures, constitutions. (Angell, quoted ibid.)

While apparently echoing realist sentiments, the key difference is the liberal belief that humans are capable of positive *progress* in political and social spheres, which includes building cooperative relations in the interests of maintaining peaceful and productive relations in the international sphere. This was reflected, in the immediate aftermath of the First World War, in the establishment of a major institution of international governance in the form of the League of Nations.

By this stage, as one commentator notes, internationalists had developed a more systemic explanation of the role of anarchy in the tendency to interstate warfare and a better understanding of how the absolute sovereignty of states, on the one hand, and the lack of an arbiter between them, on the other, required an institutional ordering of international relations (Sylvest, 2005, 282–3). This was accompanied by a belief that the success of institution-building required the development of an 'international mind'. The first holder of the Woodrow Wilson Chair at Aberystwyth, Alfred Zimmern, held that this intellectual construct was essential to the progress of humanity, asserting further that the 'international mind and the logic of internationalism embodied in the League of Nations were not the products of some utopian musings but reflections of a deeper reality' (cited in Morefield, 2005, p. 128).

As we have seen, liberal internationalism had been developing over several centuries in European and American intellectual thought and came to incorporate a strong association with ideas of international law, which in turn required a form of institutionalization. Although an association between law and peace – rather than law and war – can be traced to the time of Grotius, more effort had actually been expended on refining the laws of war. It is said to have taken the massive shock of the First World War to achieve a major focus on the conditions for *peace* (Rich, 2002, p. 118). This led proponents of the League to draw on and further elaborate the moral dimensions of earlier liberal thought (Sylvest, 2005, p. 265). Thus liberal internationalism 'attempted to counter *realpolitik* through a moral, ethical approach to international order, with a concern to stress international justice and provide an alternative to power politics' (Pugh, 2012, p. 3).

Liberal internationalism came to be closely associated with the American wartime president Woodrow Wilson (1856–1924), a key figure in the founding of the League. He had led his country into war to 'make the world safe for democracy' and to establish peace 'upon the tested foundations of political liberty'. This cause, Wilson said, was not pursued for selfish ends: 'We desire no conquest, no domination . . . We are but one of the champions of the rights of mankind' (Wilson, 2005, p. 256). This statement made clear the centrality of democracy and liberal political institutions to his particular conception of liberal internationalism, otherwise known as 'Wilsonianism' or 'Wilsonian idealism'. This approach is frequently contrasted with a doctrine of isolationism which had sought to keep the US out of 'entangling alliances'. Wilson, however, argued that the League of Nations was a 'disentangling alliance' (Price, 2007, pp. 33–4).

Wilson went on to deliver to the US Congess his famous 'Fourteen Points' address, which opened with similar sentiments and then outlined a 'program for the world's peace', the final point of which declared that 'A general association of nations must be formed under specific covenants for the purpose of affording mutual guarantees of political independence and territorial integrity to great and small states alike' (Wilson, 2005, p. 263). The League was established by the 1919 Treaty of Versailles and incorporated many of Wilson's Fourteen Points, including provisions for more open diplomacy, international covenants, navigating in international waters, lowering trade barriers, armaments reduction, and the readjustment of various borders in Eastern Europe and in the now defunct Ottoman Empire (Lawson, 2012, pp. 63–4).

It has been observed that many of the provisions represented an attempt to implement key aspects of a century and a half of liberal thought and an assumption that the principal states involved would be liberal democracies. This reflected 'confidence in the power of reason and public opinion and the underlying harmony of interests; and rejection of the balance of power as the guiding principle of the new international order' (Richardson, 2001, p. 64). And so the time appeared right for the progressive march of history and civilization led by the morally upright nations of the world. These were, of course, the victors in the war who had proceeded to draw up the Versailles Treaty.

From the start, plans for the future of world peace, which included the establishment of the League of Nations, were beset by numerous problems. The US Senate reverted to an isolationist stance and could not be persuaded to sign up to League membership, most of the larger member states had other agendas to pursue, and virtually all lacked commitment to the League's basic principles. The terms of the treaty were particularly harsh with respect to Germany, creating conditions, later exacerbated by the Great Depression, which provided fertile ground for Adolf Hitler's rise to power, with all its devastating consequences.

Another important idea given expression in the postwar settlement was that of self-determination. Although it had not been a key element of liberal internationalism to that time, the practical circumstances of postwar Eastern Europe in particular brought it to the fore. Richardson (2001, p. 64) says that national self-determination was, *prima facie*, a case of 'liberalism from below', since it implied that crucial decisions were to emanate from the people as a whole. But, in practical terms, some people were considered more advanced than others, and so Czechs, for example, were elevated in status over Slovaks. This reflects what Richardson identifies as 'elitist liberalism' – the 'liberalism of the powerful' – and has been linked, incidentally, to notions such as 'soft power', which in turn derive from claims to social or cultural superiority (ibid., pp. 64–5).

Such notions of superiority certainly underpinned the failure to apply the doctrine of self-determination to colonized peoples at that time. It would take another world war before this essentially liberal idea was extended to all. The idea of national self-determination, however, rests not merely on liberal democratic principles of consent by the governed to those who govern them. The fusion of nation with state is quite obviously the ultimate expression of nationalism – an ideology which can be anything but liberal or democratic, as illustrated by the rise of Nazism and fascism in Germany and Italy in the interwar years. Nazism, or National Socialism, in particular was based on primordial notions of 'blood and soil' and the Teutonic racial superiority which underpinned Hitler's plan for world domination. Cassells (1996, p. 168) says of the latter that such plans were 'utopian at best, lunatic at worst'.

As the 1930s unfolded it was not Hitler's schemes that attracted the epithet 'utopian' but, rather, the efforts of liberals to build a peaceful world order institutionalized through an authoritative organ of global governance underpinned by international law. As we have seen earlier, twentieth-century classical realism appears to have arisen as a direct critique of liberal ideas, and writers such as E. H. Carr gave the terms 'utopian' and 'idealist' a very negative connotation. It has been said that the realist challenge to liberalism was to make clear that 'wishing for peace does not make it occur' and that the basic laws of human nature and behaviour had been ignored by liberals of the interwar period (Vasquez, 1998, p. 43). This view, however, is something of a caricature of liberal thought.

At a more practical level, wartime leaders such as Winston Churchill and Franklin D. Roosevelt, who were as close to the realities of power politics as anyone could be, certainly embraced the idea that international institutions were essential for international peace and security. Case study 5.1 shows the extent to which liberal principles are embodied in the UN.

Human Rights, Self-Determination and Humanitarian Intervention

The mission of the UN in several other key areas reflects a clear normative orientation and commitment to human rights, decolonization, and social and economic development. The Universal Declaration of Human Rights proclaimed in 1948 sets out high moral principles to be observed by member states regarding the treatment both of their own citizens and of others. Much of the concern with human rights at this time was generated by the atrocities committed during the war against ordinary civilians – men, women and children. These atrocities were due not so much to the absolute callousness of individuals in a time of war, although that is an all too common occurrence, but to the abuse of state power on a massive scale leading to genocide and mass murder.

Since that time, such abuses have continued, and not necessarily

Case Study 5.1   The United Nations and Liberal Institutionalism

Well before the Second World War ended, plans were under way for a new organization to replace the League, although a number of its provisions were retained as the blueprint for the United Nations organization emerged. The UN Charter itself reflects strong liberal principles, its preamble opening with the declaration:

We, the people of the United Nations [are] determined

- to save succeeding generations from the scourge of war, which twice in our lifetime has brought untold sorrow to mankind, and
- to reaffirm faith in fundamental human rights, in the dignity and worth of the human person, in the equal rights of men and women and of nations large and small, and
- to establish conditions under which justice and respect for the obligations arising from treaties and other sources of international law can be maintained, and
- to promote social progress and better standards of life in larger freedom.

(www.un.org/en/documents/charter/preamble.shtml)

This, and the remainder of the preamble, clearly reflects a liberal vision of the world both as it *could* be from a practical point of view and as it *should* be from a moral standpoint. The nineteen chapters of the Charter constitute an international treaty setting out the rights and obligations of member states in terms of the purposes detailed in the preamble. It has been argued, however, that the Charter, taken as a whole, is more than just a treaty or the constitution of the UN as an organization. For all intents and purposes, it is the constitution of the international community itself (Fassbender, 2009, p. 1).

Membership of the UN is open to all states, regardless of size or status or the character of their domestic political institutions, and all have equal voting power in the General Assembly. The powers of the latter, however, are rather circumscribed, and it is the Security Council, and especially its five permanent members, consisting of Britain, France, the US, Russia and China, which wields the most significant power.

The Security Council is sometimes regarded as reflecting a distinctly realist orientation to international politics because it embodies great power privilege in the most vital areas and its decisions are binding on the membership as a whole, going far beyond the remit of its predecessor in the old League, which had proved ineffectual in dealing with great power conflict. Certainly, this privilege is regarded as 'exceptional in the landscape of international organizations' (Krisch, 2010, p. 135). It can be argued, however, that the power awarded to the five permanent members does not compromise liberal principles but, rather, reflects the fact that liberal institutions can and do embody mechanisms attuned to the realities of power politics.

during times of war. The numbers of ordinary people killed in the USSR under Stalin, in China under Mao and in Cambodia under Pol Pot, whether by direct violence or starvation, dwarf the numbers killed in the death camps of Nazi Germany. One study of the phenomenon of 'democide' – the mass murder by governments of their own citizens – argues that 'power kills' and that, the more power a state has, the more likely it is to use it both against others *and* against its own people (Rummel, 1994, p. 2).

The argument is further extended to encompass the democratic peace thesis: 'Never has there been a war involving violent military action between stable democracies' and, although democracies have fought non-democracies, 'most wars are between non-democracies' (Rummel, 1994, p. 2). We return to the democratic peace thesis later, but here we should note the link posited between the domestic character of states (i.e., whether they are democratic or non-democratic) and their behaviour in both the domestic and international spheres. This is a central aspect of liberal international theory with clear links to Kant's endorsement of republics as 'prone to peace'.

Genocide and mass murder are also issues for humanitarian intervention, human security and the 'responsibility to protect' in the contemporary period. It has been argued that humanitarian intervention, which may entail an assault on state sovereignty, is morally justifiable in certain cases, and that the justification rests on a standard assumption of liberal political philosophy – that the major purpose of states and governments is, in the final analysis, to protect their people from harm (Tesón, 2001, p. 1). This accords with the idea of the 'responsibility to protect' (R2P) formulated by the UN, an essential pillar of which is that it is the primary responsibility of states to protect their own people from the crimes of genocide, crimes against humanity, war crimes and ethnic cleansing. At the same time, it is the responsibility of the international community to assist states to fulfil their obligations in these respects, as well as to 'take timely and decisive action, in accordance with the UN Charter, in cases where the state has manifestly failed to protect its population from one or more of the four crimes' (Bellamy, 2010, p. 143).

All this is consistent with the idea of 'human security', a concept also developed within the UN. Human security is often contrasted with a notion of state security in which the sovereign rights of the state as such take precedence over those of its individual citizens. Liberals, with their emphasis on individual rights, find the latter position morally untenable. When it comes to practical action, although an act of humanitarian intervention is not without risk to innocent human lives, a legitimate case can be made if it is clear that a failure to intervene would result in significantly greater harm. This provides the essential normative context for a legitimate act of intervention which appears to fit squarely with Kantian liberal philosophy (see Lawson, 2012, pp. 92–5).

One theorist maintains that, unless it has some specific interest, neither realist nor liberal theory offers a good explanation for why a state should intervene. Martha Finnemore argues that, from a realist perspective, states would intervene only if there was a prospect of gaining some geostrategic or political advantage. Neoliberals, on the other hand, might look to economic or trade advantages. Even liberals of a more classical or Kantian type 'might argue that these interventions have been motivated by an interest in promoting democracy and liberal values' (Finnemore, 2003, pp. 54–5). However, Kantian liberals concerned with morality would no doubt object to the discounting of liberal theory as being driven by *interests* rather than by a moral imperative. In any event, Finnemore (ibid.) argues that an explanation of the normative context for action is to be found in a constructivist approach rather than a liberal one. We discuss constructivism in chapter 7.

Another set of issues concerning human rights which has featured in international debates since the UN Charter was first drawn up arises from two different categories of rights: civil and political rights, on the one hand, and economic, social and cultural rights, on the other. The former are sometimes seen as possessing a typically Western liberal character unsuited to the cultural context of non-Western countries, where the emphasis is not on the individual as a bearer of rights but on groups or collectives. This is often accompanied by arguments that the very idea of what it is to be 'human' may vary from one cultural context to the next.

The latter view is sustained by a doctrine of cultural relativism allied to a doctrine of ethical relativism, both of which have worked to undermine the liberal conception of universalism essential to human rights and in which 'the human' stands as a singular essential concept, not one that varies according to context (see Lawson, 2006, p. 49). These contrasting positions are often labelled *cosmopolitan* (reflecting the universalism of liberal human rights approaches) as opposed to *communitarian* (reflecting the notion that moral standards arise only within specific cultural communities and cannot necessarily be applied outside of those communities).

The most vocal proponents of the communitarian view have come from a number of Middle Eastern and African countries and parts of

East Asia, especially China. It is no coincidence that the countries most dismissive of the liberal or cosmopolitan view of human rights are also authoritarian in their domestic politics. Some of these countries have also deployed the argument that economic, social and cultural rights are more important for poorer, underdeveloped countries than the right to vote. This stance is more likely to be articulated by those with left-wing authoritarian regimes. In contrast, right-wing authoritarianism is more likely to deploy the idea that the wealth of privileged classes will 'trickle down' to those below. The logic of this position, which accords with economic neoliberalism, is that, the wealthier the elite become, the more there will be to trickle down. This scenario, however, remains one in which the gap between rich and poor remains significant, while in the left-wing scenario it is supposed to close. It is interesting to note that, since China has shifted from left-wing authoritarianism to a version of capitalist authoritarianism, albeit under a party which still calls itself 'communist', the gap between rich (mainly urban) and poor (mainly rural) has indeed grown much wider (see Chu, 2013). We discuss the cosmopolitan/communitarian divide further in chapter 9.

An early division of opinion within the UN on the two different clusters of rights led to the development of separate covenants for each, and so in 1976 the International Covenant on Civil and Political Rights (ICCPR) and the International Covenant on Economic, Social and Cultural Rights (ICESCR) entered into force. The US has not ratified the latter, while China's position is the reverse, having ratified the ICESCR but not the ICCPR. Just to make the point that 'the West' is not a unified entity on all such matters, and that what the US does or does not do is not necessarily representative of this entity, the UK, Australia and Germany, among a number of other Western nations, have either ratified or acceded to both covenants. However problematic the politics involved, the covenants represent a significant attempt to advance the codification of human rights and to establish an international legal framework to support them.

Decolonization and problems of social and economic development in what was commonly called the 'Third World' – the latter consisting mainly of former colonies and characterized by relatively low standards of economic development – but is now usually referred to as the 'Global South' raised further issues for liberal international theory in the post-war period. Decolonization meant, first and foremost, the liberation of subject peoples from colonial rule. The form that liberation was to take in terms of 'self-determination', however, was to set up new states largely on the basis of pre-existing colonial boundaries. These often did not accord with the way in which 'peoples' were actually distributed across territories. The extent of self-determination which the UN endorsed extended only to liberating people within those boundaries, and minority groups which found themselves once again subjugated to another dominant group seemed to have no further right to self-determination (see Emerson, 1971).

For the former groups, secession proved extraordinarily difficult in the Cold War period, Bangladesh being the only country to break away successfully (from Pakistan) and achieve separate sovereign statehood. Since the end of the Cold War the incidence of secession has become much more common, thereby establishing a more robust practical manifestation of the right to self-determination and which therefore appears to fulfil certain liberal principles. However, as Griffiths and O' Callaghan (2002, p.83) observe, 'which groups get to enjoy self-determination and which do not remains in large part a function of violence and the visibility of particular political struggles.'

Neoliberalism in the Postwar Period

Even while liberal principles seemed to dominate the world of institution-building in the postwar period, realist approaches nonetheless gained a strong intellectual following. As we have seen, Morgenthau's classical realism was highly influential in the immediate postwar period, followed by the more streamlined but equally influential school of structural realism initiated by Waltz. A principal target of both classical and structural realism was liberal thought and its alleged utopianism. But, just as institution-building made a significant comeback in the 'real world' of international politics in the form of the UN and other international institutions, liberal theory also made a comeback in the world of ideas.

One important liberal argument which began developing from the late 1960s was that the structure of the international system, far from becoming solidified in the state-centric form depicted by realism, was actually becoming much more flexible, especially with the increasing permeability of state boundaries, which made any rigid distinction between the domestic and international spheres unsustainable. These ideas focused on the phenomena of transnationalism, multilateralism and the interdependence of states as well as the variety of actors – both state and non-state – that play a role in the international system. Because of this broad focus on a plurality of actors and complex interactions, this new approach was sometimes called 'pluralism' (Little, 1996, p.66).

Two liberal theorists writing in the early 1970s, Robert Keohane and Joseph Nye, while agreeing with realists that survival is the primary goal of states and that in the most adverse circumstances force is required to guarantee survival, argued that states pursue many other goals for which alternative tools of power and influence are far more appropriate, and many of these are to be found largely in the sphere of economics. Furthermore, shifts in the balance between military and economic power are generally accompanied by the increasing complexity and diversity of actors, issues and interactions. These developments, in turn, are accompanied by a broadening agenda for foreign policy resulting from an increased sensitivity to the domestic concerns of other states and increasing linkages between various issues (Keohane and Nye, 1973, p.162). The clear message of this form of neoliberalism is that international theory in the postwar world cannot be simplified to the extent envisaged by structural realism. Thus, whereas parsimony in theory is a virtue for structural realists, for liberals it is a handicap.

Two significant works by liberal theorists followed in the early 1980s – Stephen Krasner's edited collection on *International Regimes* (1983) and Robert Keohane's *After Hegemony: Cooperation and Discord in the World Political Economy* (1984). Krasner's preface reviews the development of liberal international theory from the early 1970s, which, he says, began with 'a concerted attack on state-centric realist approaches' and the introduction of perspectives 'suggesting the importance of transnational and transgovernmental actors in the international system'. This emphasized the point that the world was to be understood as increasingly complex and *interdependent* – a concept which challenges the realist 'billiard board' model of states in the international system. Further, while the formal trappings of sovereignty remained, 'states could no longer effectively exercise their power because they could no longer control international economic movements, at least not at acceptable costs' (Krasner, 1983, p.vii). This has become a central theme in certain analyses of globalization which emphasize the decline of the state as the major actor in world politics.

Krasner's work also highlights the extent to which international regimes have come to play a key role in structuring interactions in the international sphere. Defining regimes as 'sets of implicit or explicit principles, norms, rules, and decision-making procedures around which actor's expectations converge in a given area of international relations'

(1983, p.3), Krasner shows that these operate in a variety of spheres, including security, trade and finance, and, through the introduction and institutionalization of principles, norms and rules in these areas, operate to modify greatly the dynamics of anarchy and power politics.

Keohane's work further elaborates the theme of institutionalization and is directed explicitly against the realist assumption that world politics is akin to a state of war. If this is so, argues Keohane, then institutionalized cooperation based on shared purposes would not exist except as part of a larger struggle for power, and the diverse patterns of international agreement on issues such as trade, finance, health and telecommunications and other such matters simply would not exist. The fact that these do exist highlights the functions performed by international institutions (Keohane, 1984, p.7). But he also sounds a warning concerning 'excessively optimistic assumptions about the role of ideals in world politics'. The more sophisticated institutionalists, he says, do not expect that cooperation will always prevail, but interdependence nonetheless 'creates interests in cooperation' (ibid., p.8). Even with hegemonic decline, the patterns of cooperation already established were likely to persist, as long as states perceived their interests to be invested in them (ibid.). Krasner's work clearly emphasizes interests rather than values and so differentiates a utilitarian form of liberalism from a moral one. This also accords with the distinctively positivist style of much neoliberal theorizing, which has characterized the research programs of scholars in the US, in particular, in much the same way as it has influenced realist approaches.

Liberal Political Economy from Keynesianism to Neoliberalism

Some of the key economic institutions that evolved in the postwar period were influenced by ideas of liberal political economy developed in the earlier part of the century. As noted above, Keynes had founded a highly influential school of liberal economics which saw the emergence of new macroeconomic approaches. While promoting free trade and other liberal goods, these approaches also emphasized the important role of strategic government action, especially with respect to stimulating the economy through public spending during times of recession. His *General Theory of Employment, Interest and Money*, first published in 1936, provided a 'classic vindication of a mixed economy', in which the state assumes responsibility for investment and consumption while production is left to private enterprise (Eccleshall, 2003, p. 38). Keynes thus shifted away from the laissez-faire approach advocated by classical economics to a system of managed, regulated capitalism. Keynesian ideas, which represent a form of *social* economic liberalism, continued to be highly influential in the UK until at least the 1970s, as did the liberalism of President Franklin D. Roosevelt (1882–1945) in the US. His 'New Deal' measures, instituted in the wake of the Great Depression, saw government take on more social responsibilities as well as playing a greater role in regulation.

Roosevelt and Keynes were both influential in the building of the postwar international economic order which included such institutions as the International Monetary Fund (IMF), what is now known as the World Bank, and a precursor to the World Trade Organization (WTO), the General Agreement on Tariffs and Trade (the GATT). These had been planned at a meeting of allied nations at Bretton Woods in New Hampshire in 1944. Although participation was officially broad-based, US imperatives dominated, and the system that emerged reflected this (Lawson, 2012, p. 68). In general terms, the basic institutional framework produced in the early postwar period reflected the need for capitalist states to grapple with issues of both domestic and international stability, resulting in what John Ruggie terms the compromise of 'embedded liberalism' (Ruggie, 1982, p. 392–3). This offered an institutional framework through which capitalist countries could attempt to reconcile 'the efficiency of markets with the broader values of social community' (Ruggie, 2008, p. 2).

By the 1970s, however, there was a growing backlash against government regulation and intervention, triggered by events such as the disaster of the Vietnam War, the oil crisis, and the descent of industrial relations in the UK into a veritable quagmire (Jones, 2012, p. 1). The period which followed saw the rise of a conservative form of liberalism which flourished under Margaret Thatcher (UK prime minister from 1979 to 1990) and Ronald Reagan (US president from 1981 to 1989), in particular. This brand of economic 'neoliberalism' promoted the subordination of the social to the economic, with a minimalist role for governments in either sphere. The basic ideas behind this had been formulated by Friedrich von Hayek (1899–1992), who condemned almost any form of intervention as 'socialist'. Instead, Hayek promoted the idea of 'spontaneous order' as emerging *naturally* from unfettered social and economic forces, thereby producing the best possible equilibrium (Lawson, 2012, p. 128). He further condemned all attempts at central planning as futile: it was simply impossible for people to acquire sufficient knowledge to construct a coherent order and make rational decisions on behalf of everyone (Jones, 2012, p. 60). This actually reflects a very conservative view of human capabilities as limited when it comes to larger-scale planning. Following Hayek, the best-known figure in the post-1960s neoliberal thought was Milton Friedman (1912–2006), a powerful public intellectual in the US who also propounded ideas about winding back government to let economic forces find their 'natural' way (ibid., p. 201).

In accord with this style of thinking, Thatcher and Reagan both implemented programmes of privatization and deregulation aimed at reducing the power and role of government, not just in their own countries but worldwide. Under these influences, economists and policy-makers in the IMF, the World Bank and the WTO, as well as the EU, came to reflect the ascendancy of neoliberal ideology. The 1980s and 1990s are now notorious for 'structural adjustment' policies which included regimes of tax reform, liberalization, privatization, deregulation and property rights imposed on developing countries and summarized in the term 'Washington consensus' (Jones, 2012, p. 8). These two decades of 'reform', however, produced deepening inequalities between much of the developed and the developing world.

But the problems of neoliberalism cut deeper than this, and the developed world proved no less vulnerable in the longer run, as witnessed by the 2008 global financial crisis, which demonstrated only too clearly that unregulated markets are not self-correcting after all. George Soros, a prominent Hungarian-American businessman (albeit one with strong philanthropic credentials and liberal-left views on certain issues), is worth quoting at some length on this topic. Especially noteworthy are his observations on the attempted modelling of economic theory on the natural sciences.

Key Quote: George Soros and the Myth of the Self-Regulating Market

Economic theory has modeled itself on theoretical physics. It has sought to establish timelessly valid laws that govern economic behavior and can be used reversibly both to explain and to predict events. But instead of finding laws capable of being falsified through testing, economics has increasingly turned itself into an axiomatic discipline consisting of assumptions and mathematical deductions . . . Rational expectations theory and the efficient market hypothesis are products of this approach. Unfortunately they proved to be unsound. To be useful, the axioms must resemble reality. . . . rational expectations theory was pretty conclusively

> falsified by the crash of 2008 which caught most participants and most regula-
> tors unawares. The crash of 2008 also falsified the Efficient Market Hypothesis
> because it was generated by internal developments within the financial markets,
> not by external shocks, as the hypothesis postulates.
>
> The failure of these theories brings the entire edifice of economic theory into
> question. Can economic phenomena be predicted by universally valid laws? I
> contend that they can't be, because the phenomena studied have a fundamen-
> tally different structure from natural phenomena. The difference lies in the role of
> thinking. Economic phenomena have thinking participants, natural phenomena
> don't. The thinking of the participants introduces an element of uncertainty that
> is absent in natural phenomena. The uncertainty arises because the participants'
> thinking does not accurately represent reality . . . (Soros, 2010)

More than half a decade on, however, there is no sign that economic
neoliberalism is on the back foot. This has led one author to ask why,
given the obvious failures of neoliberalism that precipitated the crisis
of 2008 and its ongoing effects, neoliberalism seems to have emerged
stronger than ever (Crouch, 2011, pp. vii–viii). Part of the answer lies in
the fact that governments have colluded in supporting the corporate
world, as evidenced by massive bailouts of financial institutions followed by 'austerity measures'. This further suggests that neoliberalism is
devoted not nearly as much to free markets as the rhetoric suggests but,
rather, 'to the dominance of public life by the giant corporation'. The
latter has been accommodated, rather than resisted, by governments,
which also appear to accept the idea that these institutions are simply
'too big to fail' (ibid., pp. viii–ix).

One reason for the apparent lack of alternatives to contemporary
global capitalism, despite all its problems, may be attributed to the
notion that, with the collapse of capitalism's major contestant, communism, there was simply no serious competitor left. This was the message
proclaimed by one liberal commentator on world politics as the Cold
War was drawing to a close and the Soviet Union was on the brink of
collapse.

'The End of History', the Democratic Peace and Soft Power

The end of the Cold War, the failure of Soviet communism and the collapse of the bipolar world seemed to open the way for the fulfilment
of the liberal ideal of world order. And the idea that history had run
its course as far as the battle of ideologies was concerned emerged as a

dominant theme. This view was put forward most famously by Francis Fukuyama, even before communism was quite dead. In the summer of 1989, just before the fall of the Berlin Wall, Fukuyama published an essay entitled 'The End of History' in which he declared that historical progress, understood in terms of the quest for human freedom, had reached its final destination with the triumph of liberal democracy and capitalism over the illusory promises of communism, which now joined hereditary monarchy, fascism, and other autocratic forms of government that had been tried and found severely wanting.

Key Quote: Francis Fukuyama and the Triumph of the West

The triumph of the West . . . is evident first of all in the total exclusion of viable systematic alternatives to Western liberalism. . . . What we may be witnessing is not just the end of the Cold War, or the passing of a particular period in post-war history, but the end of history as such: that is, the end point of [humanity's] ideological development. (Fukuyama, 1989, p. 3)

Fukuyama acknowledged that modern democracies and capitalist economic systems were far from perfect, with problems of crime and social injustice still unresolved. Nonetheless, he argued that such ongoing problems simply reflected the incomplete realization of modern democracy's basic principles of liberty and equality rather than any real defects in the principles themselves. So, while other forms of government had fatal flaws that led to their eventual demise, liberal democracy was evidently free of serious internal contradictions. Fukuyama recognized, however, that neither violent nationalisms nor religious fundamentalisms had withered away with the end of the Cold War but were likely to remain a leading cause of conflict for some time to come in places that were still stuck firmly in history.

Fukuyama sought to locate his arguments within a framework provided by the German philosopher G. W. F. Hegel. Despite the fact that Hegel occupies an ambiguous position in liberalism (see Bellamy, 1987), his notions of history as progress leading to the emergence of rational political communities were congenial to liberal thought and well suited to Fukuyama's purpose. But, as Brown (1991, p. 86) points out, Fukuyama's weakest point lies in the assumption that there are 'grand stories actually written into the fabric of history', an assumption which can scarcely be taken for granted.

One 'grand story' with which Fukuyama's essay resonated was the American narrative of 'manifest destiny', with its inherent notion of cultural superiority. With its origins deep in the history of America's early settlement, and carried forward through such notions as Woodrow Wilson's mission to make the world safe for democracy, America's manifest destiny appeared to be fulfilled with the triumph in the great struggle against the 'evil empire' of the Soviet Union (see Stephanson, 2005). It also fed into the idea that the US was poised to assume global leadership for the foreseeable future, as reflected in the establishment of the conservative Project for the New American Century, founded in the Clinton era, which aimed, among other things, to promote 'America's unique role in preserving and extending an international order friendly to our security, our prosperity, and our principles' (Project for the New American Century, 1997). Among the signatories to the Statement of Principles were Jeb Bush, Dick Cheney, Donald Rumsfeld, Paul Wolfowitz – all closely associated with George W. Bush – and Francis Fukuyama himself. But, while the Project's mission may pass for some as a liberal vision of world order, it is more closely related to the brand of neoconservatism discussed in chapter 3.

The apparent triumph of liberal democracy as a form of government, however, did inspire more mainstream liberal thinking on the democratic peace thesis. As we have seen, the early foundations for this had been laid by Kant and propounded by Woodrow Wilson in the context of America's participation in the First World War. Just before the end of the Cold War, the liberal theorist Michael Doyle reopened the intellectual debate, inspired partly by some of Ronald Reagan's claims in the context of the Cold War but owing much to Kant's vision of liberal republicanism, which held that relations of peace tended to prevail among liberal democratic states. This finding not only 'offers the promise of a continuing peace among liberal states' but, as the number of liberal states increases, 'announces the possibility of global peace' (Doyle, 1986, p. 1156). Doyle argues further that 'Kantian republics' are capable of maintaining peace among themselves not just because they are cautious, but because they are also 'capable of appreciating the international rights of foreign republics . . . who are our moral equals' (ibid., p. 1162). The relations with non-republics, however, are quite different, as shown in case study 5.2.

Russett proposes that a better alternative to forced regime change is 'democracy by example and peaceful incentives' (2005, p. 406). This accords with Joseph Nye's well-known formulation of 'soft power', which holds that proof of power lies not in the possession of material resources as such but in the ability to shape the behaviour of other states. In a

Case Study 5.2　Democratic Peace, Democratic War and US Interventionism

The proposition that democracies are *no less* prone to going to war against non-democracies appears to have been borne out in the post-Cold War period. Defining exactly what 'going to war' means is not always straightforward, but for present purposes it is taken to mean armed interventions, examples of which include US or US-led interventions in Somalia, the Balkans, both Gulf wars (against Iraq) and Afghanistan. These join a long list of other interventions and incursions by the US in its post-Second World War history, illustrating the extent to which the world's most powerful democracy sees its international role in terms of armed activism.

The most controversial action in the early post-Cold War period was the war launched against Iraq in March 2003 by a US-led 'coalition of the willing', consisting of some thirty countries. These included the UK, led at the time by a rather bellicose Tony Blair. Australia, under a conservative government, also participated. Notable for their absence from the coalition were NATO alliance members Canada, Belgium, Norway, France and Germany (BBC, 2003a). It is also in relation to this particular war that the democratic peace thesis was invoked most clearly as a justification, although this came after the invasion.

Initially, the justification focused almost exclusively on the claim that Iraq possessed weapons of mass destruction and posed an imminent threat to the national security of the US, the UK and allies in the region. This appeared to be a largely 'realist' argument but, as we saw earlier, leading realists in the US were strongly opposed to US intervention, arguing instead for containment. The UN Security Council did not buy the argument either, and so the invasion of Iraq remains highly suspect in terms of international law.

After it was confirmed that Iraq did not possess weapons of mass destruction after all, justification for the invasion turned to other possible sources, and the democratic peace thesis provided a suitable theme – much to the discomfort of theorists who supported it. One author, noting George W. Bush's inclination to use democratic peace as an *ex post* justification of the invasion of Iraq, said that Bush's 'model of "fight them, beat them, and make them democratic" is irrevocably flawed as a basis for contemporary action', while, on a practical level, the conditions in Iraq were scarcely promising, 'even if the occupation had been more competent in its execution' (Russett, 2005, pp. 395–6).

Another defender of the democratic peace theory, writing well before the war in Iraq but with an eye to previous ill-judged interventions, acknowledges the problem of 'liberal imprudence' in attempting to impose democracy by force:

> Liberal republics see themselves as threatened by aggression from nonrepublics that are not constrained by representation. Even though wars often cost more than the economic return they generate, liberal republics also are prepared to protect and promote – sometimes forcibly – democracy, private property, and the rights of individuals overseas against nonrepublics, which, because they do not authentically represent the rights of individuals, have no

rights to noninterference. These wars may liberate oppressed individuals over-
seas; they also can generate enormous suffering. Preserving the legacy of the
liberal peace without succumbing to the legacy of liberal imprudence is both
a moral and strategic challenge. (Doyle, 1986, pp. 1162–3)

complex, interdependent world in which a multiplicity of actors and
forces operate and interact, the clear message is that the realist view of
power is simply too limited (Nye, 1990). The message, addressed largely
to an American audience, was that image mattered at least as much as
material power.

Nye later defined soft power as the ability to attract and persuade in
order to achieve one's purposes, as distinct from employing coercion or
manipulative economic tactics. He warned, however, that arrogance can
turn attraction to repulsion, the consequences of which are very significant for US influence and security. This message seemed all the more
important in the wake of 9/11 and the wars in Afghanistan and Iraq (Nye,
2004, p. x). A major concern at this stage was the extent to which anti-
Americanism was on the rise, with international opinion polls showing
that US foreign policy had had a decisively negative effect on popular
attitudes (ibid., p. 127). While America's military and economic power
remained superior to all others, certainly its soft power had declined
sharply.

The idea of 'soft power' is now widely recognized as a key element in
public diplomacy. It has more recently been supplemented by notions of
'smart power', developed in the post-Iraq War period when it appeared
that the Bush administration's national and security policy was *not*
smart. Rather, by provoking unprecedented resentment around the
world, it had in fact compromised the diplomatic and security interests
of the US. This was contrasted with the quality of leadership in a number
of other countries, including China, where much more sophisticated
instruments of power had proved effective in various issue areas (Wilson,
2008, p. 111). Even so, smart power involves an intelligent combination
of soft *and* hard power to advance an actor's strategic purposes (ibid.,
p. 115). This represents not a repudiation of realist premises but, rather,
a combination of realist and liberal perspectives in what its proponents
see as a more efficacious way forward for US foreign policy in the
contemporary period.

Conclusion

From the early twentieth century to the present day, liberal international theory has attempted to make sense of, and offer prescriptions for, a wide-ranging set of issues in world politics. From an initial concern with the causes of major warfare and the conditions for peaceful interstate relations, the agenda for this body of theory has expanded to include issues of human rights, humanitarian intervention and the responsibility to protect, together with a reconceptualization of sovereignty and security as ultimately concerned with individual people and their basic rights. At the centre of these considerations is the importance of effective international institutions in providing for structured interaction within a framework of international law. These institutions are essential for managing what liberals acknowledge to be an anarchic international sphere, but which need not lapse into an unbridled war of each against all – provided that there is sufficient commitment to those institutions. In formulating these arguments, liberals reject balance of power mechanisms along with realist assumptions that norms and values play little or no part in maintaining international order.

Classic liberal ideas, derived from Kant in particular, provided the basis for theory and practice in the building of international institutions, for underpinning the democratic peace thesis, and for promoting the notion that vigorous trading relations among countries inhibit the tendency to deploy violence as a foreign policy tool. These three key constraints on war, often described as the Kantian 'tripod for peace', are seen by liberals as diminishing the force of realist arguments concerning the sphere of anarchy and the free play it gives to aggressive power politics (see Russett, Oneal and Davis, 1998, 441–67). At the same time, key liberal thinkers have reformulated ideas about power in the international sphere, offering perspectives on the efficacy of 'soft power'.

Liberal theory is also deeply implicated in issues of political economy, some of which have been touched on in this chapter. It is in this field that we can observe some very divergent views, from those of social liberals such as John Maynard Keynes in the earlier part of the twentieth century to the neoliberal ascendancy of more recent times, which, despite the global financial crisis of 2008 and its ongoing effects, shows little sign of being displaced. What this highlights, among other things, is the great variety of ideas and positions within liberal thought which, like those of all the schools of theory discussed in this book, are difficult to pin down to a single set of principles free of tensions and contradictions.

The discussion has also highlighted the fact that ideas about expanding the 'zone of peace' and concepts of humanitarian intervention can also be used to justify aggressive military intervention. This point resonates with the observation of E. H. Carr that moralism often serves as a rationalization and a cloak for purely self-interested actions. Liberal supporters of the democratic peace thesis would agree. It is not difficult to see that ethical behaviour in international affairs is a very different thing from a cynical and instrumental moralism, which is why particular care needs to be taken in analysing claims made under the rubric of morality.

QUESTIONS FOR REVISION

1 How accurate is the realist claim that liberals are simply utopian in investing their hopes in international institutions?
2 In what sense did Woodrow Wilson's approach to internationalism challenge US isolationism?
3 How does the doctrine of self-determination reflect liberal views?
4 Does the structure and power of the UN Security Council reflect realist rather than liberal assumptions?
5 What is entailed in the democratic peace thesis?
6 What did Fukuyama mean by 'the end of history'?
7 What are the basic characteristics of cosmopolitan thought?
8 What is meant by the term 'soft power'?

FURTHER READING

Friedman, Rebekka, Kevork Oskanian and Ramon Pacheco Pardo (eds) (2013) *After Liberalism? The Future of Liberalism in International Relations.* Basingstoke: Palgrave Macmillan.

Gismondi, Mark D. (2007) *Ethics, Liberalism and Realism in International Relations.* Abingdon: Routledge.

Grayson, Richard S. (2001) *Liberals, International Relations and Appeasement: The Liberal Party, 1919–1939.* Abingdon: Routledge.

Parmar, Inderjeet, and Michael Cox (eds) (2010) *Soft Power and US Foreign Policy: Theoretical, Historical and Contemporary Perspectives.* Abingdon: Routledge.

Russett, Bruce (1993) *Grasping the Democratic Peace: Principles for a Post-Cold War World.* Princeton, NJ: Princeton University Press.

USEFUL WEBSITES

www.e-ir.info/2010/06/09/how-convincing-is-e-h-carr's-critique-of-utopianism/ (E-International Relations website on Carr's critique of utopianism)

http://hawaii.edu/powerkills/DP.IS_WHAT.HTM (R. J. Rummell's website on democratic peace)

https://www.opendemocracy.net/democracy-fukuyama/revisited_3496.jsp (Open Democracy website, with reflections by Francis Fukuyama, 'After the End of History')

www.hrw.org/home (Human Rights Watch website)

www.youtube.com/watch?v=s7IwHLmE7gg (short lecture by Mark Harvey on varieties of liberalism)

6

Marxism, Critical Theory and World-Systems Theory

Since the publication in 1848 of *The Communist Manifesto*, by Karl Marx (1818–1883) and his colleague Friedrich Engels (1820–1895), the influence of Marxism in both intellectual and practical spheres has been profound. There is not a single discipline in the humanities and social sciences that has not been inspired by Marxist thought, either in positive support of its precepts or as a negative critique of them. At the same time, the impact of Marxist thought – or interpretations of Marxist thought by others – on twentieth-century world history is immeasurable, from the former USSR and Eastern Europe to China and many parts of what we now call the Global South. In many of these places, however, Marxism was used as a basis for instituting repressive authoritarian regimes which Marx himself would have found repugnant. Marx once famously declared that he was not a Marxist, and if he had lived to see how his ideas were deployed in the twentieth century he would surely have distanced himself even further. In the event, the clash of ideologies between the oppressive versions of communism underpinning the regimes of the Soviet Union and its allies, on the one hand, and those which aligned themselves with the democratic West, on the other, constituted the principal engine which drove the Cold War.

Moderate forms of non-revolutionary socialism incorporating democratic principles had been developed by other theorists from the early nineteenth century, especially in France, where the early use of the word 'socialism', emphasizing the social dimensions of human life, had been used in contrast to the 'individualism' promoted by liberals. 'Communism' relates to 'community' and things held 'in common', which also contrasts with individualism. Some speculative political thought along these lines drew inspiration from the long-distance voyages made by Europeans from the late fifteenth century in which encounters with 'primitive' societies with strongly communal characteristics, and apparently lacking notions of private property, provoked critical comparisons with the 'corrupt civilization' of Europe. As we saw earlier, Rousseau believed that European civilization represented the descent of human society from an earlier, relatively benign state of existence, and his emphasis on equality provided a foundation for later socialist and communist thought (Hobsbawm, 2011, pp. 19, 22).

This chapter examines, first, elements of Marxist thought which, although not providing an explicit theory of international relations, speak directly to issues in political, social and economic relations at a global level, and which certainly provide insights on the phenomenon of globalization. Marxist thought incorporates a critique of capitalism in general and liberal political economy in particular which remains relevant in the present period. We then examine two schools of thought which come under the broad rubric of critical theory and which carry forward some key principles of Marxist thought, namely Gramscian and Frankfurt School critical theory. Among the main ideas to be discussed in relation to critical theory are hegemony and the naturalization of power, the limitations of 'problem-solving' theory, and the fact that theorizing is itself a practice embedded in social relations and does not stand apart from it. Frankfurt School theory in particular also provides a defence of modernity and cosmopolitanism and places special emphasis on the project of human emancipation, although this is a theme underpinning all Marxist and post-Marxist approaches. Another field influenced by Marxist thought is World-Systems Theory, which has in turn been highly influential in the field of development studies, with implications for North–South relations. In adopting a macro-historical approach, World-Systems Theory also deploys the methods of historical sociology, a growing field of interest in contemporary IR which provides a macro-historical perspective on the development of the modern world across its economic, social and political dimensions.

Marx and the Emergence of Marxism

The *Manifesto of the Communist Party* stands as the best-known and probably most widely read work in the Marxist canon. It was prepared for presentation at the second congress of the Communist League in London in 1847 and outlines a political programme based on a general account of society and history and incorporating a distinctive critique of capitalism (Suchting, 1983, p. 55). After the preamble, the *Manifesto*'s opening line is the famous, resounding claim that 'The history of all hitherto existing society is the history of class struggles.' It goes on to sketch, first, the historical nature of social hierarchy and its relations of oppression and then the extent to which the contemporary period has simplified class antagonism into 'two great hostile camps', namely, 'bourgeoisie and pro-letariat', with the former imposing control over the latter. The *Manifesto* also sketches the extent to which the interests of the bourgeoisie have effectively driven a process of capitalist globalization through exploration and colonization (although the term 'globalization' was not then used). Reproduced below are the key sections addressing these matters, which are of particular interest to IR theory and international political economy.

Key Quote   The Bourgeoisie and the World Market

The discovery of America, the rounding of the Cape, opened up fresh ground for the rising bourgeoisie. The East-Indian and Chinese markets, the colonisation of America, trade with the colonies, the increase in the means of exchange and in commodities generally, gave to commerce, to navigation, to industry, an impulse never before known . . ..

Modern industry has established the world market, for which the discovery of America paved the way. . . . [I]n the same proportion the bourgeoisie developed, increased its capital, and pushed into the background every class handed down from the Middle Ages . . ..

The bourgeoisie . . . has left remaining no other nexus between man and man than naked self-interest, than callous 'cash payment' . . .. It has resolved personal worth into exchange value [and] . . . set up that single, unconscionable freedom – Free Trade. In one word, for exploitation, veiled by religious and political illusions, it has substituted naked, shameless, direct, brutal exploitation . . ..

The need of a constantly expanding market for its products chases the bour-geoisie over the entire surface of the globe. It must nestle everywhere, settle everywhere, establish connexions everywhere.

The bourgeoisie has through its exploitation of the world market given a cos-mopolitan character to production and consumption in every country. . . .

The bourgeoisie, by the rapid improvement of all instruments of production, by the immensely facilitated means of communication, draws all, even the most bar-barian, nations into civilisation. . . . It compels all nations, on pain of extinction, to adopt the bourgeois mode of production; it compels them to introduce what it calls civilisation into their midst, i.e., to become bourgeois themselves. In one word, it creates a world after its own image. (Marx and Engels, 1969, pp.15–16)

There is of course much more to the *Manifesto*, including a critique of reformist evolutionary socialism and, finally, a call for the revolution-ary overthrow of the bourgeoisie by the proletariat. Although it is a mistranslation of the original German conclusion, the popular saying 'Workers of the world unite. You have nothing to lose but your chains!' captures the spirit and meaning of the *Manifesto*'s final message.

Other key aspects of Marx's thought are his materialist conception of history, otherwise known as historical materialism, and the notion of false consciousness. Marx had a distinct notion of 'reality', based on the *material* conditions of life as they pertained to the mode of production in capitalist society. Lenin, whose work on imperialism we examine shortly, further elaborated a materialist view in realist language, asserting that humanity in general possesses an 'instinctive, unconscious materialist standpoint' which holds 'the external world as existing independently of our minds' (quoted in Acton, 1972, p.9).

Historical materialism also proposes that economic forces provide the material basis on which all other social and political institutions, and the ideas which support them, are based. Here it is important to note that, because his work dealt with material realities, as did the natural sciences, Marx believed that it offered a truly scientific way of studying human society and its history. He was therefore a realist in one sense of the word. But, unlike the political realists discussed earlier, he believed strongly in development and progress. Marx set out some of the central ideas in his preface to *Contribution to the Critique of Political Economy*, which includes a seminal statement on the relationship between materiality and social existence and its impact on human consciousness.

Key Quote   The Social Production of Existence

In the social production of their existence, men inevitably enter into definite relations, which are independent of their will, namely relations of production appropriate to a given stage in the development of their material forces of production. The totality of these relations of production constitutes the economic structure of society, the real foundation, on which arises a legal and political superstructure and to which correspond definite forms of social consciousness. The mode of production of material life conditions the general process of social, political and intellectual life. *It is not the consciousness of men that determines their existence, but their social existence that determines their consciousness.* (Marx, 1950; emphasis added)

In accordance with the view that social existence determines consciousness (and not vice versa), the extent to which the material realities of existence become enveloped within a complex of beliefs about the superstructure are understood in Marxist thought as a form of 'false consciousness'. Marx appropriated the word 'ideology' to describe this phenomenon (Cassells, 1996, pp.2–3), although, as we have seen, it has other applications. A similar notion of 'hegemony' at the ideational, as distinct from the material, level was to be developed more fully in Gramscian theory, which we consider shortly.

From Marxism to Leninism and Maoism

Marx urged action in pursuit of a new 'socialized humanity'. He was not content to join with philosophers who had so far merely '*interpreted* the world in various ways'. 'The point is', he said, 'to *change* it' (quoted in Simon, 1994, p. 101). In this notion he was joined by other prominent thinkers and activists, including Rosa Luxemburg (1871–1919), who contributed much both to the intellectual development of Marxism and its internationalist elements and to the revolutionary movement in Europe. She was to become a severe critic of the emergent authoritarian and centralist leanings of communism as it was developing in Russia, initially under Vladimir Ilyich Lenin (1870–1924), and which, under Joseph Stalin (1878–1953), turned into the very antithesis of her own strong pro-democratic emancipatory stance. Our concern here, however, is restricted to Lenin's contribution to the critique of imperialism, which, in addition to the internationalist dimensions of his thought, has direct relevance to IR theory.

Marx had identified imperialism as a major force in world politics, and he certainly anticipated what we now call globalization in the context of his critique of capitalism. But it was Lenin who provided a more extensive assessment of imperialism as an extension of capitalism and provided a basis for later critical studies in development, underdevelopment, core–periphery relations and dependency theory, all of which are key issues in World-Systems Theory. In addition, Lenin provided an explanation for the kind of large-scale total war which had emerged in early twentieth-century Europe and which he saw as a logical outcome of the capitalist system. In a preface to *Imperialism: The Highest Stage of Capitalism*, Lenin sought to provide 'a *general picture* of the world capitalist system in its international relationships at the beginning of the twentieth century – on the eve of the first world imperialist war' (Lenin, 2010, p. ii).

Key Quote   Lenin on Imperialism and the World Capitalist System

The enormous dimensions of finance capital concentrated in a few hands and creating an extraordinarily dense and widespread network of relationships and connections which subordinates not only the small and medium, but also the very small capitalists and small masters, on the one hand, and the increasingly intense struggle waged against other national state groups of financiers for the division of the world and domination over other countries, on the other hand, cause the

> propertied classes to go over entirely to the side of imperialism. 'General' enthu-
> siasm over the prospects of imperialism, furious defence of it and painting it in
> the brightest colours – such are the signs of the times. Imperialist ideology also
> penetrates the working class. (2010, pp. 146–7)

From Lenin's critique of imperialism, which undoubtedly resonates today with criticisms of neo-imperialism and global capitalism, we turn to the fate of Marxism in the thought of the Chinese revolutionary leader Mao Zedong (1893–1976). This is another complex story at the base of which is the issue, identified by Arif Dirlik (2005, p. 7), of 'how a radical ideological tradition that emerged first in Europe ... evolved in a different historical and cultural setting'. Dirlik further observes that some may reject the idea that what Mao – and other Chinese intellectuals – developed was not *really* Marxist, because he failed to grasp the essential principles of an alien European system of thought, or simply because he was not genuinely committed to Marxist ideas and/or used them inappropriately. However, Dirlik argues that a more appropriate intellectual approach is to engage Chinese Marxist intellectual thought in its own terms (ibid.). This involves accepting that what Mao and his colleagues performed was a 'vernacularization of Marxism' in an effort to render it relevant to the Chinese context (ibid., p. 96).

Case study 6.1, on the Maoist rendering of Marxism in China, provides an insight into how far Marx's ideas were 'vernacularized'. Alternatively, it can be argued that the Maoist revolution moved away from basic Marxist principles and became simply another form of elite dictatorship.

In both China and the USSR, the commitment to revolutionary communism and the concentration of power in the hands of an unaccountable elite controlled by a single charismatic leader turned both states into dictatorships and created the conditions for the abuse of state power on a massive scale, as described previously. Although they shared much in common, the relationship between the two countries was never more than cordial at best.

From revolutionary practice we move next to the first of two streams of critical intellectual thought which emerged in Europe. Both are 'post-Marxist' in the sense that each represents a refinement of certain aspects of Marxist thought while also moving away from certain of its assumptions.

Case Study 6.1   Revolution in China

Mao established the People's Republic of China in 1949 after the revolutionary defeat of the Nationalist Party, which retreated to Taiwan. Mao subscribed to the necessity of revolution, although in China the driving force would be the rural peasantry rather than an urban proletariat. In response to those nervous of the potential violence, Mao famously declared that 'A revolution is not a dinner party . . . A revolution is an insurrection, an act of violence by which one class overthrows the power of another' (Mao, 1972, p. 11), and, further, that 'power grows out of the barrel of a gun' (ibid., p. 60). This assertion sits well with realism.

For practical inspiration, Mao looked to Leninist practice in the USSR, where it was believed that an elitist party was the only instrument through which the old order could be destroyed and a new one ushered in. At the same time, however, the party elite would embody 'the will of the masses', whose true interests they would represent (Cohen, 1965, p. 165). Two particularly disastrous policies were implemented by the Chinese Communist Party under Mao's leadership.

The first was the 'Great Leap Forward', which was meant to revolutionize agricultural and industrial production in China through a massive, rapid transformation of existing practices. A recent study estimates that as many as 45 million people died between 1958 and 1962 as a direct result of the policy – almost three times the official estimates (Dikötter, 2010, p. xii).

This episode was followed by the Great Proletarian Cultural Revolution (1966–76), which was officially designed to consolidate the revolutionary political and economic changes in China. 'Culture' was defined by Lin Biao, a leading spokesperson for this ideational revolution, as encompassing 'ideology, social consciousness, world outlook, customs, habits, political viewpoints, legal viewpoints, artistic viewpoints, motion pictures and drama, sculpture, literature, the educational system, etc.', making it a revolution 'in the sphere of social consciousness' (Lin, 1996, p. 12).

China's Cultural Revolution was to create a 'new man' to carry forward the promises of Marxist–Leninist–Maoist thought by entrenching the mindset to sustain the revolution on a permanent basis by eliminating the possibility of 'revisionism' or a return to any form of bourgeois thought. A primary political motivation for the Cultural Revolution, however, was to purge the Chinese Communist Party of Mao's critics following the disasters of the Great Leap Forward. Executions of almost half a million followed among both party members and the wider public who were deemed to be 'traitors' to the revolution (Yang, 2011, p. 52).

Although it is often said that there is no significant body of Chinese IR theory as such, Mao's thought certainly extended to the central concerns of IR – the causes of war and the conditions for peace. His method of ensuring perpetual peace, however, was rather different to that of Kant.

> War, this monster of mutual slaughter among men, will be finally eliminated by the progress of human society . . . But there is only one way to eliminate it and that is to oppose war with war, to oppose counter-revolutionary war with revolutionary war . . . When human society advances to the point where classes and states are eliminated, there will be no more wars . . . that will be the era of perpetual peace for mankind. (Quoted in Yang, 2011, p. 65).

Gramscian Critical Theory

Antonio Gramsci (1891–1937) was both a political activist and a theorist, always maintaining the necessity of the unity of theory and practice and thus of praxis – of putting ideas into action. Praxis was in fact a distinguishing feature of Marxism which was never meant to be *just* a theory but a call to action. A founding member of the Italian Communist Party, a prolific writer, and at one time its leader while also serving as a member of parliament, Gramsci was imprisoned under the fascist regime of Benito Mussolini in 1926 and remained a prisoner until his death in 1937. The prosecutor for his case actually argued, as grounds for his imprisonment, that 'We must stop this brain from functioning for twenty years' (quoted in Bellamy, 1994, p. xviii). Imprisonment, however, failed to curtail Gramsci's cerebral activity, and he produced a significant corpus of writings during his confinement. His best-known works were published under the title *Prison Notebooks* (see Gramsci, 1975), which is a compilation of fragments and notes rather than a coherent, organized work in the form of extended essays or books.

Among the concepts developed throughout these writings is that of hegemony, which Gramsci analysed in terms of consent *and* coercion, both of which are essential to its maintenance. Each balances the other, 'so that force does not overwhelm consent but rather appears to be backed by the consent of the majority' (Gramsci, 1975, p. 156). Elsewhere he writes that 'in order to exercise political leadership or hegemony one must not count solely on the power and material force that is given by government' (ibid., p. 137). So, while not at all dismissing the role of either force or economic domination, which constitute forms of *material* power, Gramsci highlights the *ideational* aspect of hegemony, otherwise referred to as *cultural* hegemony. This is usually reinforced throughout civil society in popular literature, news media, educational institutions, churches, and so on. In this way, the ideational aspects of the hegemony of a dominant and dominating class become institutionalized in the form of a 'hegemonic apparatus' (see Thomas, 2009, p. 225).

Most importantly, power that is sustained and reproduced through hegemony is made to appear 'natural' – and what is 'natural' is often taken to be 'right'. In other words, it appears 'right and natural' that those in authority, those who command the heights of political, social and economic power, and use that power to advantage, are awarded legitimacy through their own self-serving hegemonic devices. Gramsci's solution was to convince the proletariat that *they* had a right to rule (see

Childs and Fowler, 2006, p. 102). This was an essential ideational element in the broader project of the emancipation of the proletariat from the social conditions which oppressed them and which impoverished both their material and intellectual lives.

Gramsci's ideas found their way into the field of international political economy and IR more generally through the work of Robert Cox, a Canadian intellectual who spent much of his working life with the International Labour Organization. There is little in Gramsci's writings about international politics as such, but Cox found his ideas about hegemony in particular to be applicable to the understanding of international organizations and the problem of world order. Cox noted that Gramsci's notion of hegemony accorded with Machiavelli's image of power as 'half man, half beast, a necessary combination of consent and coercion', adding that, for hegemony to succeed, the consensual aspect must remain at the forefront while coercion is always latent, applied only when essential. Thus hegemony ensures conformity 'in most of the people most of the time' (Cox, 1983, p. 164).

The Machiavellian connection also makes the concept of power (and of hegemony as a form of power) available to the analysis of domination and subordination in the broader sphere of relations of world order, while maintaining the connection between power relations and their social basis. The latter is obscured when world order is cast simply in terms of relations among states (Cox, 1983, p. 164). Hegemony at the international level is not just among states, although they are important in the scheme, but constitutes 'an order within a world economy with a dominant mode of production which penetrates into all countries and links to other subordinate modes of production' (ibid., p. 171).

In addition, world hegemony is 'expressed in universal norms, institutions and mechanisms which lay down general rules of behaviour for states and for those forces of civil society that act across national boundaries – rules which support the dominant mode of production' (Cox, 1983, pp. 171–2). This directs attention to the role played by international organizations in providing a mechanism through which the universal norms of such hegemony are developed, expressed and institutionalized while at the same time co-opting elites from peripheral countries and absorbing counter-hegemonic ideas (ibid., p. 172).

Cox's insights into the nature of theory itself have also had a significant impact. In one of his best-known essays, Cox declares quite simply that 'Theory is always *for* someone and *for* some purpose.' Here his point is that theories always proceed from a particular perspective, and all perspectives derive from a certain position in time and space – a stand-point that may be defined in terms of nation or social class, domination or subordination, and so on. A sophisticated theory, however, can reflect on and transcend its own perspective, but that perspective always remains an intrinsic part of it. It follows that there is never any such thing as a theory that stands independent of any standpoint in time or space and, if any theory attempts to represent itself as such, it is all the more important that it is examined as an *ideology* (Cox, 1981, p.128).

Cox also critically analyses what he calls 'problem-solving theory', which characterizes both realist and liberal approaches. These, he says, take the world, with all its prevailing power relationships and institutions, just as they find it and seek to resolve or manage problems within the terms set by that framework (Cox, 1981, p.128). A superior approach reflects on the theorizing process itself, is aware of the perspective which generates it, considers it in relation to other perspectives, and opens the way for creating a different framework for action. This is what leads to the *critical* approach, for it is capable of standing apart from the prevailing world order to ask how that order came about, to call into question the status of existing institutions and practices, and therefore to consider whether they can be changed rather than endured as part of a fixed order of things. Critical theory is thus 'directed towards an appraisal of the very framework or action, or problematic, which problem-solving theory accepts as its parameters' (ibid., p.129).

Cox's formulation is concerned directly with problems in the 'real world', and its aims, he says, are as practical as those of the problem-solving approach. However, it opens up normative choices in a way that problem-solving theory cannot, for it envisages social and political orders different from the prevailing order while nonetheless limiting the range of choice 'to alternative orders which are feasible transformations of the existing world' (1981, p.130). Critical theory conceived in this way has elements of utopianism, but is constrained by the fact that it must reject 'improbable alternatives' in the same way as it rejects the 'permanency of the existing order' (ibid.). This resonates with E. H. Carr's notion that theory must contain elements of both utopianism and realism, and indeed Cox pays homage to aspects of Carr's thought, although he maintains a highly critical stance towards neorealism in particular. The latter, Cox argues, in addition to being wholly problem-solving within a very narrow perspective of the world, endorses a notion of common rationality, which in turn reinforces a non-historical mode of thinking that dictates a future that is always just like the past (ibid., pp. 131–2).

The theorizing of Robert Cox and others who have followed his lead, and that of Gramsci more generally (e.g., Gill, 2003; Budd, 2011), constitutes but one important strand of critical theory. The second strand to be discussed here has its origins in Germany in the work of the Frankfurt School, another post-Marxist enterprise with a strong normative project of emancipation, but with different nuances.

Frankfurt School Critical Theory

The 'Frankfurt School' is the more popular name for the Institut für Sozialforschung (Institute for Social Research) established at the University of Frankfurt in 1924. In its early years under the directorship of Carl Grünberg (1861–1940), the first avowedly Marxist professor to hold a chair at a German university, it became known as 'Café Marx' (Jay, 1996, p. 12). Other leading figures in the earlier years included Max Horkheimer (1895–1973), Theodore Adorno (1903–1969), Walter Benjamin (1892–1940) and Herbert Marcuse (1898–1979). Horkheimer replaced Grünberg as director in 1930 and shortly thereafter the Institute's concerns became rather more practical than intellectual. Its members were mainly Jewish intellectuals and, with the rise of Nazism and its virulent anti-Semitism, the School relocated in 1934 to Columbia University in New York, where it remained until its repatriation in 1950. Among its most prominent contemporary figures are Axel Honneth and Jürgen Habermas.

Throughout its history, the Frankfurt School has produced a very diverse yet distinctive set of perspectives. Like Gramsci, its theorists have been ultimately concerned with a project of emancipation, not through mere reformist measures but through transcending the whole social framework within which mechanisms of domination and subordination operate. And, also like Gramsci, they have highlighted the extent to which existing social conditions, with all their inequalities and injustices, have been made to appear natural.

Horkheimer took 'traditional theory' to be strongly imbued with positivist assumptions. While acknowledging its achievements in advancing scientific and technical knowledge, he argued that, when it came to social structure, traditional theory was content to accept existing abuses as inevitable: 'The individual as a rule must simply accept the basic conditions of his existence as given.' The critical approach, however, 'is wholly distrustful of the rules of conduct with which society as presently constituted provides each of its members . . . in virtue of which the individual accepts as natural the limits prescribed' (Horkheimer, 1972, p. 207). The task of critical theory is to show how social structures originate in human action and are therefore subject to change by rational, planned human intervention (ibid.). The critical approach therefore 'runs counter to prevailing habits of thought' which contribute to 'the persistence of the past and carry on an outdated order of things' (ibid., p. 218).

The critique of positivism was continued in one of the most important works produced by Frankfurt School thinkers – *The Dialectic of Enlightenment* – co-authored by Horkheimer and Adorno. Here they asserted that the Enlightenment, the philosophical movement which had promised to liberate human minds from ignorance, fear and superstition, had 'lapsed into positivism', with a host of dire consequences (Horkheimer and Adorno, 2002, p. xii).

Key Quote   Knowledge as Power

[K]nowledge, which is power, knows no limits, either in its enslavement of creation or in its deference to worldly master. Just as it serves all the purposes of the bourgeois economy both in factories and on the battlefield, it is at the disposal of entrepreneurs, regardless of their origins. (Ibid., p. 2)

Technology is the essence of this knowledge, which 'aims to produce neither concepts nor images, nor the joy of understanding, but method, exploitation of others, capital' (Horkheimer and Adorno, 2002, p. 2). And what humans have sought to learn from nature is simply 'how to use it to dominate wholly both it and other human beings' (ibid). Horkheimer and Adorno saw their task as rescuing the original emancipatory aim of enlightenment from the perverted belief that, once superstition had been abolished, the scientific mind could rule over 'nature'. As we see in chapter 10, this critique accords with aspects of green theory.

Habermas's early work also emphasized the need to ground both the humanities and the social sciences in a method different from the natural sciences (see Hohendahl, 1985, p. 4). While not dismissing the importance of empirical approaches, he argued that these must be complemented by an interpretive or hermeneutic approach which seeks to *understand* how actors participate in their own intersubjective lifeworlds. To this must be added the critical approach to theory which reflects on its *own* suppositions (Giddens, 1993, p. 67). Habermas came to regard Horkheimer and Adorno's position on the chances of humanity escaping the logic of domination as profoundly ambivalent, and reached the conclusion that their critique of reason ultimately undermined the very possibility of critical reflection (Hohendahl, 1985, pp. 7–8). He was also dissatisfied with the way in which they cast the Enlightenment as no more than an unsuccessful attempt to escape 'the powers of fate' (Habermas, 1982, p. 19), and he critiqued the apparent spell cast over Horkheimer and Adorno by the philosopher Friedrich Nietzsche (1844– 1900), who could see nothing but the 'imperatives of self-preservation and domination' behind claims to objective truths and universal moral- ity (ibid., p. 24). It is noteworthy that, in this respect, Nietzsche comes close to a classical realist position.

Habermas then became concerned with developing a social theory which could validate its own critical standards, thus producing a theory of 'communicative action', in which reason or rationality is conceived not as possessing some transcendental, objective character but, rather, is situated in contexts of interaction, in an intersubjective 'lifeworld' (see, generally, Habermas, 2001). This is a complex theory embedded in linguistic philosophy the details of which cannot detain us here. As far as political and international normative theory goes, however, it consti- tutes, among other things, a cosmopolitan approach which attends both to the universal and to the particular. It therefore stands in contrast to a cultural communitarianism which, in rejecting universalism, tends to overemphasize the specificities of particular cultural groups.

In much the same way, Habermas's approach is critical of postmod- ern or poststructural epistemological stances, which are equally anti- universalistic and whose relativism privileges nothing, except perhaps their own epistemologies, as discussed further in chapter 7. In the prac- tical sphere of world politics, it has been observed that one could see a basic collective lifeworld come into being in communicative action in the international realm – 'a fundamental collectivity on which states can build more elaborate forms of cooperation' (Lose, 2001, p. 195). This vision is also supported by liberal theory.

Axel Honneth supports Habermas's 'unflinching defense of enlighten- ment rationality' through a conception of reason which has the capac- ity to reflect critically on 'reason' itself, and which 'emphasizes the ongoing, unfinished nature of the project of enlightenment' (Honneth, 1992a, p. ix). In his own work, Honneth supports the general normative thrust of cosmopolitan normative political and international theory through a sophisticated analysis of such concepts as recognition and respect. Again, there is not the space here to go into detail, but we should note Honneth's point that the conditions under which rights are recognized 'inherently entail a principle of universalism, which unfolds in the course of historical struggles' (Honneth, 1992b, p. 194).

The best-known contemporary IR theorist carrying forward Habermasian theory is Andrew Linklater, who confronts, in particular, the neorealist assumption that international anarchy will be reproduced indefinitely, thereby ensuring that conflict and competition among states remain endemic in the international system, especially with respect to great power relations. This approach, he says, fails to recognize the possibilities for transforming the international system by reconstituting the kinds of political communities of which it is composed, namely, sovereign nation-states – communities which presently rest on mechanisms of inclusion and exclusion (Linklater, 1998, p. 14). Linklater takes a thoroughgoing cosmopolitan approach which draws much from the Marxist tradition as well as from Kantian principles, both of which provide the resources for a critical-theoretical modus operandi capable of countering neorealist assumptions about perpetual anarchy and conflict (ibid., p. 15).

Linklater vests particular importance in a concept of citizenship which is aimed at inclusion rather than exclusion and which would transform both domestic and international politics (1998, p. 11). The glimmerings of such a transformation are evident in the European Union, where, although national identity remains strong, the idea of European citizenship has some substance, especially to the extent that it reduces the moral significance of 'alien' status. This, Linklater says, provides an admittedly rather 'thin' conception of citizenship, but it has at least brought into being an international civil society and the possibility of a post-Westphalian state (ibid., p. 199).

Linklater also notes the problems posed for cosmopolitan and universal emancipatory projects by the decline of Western political ascendency and 'the ensuing cultural revolt against Western hegemony' (1998, p. 47). No less than any liberal project, the Marxist ideal of socialized humanity has also been regarded with suspicion, and both are implicated in negative representations of non-Western societies (ibid.). The latter societies are in fact the main subject of concern for the next form of Marxist-inspired critique to be discussed. They lie primarily in the Third World or Global South in countries that were, for the most part, products of the age of European imperialism and the spread of capitalism and whose ongoing problems with development are regarded as emanating directly from that experience.

World-Systems Theory

World-Systems analysis has been described as a set of perspectives on the social realities produced by the modern world system, defined largely in terms of the capitalist world market. This is set in historical context and is underpinned by a critique of the structures of knowledge that have developed as part of that system, including the social sciences themselves (Wallerstein, 2004, p. 1). A key assumption is that the world as a whole provides the only really meaningful framework within which any particular state, or group of states, can be understood. This requires giving up the idea that it is composed of individualized sovereign states with separate, parallel histories (Worsley, 1980, p. 300). Indeed, political struggles within as well as between states can only be explained within the broad framework of the world system (Petras, 1981, p. 148).

Four figures in particular dominate the field of World-Systems Theory – Giovanni Arrighi (1937–2009), Andre Gunder Frank (1929–2005), Samir Amin (b. 1931) and Immanuel Wallerstein (b. 1930). All were moved in one way or another by the crisis of world capitalism which began in the 1970s and which impacted on the Third World in particular. All were influenced by Marx and concerned with developing an analysis that took full account of the historical dynamics of economic systems and their impact on society and politics on a global scale. The amalgam of ideas produced by perspectives on world systems now forms an important critique of 'modernization' theory. The latter has been prominent in development studies and is often seen as complicit in equating progress with Westernization and, as a corollary, with capitalist development.

Amin's early work in the 1970s began from a concern with under-development or unequal development (relative to the industrialized North), mainly in Africa and Asia, which he saw as a product of global capitalism itself and which Marx's own analysis had touched on but not fully developed. Amin sees the dynamics which came to underpin modernity as emanating from ancient China and travelling through the Middle East to Europe, where, from the sixteenth century, a form of capitalism developed that eventually 'imposed itself through the conquest of the world' (Amin, 2011, p. 5). His analysis remains within, but further develops, the tradition of historical materialism begun by Marx and which he sees as the only way of effectively advancing the analysis of global history (ibid., p. 10). At the same time, Amin provides a radical critique of Eurocentrism which rests on an assumption that European capitalism 'is the first social system to unify the world' (ibid.,

p. 12). This critique at first seems counter-intuitive and at odds with *The Communist Manifesto*'s identification of European capitalism as a force encircling the entire globe and effectively creating the world system. Amin's analysis, however, emphasizes that, while the system *conquered* the world, it did not make it homogeneous: 'Quite the reverse, it effects the most phenomenal polarisation possible' (ibid., p. 16). This is reflected in the North–South divide.

Arrighi's approach to the analysis of world systems, and the modern world capitalist system in particular, draws inspiration from the historiographical style of the French historian Fernand Braudel (1902–1985), the leading figure in the *Annales* School, which is concerned with the analysis of social change over the *longue-durée*. In looking at the expansion of capitalist power over five centuries, Arrighi sees this as being associated not just with interstate competition for mobile capital (as emphasized by Max Weber) but also with 'the formation of political structures endowed with ever-more extensive and complex organisational capabilities to control the social and political environment of capital accumulation on a world scale' (Arrighi, 1994, p. 14).

Arrighi draws not only on Marx and Weber's insights concerning high finance but those of Adam Smith as well, especially with respect to processes of world-market formation. He says that, like Marx who followed him, 'Smith saw in the European "discoveries" of America and of a passage to the East Indies via the Cape of Good Hope a decisive turning point in world history' (1994, p. 19). As for the unfortunate consequences for native populations that followed, these were due in large measure to the superiority of European force, which enabled them 'to commit with impunity every sort of injustice in those remote countries' (Smith, quoted ibid.).

Arrighi goes on to compare Smith's observations with Braudel's on 'the fortunes of the conquering West and the misfortunes of the conquered non-West as joint outcomes of a single historical process' and the 'centrality of "force" in determining the distribution of costs and benefits among participants in the market economy' (1994, p. 19). Drawing on Gramsci, Arrighi also analyses the phenomenon of hegemony in world political and economic relations.

Key Quote Giovanni Arrighi on World Hegemony

The concept of 'world hegemony' . . . refers specifically to the power of a state to exercise functions of leadership and governance over a system of sovereign states. In principle, this power may involve just the ordinary management of

> such a system as instituted at a given time. Historically, however, the government of a system of sovereign states has always involved some kind of transformative action, which changed the mode of operation in a fundamental way. (Ibid., p.27)

Arrighi argues further that the claim of a dominant actor to represent the general or common interest 'is always more or less fraudulent', although in a true hegemonic relationship the claim is always partly true and adds a measure of power to the dominant actor (ibid., p.29).

Andre Gunder Frank's approach to the idea of world systems is to start with the present and work back. This method takes him much further back into the past than just 500 years or so, and indeed leads him to conclude that the contemporary world system has a history spanning at least 5,000 years. By looking at this broader span, Frank argues that the dominance of Europe and the West more generally can be seen as a recent and, probably, passing event – 'a thesis which poses a more humanocentric challenge to Eurocentrism' (Frank and Gills, 1993, p.3). One of Frank's key theoretical categories is the centre–periphery structure of the world system, which in turn produces a condition of dependence. This has been evident, especially in Latin America, since 1492 (ibid.). The theoretical basis for this approach is Marxist thought, which helps explain dependency and underdevelopment in poor, peripheral countries (that is, the Third World or Global South) in terms of the exploitative legacy of Western imperialism and colonialism rather than of local cultural factors to do with 'traditionalism'. Independence has scarcely improved matters for many of these countries because the underlying structures of exploitation remain, and many postcolonial indigenous elites have simply colluded with the 'core' states (generally those of the industrialized North) in perpetuating relations of exploitation. A major focus of dependency theory is therefore on 'core–periphery' relations and how these are embedded in the world system.

Wallerstein's formulation of World-Systems Theory depicts a capitalist world economy which transcends the nation-state model of separate political and economic units and is therefore not *inter*national in the ordinary meaning of the word. It forms 'a unit with a single division of labour and multiple cultural systems' (Wallerstein, 1979, p. 5). Wallerstein insists that his focus on the modern period of world capitalist economic development as a 'historically specific totality' does not mean that it fails to be 'analytically universal' (ibid., p.6). Furthermore, his world system is a *social* system with its own boundaries, structures, groups and rules of legitimation, giving it an overall coherence. Wallerstein also takes up the categories of core and periphery but adds an intermediate one in the form of the semi-periphery, a category analogous to the middle class in a domestic system which acts as a buffer between the upper and lower classes (ibid., p. 96). While the core–periphery distinction differentiates those zones concentrating on high-profit, high-technology, high-wage diversified production, on the one hand, and low-profit, low technology, low-wage, less diversified production, on the other, those countries falling in between play a different role. 'In part they act as a peripheral zone for core countries and in part they act as a core country for some peripheral areas' (ibid., p. 97).

More generally, Wallerstein argues that the deep historical method and the focused critique of World-Systems Theory not only illuminates how the capitalist world system has developed and how it works, it also shows the extent to which conventional social science in its separate disciplinary boxes has failed to grapple with the problems generated by the modern world system. Above all, Wallerstein, as with other World-Systems analysts attuned to Marxist principles, believes that the emergence of this mode of analysis reflects and expresses a 'real protest about the deep inequalities of the world-system that are so politically central to our current times' (Wallerstein, 2004, p. xi). Case study 6.2 illustrates aspects of world systems approaches generally.

There have been numerous other contributors to World-Systems Theory from different disciplinary perspectives, ranging from sociology to archaeology, anthropology, geography, politics and international relations (including political economy). Writing some three decades after its emergence, one commentator suggested that it is no longer 'a theory' but, rather, a paradigm, understood as a set of guiding assumptions that prompt certain research questions. In international relations these include a focus on cycles of war and how they stem from world systemic forces and processes (Hall, 1999, pp. 2–3). From a methodological perspective, World-Systems Theory comes under the more general rubric of historical sociology, an approach which has become of increasing interest to IR scholars who have sought to critique the ahistorical basis of neorealism in particular.

Historical Sociology

Historical sociology is concerned with the study of historical change and the identification of structures and patterns over the long term. In

Case Study 6.2 Western Hegemony and the World System

European expansion began in the late fifteenth century and reached its zenith towards the end of the nineteenth century following the Industrial Revolution and the rise of capitalism, both hallmarks of modernity. Most European powers had been involved in imperial enterprises, but the British Empire outstripped all others, controlling a fifth of the world's territory and around a quarter of the world's population.

In most places, military force had been key to imposing imperial rule, but cultural hegemony was to become an important element in maintaining it. European imperialism generally integrated states and societies around the globe on various levels – economically, politically and culturally – thereby creating the modern world system through a process of what we now call globalization, itself a phenomenon sometimes traced to the first circumnavigation of the globe between 1519 and 1522.

The colonization of North America was crucial to the long-term ascendency of European economic, political and cultural systems because it brought into being the United States of America, which emerged from a number of separate colonies, mainly British, which eventually rebelled and declared independence in 1776. The US expanded territorially via its own processes of colonization on the North American continent – and beyond in the case of Hawaii.

As it developed, the US retained certain basic elements of the dominant culture of Britain, including the English language, an education system, a capitalist economy, an industrial base and considerable military capacity. By the end of the nineteenth century it had become the world's largest economy. At the end of the twentieth century it was also the dominant global military power. Whether it will be overtaken by China by the middle of the present century remains to be seen.

For the time being, the geopolitical entity we call 'the West', consisting of the US, the UK and Western Europe (with which Eastern Europe is becoming increasingly integrated and assimilated through the EU), and the remainder of the 'Anglosphere' – Canada, Australia and New Zealand – remains ascendant. Although one major nation-state does indeed dominate in the present period, Western (rather than simply US) hegemony transcends the nation-state system, as highlighted by Wallerstein in particular.

The West as a whole clearly possesses a preponderance of material power through its economic, industrial and military base. World-System theorists generally would also highlight the fact that much of the wealth that supports that power has been generated through exploitation of peripheral countries. In addition to material power, the West exercises a broad-based cultural hegemony which is expressed in a whole variety of ways. Cultural analysts would point to the dominance of Western 'material culture' and its specific products such as consumer goods, film, literature, art, music, fashion and lifestyle amenities, from golf courses to shopping malls. These are also a means by which Western values – which tend to support Western interests – are transmitted at the ideational level, and therefore constitute a source of what Michael Mann defines as social power. This is supported by Gramscian theory as well.

In terms of political organization, the international system is based formally on the Westphalian model of state sovereignty to which virtually every political entity around the world conforms, at least technically. This has been accompanied by the equally European ideology of nationalism, which aligns particular cultural/political identities with states. As for governance, modern representative democracy as developed in the West has come to be regarded as the standard against which virtually all national systems are judged, while governance at the global level is based on models developed in Europe from the nineteenth and early twentieth centuries.

To the extent that various states around the world conform to Western models of politics, economics, industrial capacity, and so forth, they are considered 'developed'. This reflects the thoroughgoing Eurocentrism entrenched in development models. But years of development based on models devised by the World Bank and other such institutions does not appear to have diminished the wealth/poverty gap between the core countries and much of the Global South.

Insofar as development and economic growth has taken place outside the West, it appears to be creating a much wider gap between rich and poor in these countries as well. So although there are now numerous Chinese, Indian, Nigerian and Brazilian multi-millionaires, abject poverty remains deeply entrenched at the lower socio-economic strata of societies in these countries. For World-Systems theorists and critical theorists generally, emancipation from grossly unfair life conditions for these people remains a pipe-dream while ever the capitalist world economic system continues in place. Whether these conditions would change greatly with the decline of Western hegemony and the rise of other centres of power, however, is debateable.

this sense, Marx's approach to the study of social relations (incorporating political and economic relations), which examines certain patterns and structures over time, is a form of historical sociology. This does not mean that historical sociology is an essentially Marxist enterprise or that historical sociologists are by definition Marxist (or post-Marxist) in orientation, although some – such as the major proponents of World-Systems Theory – may be. Others distance themselves from both Marxism and realism (see Hobden, 1998, p. 11).

An overlap with the concerns of IR is evident in the set of issues with which historical sociology is primarily concerned. These are the emergence and development of modernity, which includes 'epochal transitions' such as the move from feudalism to capitalism, the rise of the modern sovereign state, and revolutionary movements such as the Reformation and the French Revolution, as well as broad-based social movements, including the labour movement (Delanty and Isin, 2003, p. 1). One prominent historical sociologist, Michael Mann, has focused on the 'centrality of ferocious militarism to our own Western society' (Mann, 1996, p. 221), which is of course squarely within the major purview of IR's concern with war and peace.

Mann's historical sociology rests on three general orienting principles, the first of which is that it is 'resolutely empirical' (1996, p. 221). The second is a conscious awareness of the variety of ways in which humans have organized themselves through time and space. This leads to a tendency to 'relativise rather than reify social institutions' and therefore to treat states, properly, as only one possible form of politico-military organization. Realists, Mann asserts, are especially prone to reifying modern states, 'crediting them with a solidity, cohesion, autonomy and power in society that they rarely have' (ibid., pp. 222–3). The third principle is an awareness of social and historical development over the long term, which in turn alerts us to changing social dynamics and their impact on war and peace – something which Mann acknowledges he shares in common with Wallerstein, although their approaches differ in other respects: Wallerstein accounts for the modern world system within the framework of a single driving logic; Mann in contrast identifies four intertwining logics – four 'sources of social power' – ideological, economic, political and military. All are essential to our understanding of the dynamics of states and state systems, the causes of war and the conditions for peace (ibid., pp. 222–4).

Andrew Linklater has joined in discussion of the links between historical sociology and IR, once again noting the dissatisfaction expressed by both historical sociologists and IR theorists of a critical persuasion with the realist assumption that the basic driving principles of relations between states have not changed over millennia (Linklater, 2011, p. 194). In relation to the contemporary period, Linklater also notes the importance of sociological contributions to the analysis of global political and economic structures, citing in particular the work of the sociologist Anthony Giddens (ibid.). The latter's key contribution focuses on the nation-state and violence and the dynamics of power and domination in the capitalist world economy (Giddens, 1985, p. 335).

In summary, historical sociology as a methodological approach has proved attractive to IR scholars from a variety of perspectives, many of whom have followed Marxist (or post-Marxist) concerns with the transformation of human societies over the longer term. Its proponents regard it as particularly useful in illuminating the fact that, although many aspects of human society, including particular configurations of power and privilege, may appear to occur 'naturally', a deeper historical perspective shows just how malleable societies are.

Conclusion

This chapter has explained some key aspects of Marx's thought as well as the subsequent career of many of his ideas, including the unhappy fate of Marxism in both the theory and the practice of authoritarian communism in the USSR and China, where state power was abused on a massive scale and lost all connections with Marx's essential humanitarianism. This experience has therefore led some scholars to advocate a critical approach that is explicitly post-Marxist, in the sense that it is attuned not only to the problems of capitalism in the contemporary conditions of late modernity but also to those aspects of Marxist theory that have lent themselves to exploitative domination and all its wretched consequences (Giddens, 1985, p. 335).

Although we have not examined democratic socialism in detail, it is nonetheless worth noting that evolutionary rather than revolutionary socialism proved influential in Western Europe and Scandinavia, where states developed policies attuned to principles of social democracy, emphasizing a commitment to the provision of public goods and welfare assistance. Democratic socialism also had some impact in settler colonies such as Canada, Australia and New Zealand. In the US, however, it made much less headway against a strong tide of individualist liberalism, which remains a dominant force in contemporary politics and society.

The development of critical theory in both Gramscian and Frankfurt School modes aimed to further the cause of human emancipation from unfair social, political and economic conditions, and in this sense remained strongly attuned to Marx's humanitarianism while moving away from a one-dimensional historical materialism. These forms of critical theory have also been important in highlighting the role of ideational power, which operates alongside material power, with Gramscians in particular developing a sophisticated conceptualization of hegemony. Early Frankfurt School theorists also addressed ideational issues, providing insights into the relationship between knowledge and power, while later work by Habermas in particular has extended the purview of critical theory through the development of a theory of communicative action, which is essential to dealing with a culturally and socially diverse world. It has also contributed to the refinement of method, not simply through a wholesale rejection of positivism but through including interpretive methods along with the explicitly critical element of self-reflection on one's own perspectives.

The project of human emancipation has, in addition, been pursued vigorously by the various proponents of World-Systems Theory. Their concerns have been focused largely on the non-Western world and therefore have particular relevance for North–South relations in contemporary world politics in general and international political economy in particular. Their critiques of the world system are also based in a broader sociological tradition of thought concerned with power, control and inequality as well as with social order more generally and how it may be changed (see Slattery, 2003, p. vi). These perspectives, along with increasing attention to the methodological tools of historical sociology, have exposed some of the limitations of traditional IR theory in both its liberal and realist manifestations. The emphasis on the *social* as well as the political and economic dimensions of human interactions at all levels – including international relations – is further explored in the next chapter.

QUESTIONS FOR DISCUSSION

1   What inspiration did early European socialists find in the discovery of 'primitive' people?
2   Why is Marx's conception of history called 'materialist'?
3   In what sense is imperialism an extension of capitalism?
4   To what extent did the Russian and Chinese revolutions succeed or fail in realizing Marx's vision of a communist society?
5   What did Gramsci mean by the term 'naturalization of power' and how does it relate to his conception of hegemony?
6   On what grounds does Robert Cox criticize 'problem-solving theory' as exemplified by realism and liberalism?
7   On what grounds does Jürgen Habermas defend Enlightenment values?
8   What basic methodology do World-System(s) theorists and historical sociologists share in common?

FURTHER READING

Ayers, Alison J. (2013) *Gramsci, Political Economy and International Relations Theory*. Rev. edn, New York: Palgrave Macmillan.

Lachmann, Richard (2013) *What is Historical Sociology?*. Cambridge: Polity.

Leysens, Anthony (2008) *The Critical Theory of Robert W. Cox: Fugitive or Guru?*. New York: Palgrave Macmillan.

Miliband, Ralph (2006) *Marxism and Politics*. Delhi: Aakar Books.

Spegele, Roger D. (2014) *Emancipatory International Relations: Critical Thinking in International Relations*. Abingdon: Routledge.

USEFUL WEBSITES

www.marxists.org (Marxists Internet Archive)

www.internationalgramscisociety.org (International Gramsci Society)

www.youtube.com/watch?v=2pzfy2izu44 (Herbert Marcuse on the Frankfurt School)

http://sociology.emory.edu/faculty/globalization/theories01.html (Globalization/World-System Theory website)

www.youtube.com/watch?v=5UUjYzrjHn4 (lecture by Immanuel Wallerstein)

7

Social Theories of International Relations

Social theories of international politics emerged at a time when neo-realism and neoliberalism dominated the discipline, offering scholars only a limited range of perspectives on issues and problems in the field. Since the late 1980s, however, social theory has had a major impact, primarily in the form of social constructivism. We saw earlier that critical theory has important constructivist elements too, although these are attuned primarily to a critique of capitalist society. Feminist and gender analysis, insofar as they adopt constructivist perspectives, also critique particular aspects of social and political life. Constructivism is therefore an approach that lends itself to more than one school of thought. This suggests that it should be understood not so much as a theory in and of itself but more as a lens through which we may better analyse any given object of enquiry. In international politics, these objects range from anarchy and sovereignty to financial institutions and trade regimes and from gender issues to the condition of the postcolonial world.

Although constructivism is a relative latecomer to the field of IR theory, it has an important precursor in the English School. This school had emerged much earlier in the post-Second World War period, bringing ideas of sociality and the role of norms and values to bear on problems of order and justice in the international sphere. The English School has experienced a revival in recent years, partly on account of the rising tide of social constructivism in the discipline more generally.

A very different and much more radical version of constructivism is provided by postmodernism/poststructuralism. These are strongly opposed to the universalist premises of realism, liberalism, Marxism and post-Marxism and are highly critical of the 'Enlightenment project' and the more general phenomenon of modernity. Postmodern/poststructural approaches also offer a more radical account of the relationship between power and knowledge, an account that rests on an equally radical approach to epistemology which denies any firm foundations for certain knowledge.

A brief explanation of the rather awkward use of the combination 'postmodern/poststructural' is warranted here. Although it has become common for IR theorists in the genre to favour the term 'poststructural' and to consider 'postmodern' somewhat passé, it is difficult simply to disregard the latter term without at the same time erasing much that has been conveyed by that particular label, as well as the fact that there is considerable overlap between the two terms. To the extent that they can be distinguished, the most straightforward way of doing so is to describe postmodernism as a theory of society, culture and history and poststructuralism as a theory of knowledge and language (Agger, 1991, p. 112). They are both, in any event, a species of social theory, a field within which all the variants discussed in this chapter are embedded. This is followed by an examination of the notion of the 'social construction of reality' as it emerged in European sociology and which underpins virtually all versions of constructivism.

Social Theory

Social theory provides the analytic framework for sociological studies in the same way that political theory does for political studies, although social theory in a broad sense underpins all the social sciences. It examines 'meaning, values, intentions, beliefs and ideas realized in human social behaviour and in socially created events and symbolic objects such as texts and images' and which emerge from 'contexts of intentional agency by human actors in definite cultural and historical situations' (Harrington, 2005, p. 5). In its early years, social theory gave rise to notions such as functionalism and structuralism, which in turn derived from the idea that society could be studied only as a whole (i.e., holistically) and not just as the sum of its component parts. Structuralism and functionalism focus on the interrelationship of the various parts, and structuralists in particular are concerned with identifying underlying social structures which shape people's thoughts and actions and of which they are not necessarily aware. Structuralists have also used linguistic theory to help make sense of certain social phenomena (ibid., p. 4).

Alternative approaches are found in various 'interpretive sociologies' which hold, in opposition to structuralism and functionalism, that people's actions are not simply the product of social structures imposed on them but, rather, that people actively interpret the realities surrounding them and act accordingly (Harrington, 2005, p. 5). Another development has been 'structuration theory', which does not award priority either to the individual actor or a social totality but looks at how social practices are reproduced by actors across space and time (Giddens, 1984, p. 2). This raises the relationship between structure and agency. Structuralist and functionalist approaches generally award primacy to the social structure within which individuals must operate. Social structure is not created anew by each generation but has continuity through time, more or less determining social existence. This reflects the holistic approach noted above. The contrasting perspective awards primacy to individuals, who, as active agents, are seen as capable not just of acting within an existing social system but of changing that system. This kind of approach is known as methodological individualism. Structuration theory, as suggested above, is inclined to synthesize or conflate structure and agency.

There is also a critical realist approach to social theory, which argues for the 'reality of the life of the mind' – of our evaluations, beliefs, desires, intentions and commitments. These 'internal deliberations' do not have the properties of material objects that we can see, touch and feel, for materiality is not the same as reality. Rather, the reality of an agent's subjective, ideational world of the mind is known by its effects, and it is through these effects that we can apprehend the ontological status of the subjective mind (Archer, 2003, pp. 35–6). Thus there are 'different modes of existence of different types of entities in the world . . . mountains, plants and chairs have an objective mode of existence, whereas desires, thoughts and feelings have a subjective mode' (ibid., p. 36). This approach, also known as social realism, highlights the interdependence of structure and agency but does not conflate them. Indeed, critical realism suggests that 'it is the generic defect of conflation to withhold causal powers from either structure or agency' (Archer, 2000, p. 307).

The Social Construction of Reality

The notion that what we perceive as 'reality' is socially constructed rather than given by nature owes much of its currency to a school of social theory concerned with the 'sociology of knowledge', which seeks to show how certain social structures give rise to particular systems of knowledge. This is implicit in Marx's notion that people's consciousness is conditioned by their social existence, and not the other way around, but the idea received a more explicit formulation in the work of the French theorist Émile Durkheim (1858–1917), widely regarded as the founder of the academic discipline of sociology. Durkheim's work is sometimes described as 'social realism', in the sense that social phenomena are as real as 'things' (material objects) and should be studied as such. The sociology of knowledge was further developed by the German-Hungarian sociologist Karl Mannheim (1893–1947), partly in collaboration with the German philosopher Max Scheler (1874–1928), who has been credited with first coining the phrase (see Berger and Luckmann, 1991, p. 4).

Although Mannheim drew on Marx's theory of ideology, he rejected the claim that ideology was necessarily a *deliberate* distortion of reality with a purely instrumental intent based on class interest. As a later commentator noted, 'ideas are the outcome of profound interests which *unwittingly* tincture and distort every phase of man's thought' (Merton, 1937, p. 494; emphasis added). Mannheim's work therefore focused on how particular social settings give rise to ideas which are then promoted by certain interests and come to be accepted by society at large, although not necessarily in some grand conspiratorial fashion. Mannheim further observed that people 'do not confront the objects of the world from the abstract levels of a contemplating mind as such, nor do they do so exclusively as solitary beings. On the contrary they act with and against one another in diversely organized groups, and while doing so they think with and against one another' (Mannheim, 1954, p. 3).

The more specific formulation of the social construction of reality came with a book by Peter Berger and Thomas Luckmann, first published in 1966, which held simply that reality is socially constructed and that the task of the sociology of knowledge is to analyse the processes through which this takes place. 'Reality' is a quality of phenomena that we take to have an existence independent of our own volition – that is, we cannot 'wish them away'. 'Knowledge' is the certainty that the phenomena are real, and that they possess specific characteristics (Berger and Luckmann, 1991, p. 1). Sociological interest in issues of 'reality' and 'knowledge' is justified by the very fact of their social relativity, which is evident when one considers the extent to which perceptions of reality, and what counts as knowledge, differ according to one's social location (ibid., p. 3). On the question of how social order arises, Berger and Luckmann propose that it is an entirely human product or, rather, an ongoing human production which, in its empirical manifestations, is *not* biologically determined.

Key Quote   The Production of Social Order

Social order is not part of the 'nature of things,' and it cannot be derived from the 'laws of nature.' Social order exists *only* as a product of human activity. No other ontological status may be ascribed to it without hopelessly obfuscating its empirical manifestations. Both in its genesis (social order is the result of past human activity) and its existence in any instant of time (social order exists only and insofar as human activity continues to produce it) it is a human product. (Ibid., pp. 51–2)

In further developing their argument, Berger and Luckmann highlight the fact that social interactions and their meanings become habitualized, so that ordinary activities, situations and interactions need not be interpreted anew each day, although this by no means precludes innovation. Habitualization, which precedes institutionalization, occurs on the basis of the 'typification of interactions' over time and in the course of a shared history, and so an understanding of the historical process through which the institution was produced is the key to understanding the institution itself. In addition, the very fact that institutions exist indicates the extent to which they 'control human conduct by setting up predefined patterns of conduct' (Berger and Luckmann, 1991, p. 55). While this institutionalized world is an objective social reality, it is not fixed. Rather, it is a dynamic and ongoing human production which is transmitted to each new generation through processes of socialization while remaining subject to the dynamics of social change (ibid., p. 61).

In addition to building on the work of Marx, Durkheim, Mannheim and others, Berger and Luckmann drew on a related school of sociological thought known as symbolic interactionism, developed primarily in the US by George Herbert Mead (1863–1931) and elaborated by Herbert Blumer (1900–1987). Symbolic interactionism was concerned to show the extent to which humans act towards things, including other humans, on the basis of meanings and interpretations which are themselves derived from social interaction. The meaning attributed to the status of other humans such as 'friend' or 'enemy' or to institutions such as 'government' or 'school', for example, are produced only *within the specific context of social interaction* and are not exogenous (see Blumer, 1986, p. 2). This is sometimes referred to as 'situated knowledge'. However, all this begs the question of what exactly constitutes 'the context' within which intersubjective meanings are developed. This is no straightforward matter, as there are no rules for determining the nature of contexts, where the boundaries of contexts may be drawn, and how transcontextual interactions operate (see Lawson, 2008).

These issues aside, general developments in theories of socially situated knowledge outlined above, from Durkheim through to Berger and Luckmann, Mead, Blumer and others, created a highly influential strand of social theory which was to be picked up by IR scholars from about the late 1980s onwards. This interest emerged at a time when theoretical debates in the discipline had been dominated by the so-called neo–neo debate between neorealists and neoliberals, each advancing more and more sophisticated positions on such topics as relative versus absolute gains. The concern of the emerging school of constructivists was not so much with the details of these debates, or with mounting challenges to their specific findings, but with what a focus on such issues tended to preclude or ignore, namely the 'content and sources of state interests and the social fabric of world politics' (Checkel, 1998, p. 324). In pursuing a constructivist approach to theory, however, its proponents drew not only on elements of social theory produced by sociologists but from an approach to the study of international politics by a group of scholars in the UK known as the English School, who had taken an explicitly social approach to the analysis of what they called 'international society'.

The English School

From the late 1950s a number of scholars came together to form the British Committee on the Theory of International Politics. This group was to provide the foundations for what became known simply as the 'English School' (see Dunne, 1998). A series of papers, articles and books produced by members of the group addressed questions of how the sphere of international anarchy can actually produce a stable order, in turn creating conditions conducive to the realization of at least some measure of justice in this sphere. The concerns of English School theorists were therefore with structural *and* normative issues, and these overlapped with both realist and liberal concerns. The emphasis on the *social* aspects of politics in the international sphere, however, set English School theorists apart from these more conventional approaches and led them to develop new insights into the dynamics underpinning order and justice.

The idea of a 'society of states' or 'international society' came to form the centrepiece of English School deliberations, and a prominent Australian member, Hedley Bull (1932–1985), produced an extensive treatment of this idea in *The Anarchical Society: A Study of Order in World Politics* (1977). Here Bull distinguishes between a *system* of states, in which regular interaction prompts states carefully to observe and calculate the behaviour of other states, and a *society* of states, characterized by a convergence of interests, norms and values and the development of rules and institutions which provide for both order and justice.

Key Quote   The Society of States

A society of states (or international society) exists when a group of states, conscious of certain common interests and common values, form a society in the sense that they conceive themselves to be bound by a common set of rules in their relations with one another, and share in the working of common institutions. (Bull, 1977, p. 13)

The contemporary scholar Edward Keene (2002, p. ix) finds the most compelling aspect of Bull's work to be 'his lucid defence of the view that in certain respects international relations are social relations, and that order in world politics should therefore be conceived as a form of social order.' Bull's purpose in developing this approach was to challenge the popular notion that international relations could only be understood in Machiavellian or Hobbesian terms in which the 'brutal logic of *Realpolitik*' prevailed (ibid.). In rejecting one tradition of thought, a theorist is often inclined to embrace the most clearly opposing position which, in this case, is the progressivist/cosmopolitan approach of the Kantian tradition. Bull, however, sought a middle way inspired by the thought of Hugo Grotius, whose work had provided at least an incipient notion of international society (see Kingsbury, 1997–8).

Methodologically, English School theorists were highly sceptical of the claims of positivism and of attempts to mimic the natural sciences. Some, such as Martin Wight (1913–1972), pioneered an interpretive approach which drew on philosophy, diplomatic history and law. Utilizing Grotian ideas, this viewed the aspiration for international order as one based squarely on reason. In other words, the desire to establish and maintain a society of states which both brings order to the anarchical sphere of international relations and mitigates the tendency to violent conflict is an eminently *rational* one. Even so, English School theorists remained acutely aware that the society of states is 'threatened by the ever-present realities of the "state of war"' (Dunne, 1998, p. 8). This, together with an emphasis on states as the major actors in world politics, has sometimes seen English School theorists branded as essentially realist in orientation. But their emphasis on norms, values and the *social* rather than the *systemic* nature of international relations undermines such claims.

An important debate within the English School which remains highly relevant to normative issues in world politics, especially in relation to human rights discourses and humanitarian intervention, revolves around two distinct positions, known as 'pluralism' and 'solidarism'. Each takes a contrasting approach to how norms, values and rules should be understood in the context of a society of states and whether or not action should be taken against those states abusive of human rights. Both also map directly on to two contrasting approaches in contemporary normative international theory – communitarianism and cosmopolitanism – and tend to reflect realist and liberal perspectives respectively.

I have elsewhere described communitarian approaches as asserting the cultural specificity of values and norms against universally valid moral precepts. Further, if it is taken as self-evident that ethical systems represent constructions of reality based on particular, culturally informed world views, and if culture itself is highly variable, then ethical systems can only ever be relative (Lawson, 2006, p. 45). When applied to the international system, states are frequently viewed as the containers of culture, thereby enhancing the normative force of state sovereignty. The pluralist approach also emphasizes the fact that, internally, different states possess very different norms and values which are derived from their own cultural heritage. This fact renders any overarching international morality as rather 'thin' in that it is limited to supporting relations in a society of states based on mutual tolerance and peaceful coexistence. To achieve this, each state must simply get on with managing its own domestic concerns while tolerating or ignoring practices in other states that may well be morally repugnant according to its own norms and values. To do otherwise undermines the doctrine of non-interference in the affairs of a sovereign state and invites conflict and strife. This pluralist position has been described as leaning towards a realist form of rationalism in which prudential, instrumental considerations concerning stability and order in the society of states trump deeper moral concerns about human rights (Buzan, 2004, p. 47). Order therefore takes precedence over justice.

Cosmopolitanism, on the other hand, rejects the proposition that moral standards can be located only within specific cultural and political communities. It promotes ethical principles that transcend both cultural *and* nation-state boundaries and seeks to establish an overarching ethical basis for global order, and it does so on the basis that all humans share certain attributes and needs, which in turn creates a common moral bond (Lawson, 2006, p. 48). These ideas inform the solidarist approach and its more Kantian (liberal) form of rationalism, which proposes that the norms and values of international society must be underpinned by a much more robust cosmopolitan conception of the unity of humanity which respects individual human rights. Thus solidarism 'focuses on the possibility of shared moral norms underpinning a more expansive, and inevitably more interventionist understanding of international order' (Buzan, 2004, p. 114).

Solidarism therefore raises more complex questions for moral action in world politics in cases where great suffering is occurring but where intervention may do more harm than good. It has also been pointed out that those supporting a solidarist position on intervention must guard against 'the evil of unilateralism masquerading as solidarism' (Linklater and Suganami, 2006, p. 272). In summarizing the pluralist/solidarist debate, Buzan argues that the respective positions should not be understood as mutually exclusive but, rather, as 'positions on a spectrum representing, respectively, thin and thick sets of shared norms, rules and institutions' (Buzan, 2004, p. 139). The question is, how do these issues play out in 'real world' situations? Case study 7.1, on the Rwandan genocide and the responsibilities of the international community, provides some insights.

While little work was carried out in the 1980s by scholars identifying themselves as English School theorists, the end of the Cold War and other developments in the discipline of IR saw a resurgence of interest in its principal themes, and a new generation of scholars began to elaborate these. In addition to identifying themselves as sharing a common tradition of concern with the idea of international society, and therefore the social nature of the international sphere, such scholars share both a common methodological orientation to an interpretivist as opposed to a positivist mode of enquiry and a commitment to international theory as explicitly normative in orientation (Bellamy, 2004, p. 5). This is reflected in Andrew Hurrell's study of how stable order, along with the institutionalization of key values such as democracy and human rights, can be achieved in a global society of states and in which the interrelated domains of the market and civil society are also fully implicated in the production of social order (Hurrell, 2007).

Case Study 7.1　Humanitarian Intervention and the Rwandan Genocide

The Republic of Rwanda is a relatively small but populous state located in central east Africa. Independent since 1962, Rwanda was previously colonized, first by Germany until the First World War, then by Belgium under a League of Nations mandate and, finally, following the Second World War, as a UN trust territory. Ethnic tensions between the Tutsi minority and Hutu majority escalated in the pre-independence period and erupted in violent episodes both before and after independence. These tensions were exacerbated by population growth, which put much pressure on land. Civil war broke out in 1990. Although a peace agreement was reached in 1993, it barely contained hostilities. Hutu President Habyarimana and his supporters were imbued with a virulent racial nationalism and were unwilling to accommodate minority Tutsi demands. Habyarimana died in April 1994 when his plane was shot down as it approached Kigali airport. It is still not known whether Tutsi or Hutu extremists were responsible, but Hutus blamed Tutsi operatives.

On 6 April 1994, Hutus began slaughtering both Tutsis and moderate Hutus in an orgy of violence that lasted 100 days and left approximately 800,000 men, women and children dead.

The role played by the media in the slaughter was significant. One extremist Hutu newspaper had for several years been fanning the fires of ethnic hatred against Tutsis. When the killings began, a TV station urged 'loyal' Hutus to 'crush the cockroaches' – i.e., the Tutsis. Hutus who refused to kill Tutsis were themselves killed.

Although there had been credible warnings of a genocide well before it occurred, little preventive action had been taken. And once it started no outside power attempted to intervene in what turned out to be a deliberate, systematic attempt at extermination of a particular racial, ethnic or cultural group. This is despite the 1948 UN Convention on the Prevention and Punishment of the Crime of Genocide, which holds that 'genocide, whether committed in time of peace or in time of war, is a crime under international law' which the contracting parties 'undertake to prevent and to punish'. (UN, 1948).

A contingent of Belgian peacekeepers had been present in the capital early in the episode but were withdrawn after ten of their number, attempting to protect the moderate Hutu prime minister, were killed by Hutu extremists. Peacekeepers in other locations, also sent to monitor the 1993 peace agreement, withdrew when the violence escalated. Although the peacekeepers encountered heavy criticism for their departure, one explanation is that they were not authorized or equipped to use military force. But the UN Security Council could have strengthened the mandate of the forces already there as well as providing reinforcements.

The US and France subsequently came in for especially heavy criticism – the US for a gross failure of political will and France for supporting the Hutus. The US had lost a number of soldiers in Somalia in 1993 and was reluctant to get involved in another African theatre of conflict. Whatever the reasons for UN inaction, there is no escaping the fact that little or nothing was done to prevent an episode of mass murder that went on for 100 days.

How do we analyse this particular incident in late twentieth-century history in terms of the contrasting approaches provided on intervention by pluralists and solidarists, or communitarians and cosmopolitans? What would pluralists and communitarians have to say about the cultural embedding of ethical norms within the Rwandan context in such an egregious case of human rights abuses? Should the state of Rwanda have been left to its own sovereign devices, which is more or less what actually happened for over three months?

If, in rejecting such approaches, we adopt a solidarist or cosmopolitan principle and declare that *someone* should have intervened in a case such as this, we must also address the question: who would authorize an intervention and who should carry it out? The issue of authorization seems relatively simple – the UN. But exactly who should carry it out is more problematic. The US and its NATO allies have intervened in a number of serious conflicts on the grounds that they are protecting innocent civilians – Libya in 2013 being a recent case – but they have often been criticized for doing so only when it suits their interests.

There is also the issue of what general rules should govern any such intervention. Every case is different, and there is little agreement on how a general rule should be formulated or applied to cover varying circumstances. Also, some states may be willing and able to carry out an authorized intervention, but at other times they may not be so willing. Following Somalia, the US was extremely unwilling to commit troops abroad in such situations, at least until the (unauthorized) invasion of Iraq in 2003. Action in Libya was limited to air strikes, and no NATO military personnel were deployed on the ground. In the case of Rwanda, the US was even reluctant to recognize what took place *as* a genocide at the time, because doing so would have placed it under an obligation to act.

These are just some of the problems we encounter when trying to work through all the implications of 'hard cases'. It is therefore difficult to disagree with the conclusion that, while there may well be 'a pragmatic solidarism in international society in which there is agreement about norms of behaviour', there is still 'no likelihood of agreement about how those norms apply to particular cases' (Bellamy, 2003, p. 20).

Constructivist IR

It was noted earlier that constructivism does not constitute a theory of IR as such, at least not in the same way as realism, liberalism, Marxism and critical theory do. Constructivism is more of a *meta*theoretical enterprise, offering not a specific theory *of* international politics as such but, rather, an analysis of the way in which theories themselves are produced. But, more than that, it offers a distinctive way of theorizing 'reality'. It has certainly impacted very significantly on the way in which we think about theory in general, about how actors in world politics acquire perceptions of selves and others, and about how identities and interests are shaped and reshaped according to shifting contexts. Constructivism therefore emphasizes the *ideational*, although this is not at the expense of dismissing the *material* as relevant. One leading constructivist says that, unlike neorealism and neoliberalism, which drew on earlier, 'classic' forms of theory, constructivism has no direct antecedents in IR theory, although the English School, with its emphasis on values and rules and institutions, was a significant influence on a number of scholars associated with the constructivist enterprise (Ruggie, 1998, p. 11).

Other influences came from scholars such as Karl Deutsch (1912–1992) and Ernst Haas (1924–2003), who 'anticipated' a form of modernist constructivism. Deutsch, for example, initiated research on 'security communities' in the international sphere which emphasized social transactions and social communication in the development of peaceful transnational collective identities, while Haas promoted a form of neofunctionalism which examined international cooperation based on social learning and collective identity formation, as exemplified by European integration (Carlsnaes, Risse and Simmons, 2012, pp. 118–19). There was also the increasing influence of continental philosophy and, in particular, the radical constructivism of postmodern/poststructuralist approaches, which we consider shortly. This contributed to an 'intellectual ferment' of theoretical possibilities in a new period also characterized by postpositivism (see Lapid, 1989).

'Constructivism' as a term made an explicit appearance in IR with Nicholas Onuf's pioneering work *World of our Making: Rules and Rule in Social Theory and International Relations*, first published in 1989. Onuf observed that, while IR theory had experienced a revival from the mid-1970s (referring here largely to developments in neorealist/neoliberal theory in the US), more spectacular changes had been occurring in other fields. The common point of departure for these 'was a repudiation of the positivist model of science as a canonical characterization of theory and its relation to methods of inquiry' (Onuf, 2013, p. 10).

For Onuf, 'international relations form a bounded and distinctive social reality.' And what makes this particular set of social relations distinctive is that they are manifestly political relations even while lacking the element of authority (sovereignty) with which traditional political science has long been concerned (Onuf, 2013, p. 6). A key argument is that all social relations, including international relations, are characterized by the presence of rules which in turn give substance to *rule*, an argument that throws doubt on the assumption that the distinguishing feature of the international sphere is in fact anarchy. This is a clear departure from English School theory, which maintains anarchy as the primary feature of international politics, although 'rule' and 'order' bear close comparison. Onuf is especially concerned to undermine the Hobbesian opposition of anarchy and authority on which international relations and political science are separately constituted as disciplines. *Rule* is the distinctive feature of political society, which is taken to include international relations no less than civil society (Onuf and Klink, 1989, p. 149).

Elsewhere, however, Onuf claims that anarchy is 'rule by no one in particular, and therefore by everyone in association, as an unintended consequence of their many, uncoordinated acts' (Onuf, 2013, p. 23). But if anarchy is 'absence of rule', which is its literal meaning, then it is hard to escape the conclusion that Onuf is simply redefining anarchy, or rather turning it on its head. Perhaps it is more persuasive to argue that the sphere of international relations is *not* actually anarchic precisely because it is constituted through rules and *rule*, even though that rule is not embodied in a single sovereign authority. This is consistent with his argument that rule is the distinctive feature of political society, and that international relations constitutes such a society even in the absence of a single source of sovereign authority.

Similar arguments concerning rules, norms and the relationship between structure and agency have been advanced by Rey Koslowski and Friedrich Kratochwil, who, in their critique of neorealism in the wake of the unexpected collapse of the Soviet Union and the bipolar world order – which neorealism had not predicted – argued that, 'in all politics, domestic and international, actors reproduce or alter systems through their actions.' It follows that international systems exist not because their structures are immutable, but because their structures depend on the practices of actors for their reproduction. When fundamental changes occur, they do so in response to changes in the beliefs and identities of domestic actors, who thereby alter 'the rules and norms that are constitutive of their political practices. And so where distinctive patterns do emerge, they can be traced and explained, although they are unlikely to exhibit predetermined trajectories to be captured by general historical laws' (Koslowski and Kratochwil, 1994, p. 216).

The meaning and interpretation of anarchy was taken up by another leading constructivist, Alexander Wendt, in his seminal article 'Anarchy is What States Make of It' (Wendt, 1992). Noting first the extent to which debates – mainly between realists and liberals – had, by the early 1990s, come to revolve around structure, process and institutions, Wendt posed three key questions: does anarchy really force states into competitive power politics; can international regimes (institutions) overcome the logic inherent in structural assumptions about anarchy; and what exactly is immutable in anarchy, and what is amenable to change? (ibid., p. 391). In critiquing realist and liberal approaches, Wendt points out that both take 'the self-interested state as the starting point for theory', while realism, in particular, leaves no space for the consideration of interest- or identity-formation (ibid., p. 392).

It is a concern with the latter, and the extent to which these are socially constructed subjectivities, which leads Wendt to categorize his own work as constructivist while arguing that other constructivists to date had not taken the causal powers of anarchy seriously.

Key Quote   Anarchy is What States Make of It

Self-help and power politics do not follow either logically or causally from anarchy and that if today we find ourselves in a self-help world, this is due to process, not structure. There is no 'logic' of anarchy apart from the practices that create and instantiate one structure of identities and interests rather than another; structure has no existence or causal powers apart from process. Self-help and power politics are institutions, not essential features of anarchy. *Anarchy is what states make of it.* (Wendt, 1992, pp. 394–5; original emphasis)

An important theme, continued in Wendt's later work, is the extent to which ideational factors – which arise from and are mediated by social processes – are just as important as, if not more so than, material factors, for it is at the ideational level that meaning is created and identities are formed. Wendt invites us to consider, for example, that a gun in the hands of a friend is very different from a gun in the hands of an enemy (Wendt, 1996, p. 50). But, as I have noted elsewhere, if your friend happens to be former US Vice-President Dick Cheney, who famously shot a companion during a hunting expedition in 2006, you may rethink the meaning of that gun, as well as the identity of 'friend' (Lawson, 2012, p. 50). The US gun lobby slogan also puts another spin on the issue when it declares that 'Guns don't kill people; people kill people.' In an interesting article on the topic of gun violence in the US as compared with other countries, an obvious link was found between high levels of gun ownership and gunshot fatalities. In Switzerland, however, there is a higher rate of gun ownership than in most other OECD countries but a relatively low homicide rate. The conclusion drawn by the author supports a constructivist perspective: 'culture and institutions matter to the relationship between guns and violence' (Kenny, 2013).

Wendt's book-length study *Social Theory of International Politics* (1999) looks in greater depth at the social construction of the international system. While maintaining a strong state-centric approach, Wendt's emphasis on ideational rather than material forces, his proposition that identities and interests are constructed through shared ideas and not given by nature, and his holistic rather than individualistic ontology are all aimed critically at neorealist theory. But neoliberalism comes in for criticism too, especially with respect to the tendency it shares with realists to reduce social structures to individuals, resulting in an 'undersocialized' approach to theory (1999, pp. 1–4). At the same time, Wendt suggests that the tendency of some critical theorists to 'eschew state-centric theorizing' simply will not do. One purpose of his own work, he says, is to show how state-focused theory can in fact 'generate insights that might help move the international system from the law of the jungle toward the rule of law' (ibid., p. 10). This ambition is obviously shared by liberal theorists.

Despite the critique of neorealism in particular, Wendt remains committed to a form of 'scientific realism' – 'The state and state system are real structures whose nature can be approximated through science' such that 'theory reflects reality, not the other way around' (1999, p. 47). This puts Wendt on the 'thin' side of constructivism, which is essentially modernist in orientation and does not entail repudiating positivism altogether. One critic argues that Wendt only succeeds in undermining the neorealist reification of anarchy by reifying the state instead (Weber, 2009, p. 80).

The 'thin constructivism' of Wendt and others in the modernist camp tends to place them somewhere between the rationalist cluster composed mainly of neorealists and neoliberals, with their essentially positivist and materialist philosophies of science, and the 'thick constructivism' of postmodern/poststructuralist approaches, as well as some Frankfurt School critical theorists and feminists who share a commitment to an interpretivist sociology of knowledge and a relativist philosophy of science (Adler, 1997, p. 321). A particular strength of a middle-ground position is said to be its capacity to be both critical *and* problem-solving. Thus it is capable of standing apart from the prevailing world order and asking how it came about, while also maintaining a pragmatic, problem-solving orientation to the reality of the socially constructed world in which we find ourselves (ibid., p. 334).

The Postmodern/Poststructuralist Turn

Postmodernism arose initially as a literary, intellectual and artistic movement and made its way into philosophy in the late 1970s. The very term presupposes the 'modern' while the 'post' signals something that goes beyond or transcends modernity. It is not simply a critique of all that modernity stands for – science, technology and progress based on rationality and certain knowledge – but rather a challenge to many of the assumptions underpinning it. Since the study of politics in any sphere is concerned with the machinations of power, postmodern approaches in their application to politics are concerned with how power operates, especially through versions of reality produced via certain knowledge claims.

One commentator says not only that postmodernism is almost possible to define in precise terms, but that the effort to do so reflects exactly the kind of rationality that postmodernism sets out to challenge. Whereas scientific reason or philosophical reasoning seek logic, clarity and precision, postmodernism 'often seeks to grasp what escapes these processes of definition and celebrates what resists or disrupts them' (Malpas, 2005, p. 4). Another suggests that postmodernism can only be described 'as a set of critical, strategic and rhetorical practices employing concepts such as difference, repetition, the trace, the simulacrum, and hyperreality to destabilize other concepts such as presence, identity, historical progress, epistemic certainty, and the univocity of meaning' (Aylesworth, 2013).

The four leading postmodern authors of the late twentieth century whom we consider below are all French, although they drew on a variety of sources in the history of European philosophy. They were also influenced by the circumstances of the times. In addition to the phenomenon of widespread social protest experienced in France in the late 1960s, there was the broader civil rights movement, feminist issues were prominent, and anti-colonial struggles and postcolonial wars such as those in Algeria and Vietnam were in the spotlight, as was the problem of communist oppression. All these issues contributed to a dynamic intellectual milieu (Campbell, 2010, p. 222).

The first major work of philosophy in the genre was produced by Jean-François Lyotard (1924–1998), whose book *The Postmodern Condition* first appeared in 1979. The focus of this study was the 'condition of knowledge', a condition Lyotard described as postmodern in accordance with 'the state of our culture following the transformations which, since the end of the nineteenth century, have altered the game rules for science, literature and the arts' (Lyotard, 1993, p. 71). He proposed to examine those transformations 'in the context of the crisis of narratives'.

Key Quote   Science, Narratives and the Discourse of Legitimation

Science has always been in conflict with narratives. Judged by the yardstick of science, the majority of them have proved to be fables. But to the extent that science does not restrict itself to stating useful regularities and seeks the truth, it is obliged to legitimate the rules of its own game. It then produces a discourse of legitimation with respect to its own status, a discourse called philosophy. I will use the term *modern* to designate any science that legitimates itself with respect to a metadiscourse of this kind making an explicit appeal to some grand narrative. (Ibid., pp. 71–2)

Lyotard described the Enlightenment narrative as one in which 'the hero of knowledge works towards a good ethico-political end – universal peace.' A consequence is that 'justice is consigned to the grand narrative in the same way as truth.' He went on to define the postmodern condition simply as 'incredulity toward metanarratives' (1993, p. 72). Although Lyotard effectively lined up a whole range of grand narratives for demolition, from Christian redemption and Romanticism to Marx's theory of history and Enlightenment progress, Perry Anderson says that the 'one whose death he above all sought to certify was . . . classical socialism' (Anderson, 1998, p. 31). Indeed, Lyotard's avowed opposition to communism also meant that capitalism largely escaped critique, although he did not actually defend it. At the time Lyotard wrote, the capitalist world was facing a major recession. This was to change during the 1980s with the rise of Ronald Reagan and Margaret Thatcher, with their right-wing 'ideological offensive', followed by the collapse of the Cold War and the Soviet Union. Far from grand narratives disappearing, the grandest of all appeared poised to triumph: 'a single universal story of liberty and prosperity, the global victory of the market' (ibid., p. 32).

In the meantime, the work of another extraordinary French scholar was gaining significant attention. Michel Foucault (1926–1984) was very much influenced by the thought of the German philosopher Friedrich Nietzsche (1844–1900), who has been described as the 'patron saint of postmodernism' (Blackburn, 2005, p. 75). For Nietzsche, 'truth', including scientific knowledge, is nothing more than a series of metaphors. These emerge in a process, first, of neural stimulations producing images, which in turn prompt a sound (a word) to represent the image. This then becomes communicated to and adopted by others. When applied to many instances of the same event, it is transformed into a concept and eventually a metaphor.

> ### Key Quote   Nietzsche on Truth
>
> What then is truth? A movable host of metaphors, metonymies, and anthro-pomorphisms: in short, a sum of human relations which have been poetically and rhetorically intensified, transferred, and embellished, and which, after long usage, seem to people to be fixed, canonical and binding. Truths are illusions which we have forgotten are illusions . . . (Nietzsche, 2010, p. 20)

Nietzsche also pioneered a 'genealogical' form of analysis which, in revealing the contingent conditions of our existence – of what is in fact arbitrary and therefore neither natural nor necessary – sought to show how claims to truth are intimately related to power. Truth thus becomes the handmaiden, not of freedom and progress, but of tyranny. Foucault further developed and refined Nietzsche's genealogical methodology, which he distinguished from history and a search for origins. Rather, genealogy attends to the 'singularity of events outside of any momentous finality' (Foucault, 2011, p. 341). Genealogy therefore avoids the tendency to combine a myriad of observations into anything resembling a 'grand narrative' (although this term is never used by Foucault). Genealogy is therefore a method rather than a production, and Foucault's aim is to problematize, through critique, what we might otherwise take for granted.

Foucault's treatment of genealogy also expands on the relationship between power and knowledge. He conceives power as consisting in relations of strategic force which are immanent in society and interwoven into every kind of relationship – from gender and kinship to broader social relations. 'Power is everywhere, not because it is all embracing but because it comes from everywhere' (Barker, 2003, p. 27). The more specific relations between power and knowledge may be observed through what power produces, and these are, in short, both the objects of knowledge and the subjects to which a particular knowledge subject relates. 'This has a major theoretico-political consequence, insofar as it challenges the foundational belief of humanism that the subject contemplates the truth from a politically neutral zone outside power' (ibid.). It follows that 'truth' is always produced within a field of power, and society itself constitutes that field.

> ### Key Quote   Foucault's Regimes of Truth
>
> Each society has its regime of truth, its 'general politics' of truth: that is, the types of discourse which it accepts and makes function as true; the mechanisms and instances which enable one to distinguish true and false statements, the means

by which each is sanctioned; the techniques and procedures accorded value in the acquisition of truth; the status of those who are charged with saying what counts as true. (Foucault, quoted ibid., p. 30)

With respect to science, this is regarded as a 'discursive formation' or 'episteme', which dictates what we can accept as 'true' while simultaneously disqualifying other knowledges (ibid.). This applies as much to the social sciences as to the natural sciences insofar as they purport to offer positive knowledge of the social world of human existence while at the same time effectively concealing the machinations of power behind the production of knowledge.

Another move in the development of postmodern/poststructural thought involved a shift away from the broader-based theorizing about society, culture, and history, exemplified in the work of Lyotard and Foucault, towards a focus on the relationship between language and knowledge. This shift was initiated largely by another highly influential French scholar, Jacques Derrida (1930–2004), through his method of 'deconstructing' texts. Because this method rejects key aspects of structuralism in philosophical linguistics, especially with respect to objectivity and universalism, it is usually labelled poststructuralist rather than postmodern. Derrida himself rejected such labels (as did Foucault), but they have tended to stick nonetheless.

Derrida's method of deconstruction focuses on the idea of 'binary oppositions' which he says are prevalent in Western thought. Deconstruction involves the identification of hierarchical oppositions – for example, good/bad, light/dark, self/other, civilized/barbarian, superior/inferior. These are fundamental to the construction of meaning because they identify not just what something is, but what it is *not*, while at the same time assigning positive or negative value to one or the other. Derrida's method is a form of critique that 'reads backwards from what seems natural, obvious, self-evident, or universal in order to show that these things have their history, their reasons for being the way they are . . . and that the starting point is not a (natural) given but a (cultural) construct, usually blind to itself' (Johnson, in Derrida, 2004, p. xvi). This appears similar to the purpose of genealogy and the 'archaeology of knowledge' which that exercise entails. The end goal of deconstruction is to dismantle the very structures of meaning and expose their premises, thereby revealing the extent to which 'objectivity' is itself a construct often allied to power (Edgar and Sedgwick, 1999, pp. 108–9).

The fourth of the French philosophers introduced here is Jean

Baudrillard (1929–2007), whose notions of hyperreality and simulacra turned the postmodern gaze in the direction of 'mediatization', the prime agents of which are film and television. These allow the simulation of some 'thing' or other through the technological mediation of images and sounds. Baudrillard contends that the 'thing' has no reality in an original form – it is 'the generation by models of a real without origin or reality: a hyperreal' (Baudrillard, 1994, p. 1). Thus what passes for reality is 'a network of images and signs without an external referent, such that what is represented is representation itself' (Aylesworth, 2013). Interestingly, Baudrillard prefaces his discussion with an epigraph which purports to be from the Old Testament book Ecclesiastes: 'The simulacrum is never what hides the truth – it is truth that hides the fact that there is none. The simulacrum is true.' The 'truth' in this case, however, is that there is nothing in Ecclesiastes that even vaguely resembles this quotation. Perhaps Baudrillard was making his point about the representation of something that does not exist in an 'original'. In one infamous development, Baudrillard seemed to overstate his case when, in reference to the first Gulf War of 1991, he declared that it simply had not taken place. Case study 7.2 explains this interesting claim and the reaction to it from critical theorists.

We can see from the foregoing that a common theme running throughout postmodern/poststructuralist analyses is the rejection of objective truth and, as a corollary, of firm foundations for knowledge. To the extent that we believe that we possess knowledge, or that we apprehend realities, these are produced through social processes – hence social constructivism underpins the postmodern/poststructuralist enterprise, although it is expressed in a rather stronger form. Further, although postmodern/poststructuralist intellectuals may well reject the whole notion of 'ideology' and 'taking a stance', the anti-science/anti-modern/ anti-Enlightenment approach evinced by authors in the genre may well be read as a form of ideology whose own foundations are constructed on an anti-truth logic.

Having provided a sketch of some of the principal philosophical ideas underpinning postmodern/poststructuralist thought in general, we turn now to their more specific manifestation in IR theory. The principal target of early postmodern IR critiques was, as with much critical and constructivist theory, neorealism. A seminal article published by Richard K. Ashley in the early 1980s made this clear enough in its title, 'The Poverty of Neorealism'. Ashley's own approach was also flagged in the quotation from yet another influential French intellectual, Pierre

Case Study 7.2 Jean Baudrillard and the War That Never Happened

In August 1990, Iraq under the rule of Saddam Hussein invaded and occupied neighbouring Kuwait with the intention of annexing it. Iraq had accumulated massive debts during a previous war with Iran, and the acquisition of Kuwait's extensive oil fields would have contributed much to reducing that debt, as well as expanding Iraqi power in the region. The UN swiftly imposed sanctions and called for Iraq's immediate withdrawal. Other states in the region, especially Saudi Arabia and Egypt, were alarmed at Iraq's behaviour and urged international action.

Iraq ignored all the demands of the UN, and on 17 January 1991 a coalition of forces, sanctioned by a UN resolution and led by the US, moved against Saddam's forces in Operation Desert Storm. In the ensuing war, now commonly known as the First Gulf War, US-led forces dropped approximately 85,000 tons of munitions on Iraq and Kuwait. Iraqi civilian and military deaths are estimated to be around 200,000. Many Iraqi deaths in the aftermath of the war have been attributed to the massive destruction of essential infrastructure. US casualties were around 300 dead.

This war was covered much more extensively by the media than previous conflicts, especially the war from the air, and was virtually continuous (albeit with many repeats of actions) from the moment it started, becoming a daily spectacle for millions of viewers around the world. (This author recalls her elder son calling on the day to say 'The war's started – we're watching it on TV'.)

Even as the bombs were falling, Baudrillard proposed that it was a simulacrum of war, 'a virtual event which is less the representation of real war than a spectacle which serves a variety of political and strategic purposes on all sides' (Patton, in Baudrillard, 1995, p. 10). Baudrillard's work incidentally, is a key source for the popular *Matrix* film trilogy and is actually shown in the first film. In explaining Baudrillard's position, Patton says:

> At the time, the TV Gulf War must have seemed to many viewers a perfect Baudrillardian simulacrum, a hyperreal scenario in which events lose their identity and signifiers fade into one another. Fascination and horror at the reality which seemed to unfold before our very eyes mingled with a pervasive sense of unreality as we recognized the elements of the Hollywood script . . . Occasionally, the absurdity of the media's self-representation as purveyor of reality and immediacy broke through, in moments such as those when the CNN cameras crossed live to a group of reporters assembled somewhere in the Gulf, only to have them confess that they were watching CNN in order to find out what was happening. Television news coverage appeared to have finally caught up with the logic of simulation. (Ibid., p. 3)

Critical theorists, however, were not amused, let alone persuaded, by Baudrillard's claims about the non-event of the Gulf War. One response by the philosopher and literary critic Christopher Norris was to deplore the flight from reason evinced by Baudrillard and to describe him as the 'purveyor of some of the silliest ideas yet to gain a hearing among disciples of French intellectual fashion', for whom there is no appeal to any standard of veracity. Rather, any truth claim, according to Baudrillard's perspective, would simply be subscribing to a 'realist ontology that clung to some variant of the truth/falsehood or fact/fiction dichotomy' (Norris, 1992, pp. 11, 13).

Norris concludes his critique by describing postmodernism's 'retrograde stance' and its 'intellectual and political bankruptcy' as effectively negating the entire legacy of critical emancipatory thought. In this he has been joined by other critical theorists, such as Terry Eagleton, who, although appreciating some of the innovative ideas produced by postmodern thinkers such as Foucault on the functioning of power, nonetheless argue that this has been at the expense of maintaining any sort of ethical basis from which to mount social critique (see Smith, 2008, p. 99). Similarly, Habermas has been concerned to rescue the very possibility of reasoned critique from what he sees as the abyss of irrationality created by postmodernism's own particular anti-modernist/anti-Enlightenment logic, which, in the final analysis, amounts to another species of conservatism (see Habermas, 1981).

Baudrillard's obituary in *The Guardian* commenced with the observation that 'Jean Baudrillard's death did not take place', but conceded that his 'simulacrum departed at the age of 77' (Poole, 2007).

Bourdieu, with which his article opens: 'The theory of knowledge is a dimension of *political* theory because the specifically symbolic power to impose the principles of the construction of reality – in particular, social reality, is a major dimension of political power' (Bourdieu, quoted in Ashley, 1984, p. 225; emphasis added).

The critique of neorealism is summed up in a scathing denunciation of its assumptions and its own totalizing project. This is worth quoting at some length to capture the flavour of Ashley's approach.

Key Quote   The Poverty of Neorealism

I shall contend that neorealism is itself . . . a self-enclosed, self-affirming joining of statist, utilitarian, positivist, and structuralist commitments. Although it claims to side with the victors in two American revolutions – the realist revolution against idealism, and the scientific revolution against traditionalism – it in fact betrays both. It betrays the former's commitment to political autonomy by reducing political practice to an economic logic, and it neuters the critical faculties of the latter by swallowing methodological rules that render science a purely technical enterprise. From realism it learns only an interest in power, from science it takes only an interest in expanding the reach of control, and from this selective borrowing it creates a theoretical perspective that parades the possibility of a rational power that need never acknowledge power's limits. What emerges is a positivist structuralism that treats the given order as the natural order, limits

> rather than expands political discourse, negates or trivializes the significance of variety across time and place, subordinates all practice to an interest in control, bows to the ideal of a social power beyond responsibility, and thereby deprives political interaction of those practical capacities which make social learning and creative change possible. What emerges is an ideology that anticipates, legitimizes, and orients a totalitarian project of global proportions: the rationalization of global politics. (Ashley, 1984, p. 228)

Although Ashley's critique of neorealism clearly takes aim at its 'structuralism', it does not reflect an explicit *post*structuralism in the mode of the French philosophers discussed above, noting that Bourdieu, frequently cited in Ashley's article, is a critical social theorist with discernible modernist tendencies. Further, Ashley is not dismissive of science as such but, rather, of the positivistic pretensions of neorealism, which he cast as 'bad science' (1984, p. 285), a position that most critical theorists and social constructivists generally would endorse.

A few years later, Ashley and another very prominent IR theorist, R. B. J. Walker, co-authored the lead article of a special journal issue subtitled 'Dissident Thought in International Studies', which is recognizably more postmodern/poststructuralist in orientation (and which opens and closes with quotes from Foucault). They draw out the fact that 'knowing' in the sense celebrated in modern culture involves constructing a controlled meaning whose truth is beyond doubt, and which therefore resists further interpretation.

Key Quote   Man Is Not the Measure of All Things

It is the figure of 'man' who is understood to be the origin of language, the condition of all knowledge, the maker of history and the source of truth and meaning in the world. . . . man may subdue history, quiet all uncertainty, clarify all ambiguity, and achieve total knowledge, total autonomy and total power. This is the promise implicit in every claim of modern 'knowledge' . . . This, too, is the promise that the disciplines of modern social science make – a promise of knowledge and power on behalf of a universal sovereign figure of 'man' whose voice a discipline would speak. And this, as it happens, is the same promise that legitimates the violence of the modern state . . . (Ashley and Walker, 1990, pp. 262–3).

One purpose here, among others, seems to be thoroughly to problematize 'man' in the humanist sense as 'the measure of all things'. And yet 'man' is, according to the logic of any version of social constructivism, and especially a postmodern/poststructural perspective, indeed the author of all 'things', for 'reality' by no means exists 'out there' in some objective realm of being but is constructed in and through the social interactions of human subjects.

If 'reality', 'truth' and 'knowledge', including moral knowledge, emerge only as a function of power, it seems that morality can only ever be relative to the particular configuration of power which gives rise to it. Postmodern/poststructuralist perspectives therefore appear to constitute a radical form of ethical relativism or, at best, offer only negative critiques of foundational theories. This is the view taken by Habermas, who, as we have seen, critiqued in particular the work of both Foucault and Derrida for their attack on the prime Enlightenment values of reason and universal morality, a position that leads not only to relativism but also to a form of anti-modern conservatism.

As I have remarked previously (Lawson, 2012), most postmodern/poststructuralist writers within IR do not see themselves as abandoning the possibility of ethics and have, indeed, been concerned to mount an ethical critique of such constructions as sovereignty, especially in relation to its exclusionary practices (see, for example, George, 1994). In this respect, they appear to share common ground with critical theorists. Linklater argues, however, that 'incredulity towards grand narratives of universal emancipation' combined with merely 'contingent moral standpoints' leave postmodern/poststructural approaches ill-equipped to tackle the serious ethical issues in contemporary world politics (Linklater, 1998, pp.64–5). On the other hand, postmodern/poststructural authors can readily point to the consequences of certain emancipatory metanarratives which, they argue, have led to practices just as oppressive as those they replaced. Liberalism, for example, emancipated people from feudalism, only to deliver them to capitalism, while Marxism replaced capitalism with Leninism and Maoism (Griffiths and O'Callaghan, 2002, pp.252–3).

If postmodern/poststructural approaches have difficulty with proposing a theory of ethics rather than simply a critique of other approaches, perhaps it is because postmodern/poststructural approaches, as with constructivism more generally, do not themselves constitute a theory as such. Nor do they attempt to do so. They certainly do not seek to examine cause and effect but, rather, to examine how the partnership between cause and effect is produced in discourse, with all its attendant power relations, and does not occupy an independent position outside of discourse. Rather than producing theory, then, the point of the postmodern/poststructural intellectual enterprise is to produce critiques of theory. In other words, it does not seek to replicate anything resembling a 'social science' but, rather, to expose the assumptions on which conventional theories have been built and to highlight the possibilities for alternative accounts of the world (Campbell, 2010, p. 235).

Conclusion

The revival of the English School, the emergence of constructivist IR and the impact of postmodern/poststructural approaches on the study of international politics reflect the considerable impact that social theory has had on the discipline over the last three decades or so. All have highlighted the starkly *a*social world depicted by neorealism, in which the anarchical structure of international politics is constructed in entirely mechanistic terms and in which there is little room for the play of social forces. Social theory approaches also tend to eschew the equally mechanistic methodology of positivism and its claims to produce objective knowledge free of the taint of subjectivities. There are, however, differences within and between the various forms of social theory as manifest in the three broad approaches to IR discussed here.

We have seen that English School theorists focus on the production of norms and values that contribute to the sociability of the international sphere. Constructivists also take account of norms and values but focus more on the identities and interests generated by international actors. They are especially concerned to highlight the relationship between the material and the ideational and to show how the *meaning* of material features of the world is produced through ideational processes.

There are no serious points of contention between English School approaches and the more general constructivist enterprise in IR, but the latter has drawn far more explicitly on social theory and the social construction of reality, highlighting more clearly the problem of locating the realities of international politics outside of the social interactions of the participants themselves. This also serves to strengthen the critiques of approaches that appeal to some standard supplied by 'nature'.

The scrutiny with which postmodern/poststructural approaches have subjected all modes of representation and exposed the contingent nature of constructs such as sovereignty, justice, order, and the like, has taken critique to another level again. Although these approaches have been critiqued in turn for their apparent denial of the very possibility of reasoned knowledge, they have nonetheless provided important insights on the power/knowledge nexus. This has particular relevance for the topics covered in the next two chapters.

QUESTIONS FOR DISCUSSION

1 How do ideas of critical or social realism and situated knowledge contribute to our understanding of the world of politics?
2 What is the difference between a *system* of states and a *society* of states in English School theory?
3 What is the relationship between pluralism and communitarianism, on the one hand, and solidarism and cosmopolitanism, on the other?
4 What is the relation between the material and the ideational in constructivist thought?
5 How does constructivist IR treat the 'logic of anarchy'?
6 How are state identities and interests 'constructed' in international politics?
7 In what sense is 'truth' the servant of power in postmodern thought?
8 Is it fair to say that the point of the postmodern/poststructural intellectual enterprise is to produce critiques of theory rather than theory as such?

FURTHER READING

Barkin, J. Samuel (2010) *Realist Constructivism: Rethinking International Relations Theory*. Cambridge: Cambridge University Press.
Edkins, Jenny (1999) *Poststructuralism and International Relations: Bringing the Political Back In*. Boulder, CO: Lynne Rienner.
Fierke, Karin M., and Knud Eric Jørgensen (2001) *Constructing International Relations: The Next Generation*. Armonk, NY: M. E. Sharpe.
Guzzini, Stefano, and Anna Leander (eds) (2006) *Constructivism and International Relations: Alexander Wendt and his Critics*. Abingdon: Routledge.
Navari, Cornelia, and Daniel Green (eds) (2013) *Guide to the English School in International Studies*. Chichester: John Wiley.

USEFUL WEBSITES

www.youtube.com/watch?v=7yQJTXWgd8k (short lecture on constructivism by Daniel Nexon)
www.oxfordbibliographies.com/view/document/obo-9780199743292/obo-9780199743292–0061.xml (bibliography of constructivism)

www.theory-talks.org/2008/04/theory-talk-3.html (interview with Alexander Wendt)

www.e-ir.info/2008/01/28/how-do-postmodernists-analyse-international-relations/ (explaining postmodern analysis in IR)

www.youtube.com/watch?v=xQHm-mbsCwk (documentary on Michel Foucault)

8

Feminism and Gender Theory

Both feminism and gender theory are concerned with how biological sex – which is conventionally understood as given by 'nature' – and the categories of masculine and feminine – which are socially constructed – are implicated in the dynamics of power. In this chapter we first consider the rise of feminism as a body of theory concerned with the role and status of women vis-à-vis men and with the various feminisms that have emerged. This pluralization indicates that feminism is no homogeneous category but rather a very diverse intellectual enterprise with conflicting strands, some of which intersect with other theories and ideologies discussed in this book. Gender theory is linked to the rise of feminism but is more expansive in devoting equal attention to problems with the construction of masculinity, as well as hierarchies within these categories. For social and political theory generally, gendered roles, gendered hierarchies, and the very notion of a simple masculine/feminine binary gender divide are of particular importance in the analysis of power.

This chapter looks specifically at the emergence of feminist IR as well as at gender issues in global political economy and the state of political representation, both of which indicate that gender parity in the political and economic spheres is still very far from being realized. Finally, we consider the gendered nature of war and the military along with the very problematic issue of sexual violence in the broader context of political violence. This sheds light on an aspect of power politics that has long been ignored in traditional IR theory.

The discussion further illuminates several themes of the book. First, it will be seen that the various versions of feminism and gender theory are strongly normative in their critique of the institution of patriarchy and conventional models of femininity and masculinity. Second, they engage with issues concerning what is 'natural' or otherwise in terms of gender and provide some rather different perspectives on the 'naturalization of power'. And, third, they challenge conventional understandings of reality through exposing the subjective, interest-laden dimensions of gendered constructions of legitimate power and authority and the implications for politics at various levels, from the local through to the global sphere.

Feminism(s) in Historical Perspective

In its most basic formulation, feminism is concerned with the right of women to be treated equally with men, implying that there are gendered *in*equalities to be addressed as a matter of justice. These inequalities are regarded by feminists as historically enshrined in patriarchal social, political and economic arrangements privileging males in numerous spheres of life while casting women as essentially inferior and therefore subordinate by nature. Patriarchy itself is an expression of power.

Key Quote   Patriarchy and Power

The term patriarchy refers to power relations in which women's interests are subordinated to the interests of men. These power relations take on many forms, from the sexual division of labour and the social organisation of procreation to the internalised norms of femininity by which we live. Patriarchal power rests on social meaning given to biological sexual difference. (Weedon, quoted in Hodgson-Wright, 2006, p. 3)

Beyond a basic understanding of feminism as a normative critique of patriarchy and a quest for justice, there have been numerous disagreements among its adherents, ranging from the essential causes of gender inequality to just what the aims of feminism should be and how these may best be achieved. These contestations are reflected in the different variants of feminism examined in this chapter.

Historically, feminism emerged in the more general context of modernity and the Enlightenment in Europe and North America, drawing inspiration from movements for liberation embodied in the French and American revolutions as well as the anti-slavery movement. Although there were antecedents, modern feminism effectively begins with Mary Wollstonecraft, whom we encountered in the earlier discussion of Marxism. Her treatise *A Vindication of the Rights of Woman*, first published in 1791, however, drew on classic liberal ideas of individual rights to attack prevailing conservative views on the 'correct' place of women in society – one which was firmly subordinate to men – as well as broader criticisms of the rigid class hierarchies common in her day. The key to liberation from the infantilized state within which woman were contained was education: 'Strengthen the female mind by enlarging it, and there will be an end to blind obedience' (Wollstonecraft, 1891, p. 56).

Wollstonecraft's liberal contemporary John Stuart Mill supported full equality for women, arguing that the 'legal subordination of one sex to the other – is wrong in itself, and now one of the chief hindrances to human improvement' (Mill, 1869, p. 1). Mill further identified the justification for male dominance in a realist/Darwinist notion that inequality emerges from the 'law of the strongest', a notion which 'advanced nations' had abandoned 'as the regulating principle of the world's affairs' (ibid., p. 10). Indeed, he suggested that the degree of civilization itself may be measured according to the degree of debasement or elevation of the social position of women (ibid., pp. 37–8). Mill also reflected on the notion, embedded in critical theory approaches, that, although mechanisms of domination and subordination always appear *natural* to those who possess them, they actually depend on custom (ibid., p. 21, 23). This clearly implies that custom, or what we now generally call culture, is itself shaped by power.

Liberal theorists were not the only voices in the debate. Socialists contributed too, most notably the French intellectual Charles Fourier (1772–1837), who foreshadowed some of Mill's arguments.

Key Quote   Progress as the Emancipation of Women

The change in a historical epoch can always be determined by the progress of women towards freedom, because in the relation of women to man, of the weak to the strong, the victory of human nature over brutality is most evident. The degree of emancipation of women is the natural measure of general emancipation. (Fourier, quoted in Shukla, 2007, p. 68)

The words 'feminism' and 'feminist' did not enter the vocabulary of English or other European languages until around the end of the nineteenth century. The fledgling social movement which had emerged by this time had been known simply as the 'woman movement'. Much of the energy of the early movement had been directed towards obtaining basic civil rights, such as the right to vote, but the arrival of 'feminism' appeared to signal a much more thoroughgoing social revolution in the drive for emancipation. From the earliest stages, arguing for the rights of women involved promoting their inherent equality with men, although most recognized a distinction between the sexes when it came to their 'natural endowments'. Some felt that men, apart from being obviously physically stronger, were fundamentally more competitive, aggressive and egocentric, while women were more peacefully inclined and possessed a greater capacity for nurturing. One commentator, writing in mid-nineteenth-century America, suggested that these qualities, combined with a superior moral capacity, were much needed to counter the 'excess of masculinity' found both in an unjust legal system and in society more generally (Frohock, quoted in Cott, 1987, p. 19). These views contrasted with conservative thought, which held that women generally possessed a diminished capacity for rational thought *and* morality, as supported by the biblical account of the temptation of Eve in the Garden of Eden as well as the fact that she was created second to Adam (Hodgson-Wright, 2006, p. 5).

The early feminist movement, now known as the 'first wave' of feminism, began in nineteenth-century Europe and North America and extended to settler colonies in Australia, New Zealand and South Africa. The campaign for suffrage saw voting rights for women introduced, with New Zealand leading the way at a national level in 1893. But the movement for equal rights was not confined to the West. In parts of the Middle East, India, China and Japan, movements emerged reflecting both the general principles of equality and the particular problems of women in those areas. In China, the issue of gender inequality achieved prominence in the mid-nineteenth century, when more general questions of reform and modernization came onto the social and political agenda. As in the West, the emphasis was on equal legal rights, as well as abolishing such practices as polygamy and foot-binding (see, generally, Yuan, 2005). At much the same time, the status of women in India began to be questioned in the context of widespread socio-religious reform. One commentator on this period notes the particularity of feminism in cultural terms but also remarks: 'It seems to be a universal phenomenon that the definition and discourse on the "nature" of "woman" originated in commentaries on religious texts, which authorize patriarchal customs' (Anagol, 2005, p. 20).

It was not until the second half of the twentieth century that a 'second wave' of feminism prompted more significant social and political changes. This second wave was situated in a post-Second World War context of social and political change which saw liberation movements of various kinds emerge, including the decolonization movement. The most important feminist text in the immediate postwar period was produced in 1949 by Simone de Beauvoir, who looked in particular at the social construction of woman as 'other'. Beginning with the observation that 'One is not born, but rather becomes, woman', she went on to suggest that 'No biological, psychical or economic destiny defines the figure that the human female takes on in society; it is civilisation as a whole that elaborates this intermediary product between the male and the eunuch that is called feminine.' In this process, the female is constituted 'as an *Other*' (de Beauvoir, 2010, p. 293; original emphasis).

Although the 'equal rights feminism' of the first wave seemed radical at the time, the second-wave quest for 'women's liberation' went further. It tackled not only continuing sex discrimination in many different areas, including unequal pay and opportunities, but also the continuing subordination of women in social life through a critique of prevailing notions of what constitutes a proper standard of femininity. Contraception and abortion rights also came firmly onto the agenda as many women demanded control of their own bodies – control now made possible by new medical technologies. In the US, women's liberation was linked to civil rights issues pursued by the black movement, although it remained mainly white and middle class. Tactics varied within and between these movements, but they shared a focus on claims to individual rights in the liberal tradition.

In Britain and other parts of Europe, women active in left-wing politics are said to have given the movement a more radical Marxist-socialist inflection (Thornham, 2006, p. 27). Whether this made a significant difference to outcomes, however, is rather doubtful. Interestingly, female leadership in Britain has actually emerged from its most conservative institutions. Three of Britain's most successful monarchs have been queens. And, under a Conservative government, Britain has recently changed the law of primogeniture to give precedence to a first-born child of either sex. The Conservative Party has also produced Britain's only female prime minister to date. In the most recent German elections, Angela Merkel was returned as chancellor at the head of Germany's conservative Christian Democratic Union party. In other parts of the world, some cultural areas generally regarded as very socially conservative have had more female heads of government or state than many parts of the West. India, Pakistan, Bangladesh and Sri Lanka have all produced female prime ministers. The US compares very unfavourably.

Second-wave feminism, which ran more or less from the 1960s to the 1980s, also revolved mainly around concerns expressed by white, middle-class women and, although seemingly more far-reaching in some ways, tended to be underpinned by liberal assumptions about equal rights and equal opportunity and was not theorized much beyond these inferences. Subsequent critiques of second-wave feminism accused its proponents of assuming that these concerns, along with their own essentialized notions of womanhood, could be projected universally, as if the concerns of working-class women, ethnic minority women, or women in the developing world were more or less the same.

This matches the critique of liberalism more generally insofar as it is accused of homogenizing, essentializing and projecting a 'universal individual' – an individual that is likely to exhibit the characteristics of its creator: white, Western, middle class, heterosexual and male. In the case of liberal feminists, the only difference is that the figure is female. Feminism was therefore under pressure to recognize differences among women and to abandon notions of a unified female subjectivity that can be liberated or emancipated through the progressive march of modernity, a vision that socialist approaches had also embraced.

But this was also the period in which 'radical feminism' became distinguished from liberal feminism and socialist feminism. Although there are variations within this version, as there are within liberal and socialist versions, radical feminists shared a commitment to exposing the deeper social bases of discrimination. According to one source, radical feminists first coined the terms 'sexism' and 'sexual politics', the latter training a critical spotlight on the institution of marriage and family life, drawing attention to the power dynamics operating within what was conventionally seen as a personal and private sphere and popularizing the phrase 'the personal is the political'. A major contention of radical feminist groups was that sexism constituted neither a natural expression of sexual differences nor simply outdated attitudes, but a whole social system 'embedded in law, tradition, economics, education, organized religion, science, language, the mass media, sexual morality, child rearing, the domestic division of labor, and everyday social interaction – whose intent and effect was to give men power over women' (Willis, 1989, p.x). These ideas were later taken up by another radical sexual political movement in the form of gay liberation (ibid.).

Another strand of feminism often associated with radical feminism, but with a distinctive set of ideas, is cultural feminism. This strand endorses the view that biological differences between women and men do indeed give rise to essential differences in character traits; women are more nurturing, peaceful, compassionate and egalitarian while men are more aggressive, violent, self-interested and hierarchical. Cultural feminism therefore effectively naturalized these differences but promoted the idea that women's inherent qualities are superior. This obviously contrasts with feminist approaches that minimize the importance of biological differences and take a social constructivist approach to gender characteristics. Another variant, emphasizing inherent equality and sameness even at a physical level, is 'Amazon feminism', which tends to idealize strong, muscular, heroic women (see Kharbe, 2009, p. 270).

A third wave of feminism, starting around the late 1980s/early 1990s, recognized that the plurality of positions in which women find themselves (working class, non-white, non-Western, etc.) meant that their concerns may differ accordingly, an approach that fits with postcolonial analysis. However, it has been pointed out that postcolonial theory 'has tended to elide gender differences in constructing a single category of the colonized' (Ashcroft, Griffiths and Tiffin, 2000, p. 84).

Yet another quite different strand of feminism to emerge with the third wave is ecological feminism or ecofeminism. As the term suggests, this is concerned with the links between the domination and exploitation of nature and the domination and exploitation of women, thereby making the environment a feminist issue. Common themes in ecofeminism are the interconnectedness of all living things (ecologism), a concern for the relationship between humans and the natural world, and a special emphasis on a 'woman–nature' connection. A major claim of ecofeminists is that the hierarchical framework supporting patriarchy damages both women *and* nature. Others object to this formulation, noting that drawing too close a relationship between women and nature amounts to another way of essentializing women and falsely naturalizing relationships (see Ford, 2008, p. 186). Cultural feminists, however, would not regard this as a problem.

An alternative account of ecofeminism holds that there is a close relationship not only between how people are treated on the basis of their gender and how the natural (non-human) environment is treated, but that class or ethnicity are implicated as well. Furthermore, it is argued that those who live on the margins are most likely to suffer the consequences of environmental degradation. The main target of critique is modern Western industrial/capitalist society. The remedy for the injustices it has perpetrated, which include the injustices of colonialism and indigenous dispossession as well as environmental degradation, lies in an approach which brings together feminist, indigenous, postcolonial and green perspectives (Warren, 1997, pp. xi–xvi). This kind of approach has led others to declare ecofeminism 'incurably neo-romantic' (Hay, 2002, p. 90).

Interestingly, although one might expect ecofeminists and deep ecologists to join hands on many issues, there has been a history of quite hostile debates between the two groups, with ecofeminists accusing deep ecologists of an inherent masculinism which fails to recognize that the oppression of nature is linked to the oppression of women. Deep ecologists, on the other hand, see ecofeminists as simply promoting another form of anthropocentrism (see Sessions, 1991). Some ecofeminists have also taken aim at mainstream feminism, especially first-wave 'masculinizing feminism', accusing it of 'complicity with the Western androcentric colonisation of the lifeworld by instrumental reason' (Saleh, quoted in Hay, 2002, p. 92). Clearly, there is no end to the permutations of feminism.

Mention must also be made of a discernible element of conservative 'post-feminism' that has emerged alongside the third wave. Post-feminism has been especially critical of so-called victim feminism, perhaps partly in response to a cultural backlash against second-wave feminists, negative portrayals of feminism in the media and elsewhere (with feminists often being cast as ugly, man-hating lesbians), and claims that women were now in fact liberated and no longer need any special ideology to sustain a cause that had been fought and won (see, generally, Gamble, 2006). We return to some of these issues in the section on feminist theorizing in IR, but first we look at the more general field of gender theory, which extends many of the insights first raised by feminism.

From Feminism to Gender Theory

Gender theory developed more or less out of feminist theory and the quest for women's equality simply because most gendered orders around the world have long privileged men over women (Connell, 2009, p. x). But gender theory has gone beyond feminism's more specific concerns and now incorporates a much broader range of issues concerning masculinity and femininity and how these mediate social and political life. While these concepts are obviously associated with biological sex, they are not the same thing. One's sex is biologically given as either male or female (notwithstanding cases of intersexuality and transsexuality) but masculinity and femininity are social constructs. This is illustrated by the fact that individuals may be described as *more or less* masculine or feminine based on their personal style or behaviour. Thus a male may be described as 'effeminate' if his style does not accord with a certain standard of masculinity, while a female may be regarded as 'butch' or at best 'androgenous' if she does not conform to socially determined norms of femininity. In other words, gender perceptions reflect certain socially acquired beliefs about how males and females *ought* to conduct themselves, and individuals *learn* their roles accordingly. Most importantly, the distinction between masculine and feminine traits is rarely value-neutral, and masculine characteristics have traditionally been valued more highly in the political and social sphere. Thus it is men who are conventionally seen as possessing strength, rationality, leadership qualities, and so on, while women are seen as vulnerable, emotional and passive (Sjoberg and Via, 2010, p.3). Once again, we can see the mechanisms of social constructivism at work along with value-laden binaries.

As with other hierarchies, there are powerful traditional understandings of gender roles that link them closely to biology and which therefore 'naturalize' them. The biological fact that women give birth and produce milk to feed their infants has been taken to mean that women are naturally suited to a life of child-rearing (well beyond the infant stage) and the domesticity this entails. This can then be used to justify girls having more limited access than boys both to education and to paid employment in adulthood (Rahman and Jackson, 2010, p.4). Then there are the problems of those who do not meet conventional standards of masculinity or femininity and who, as a consequence, it is assumed, do not meet conventional norms of sexuality. Effeminate males are frequently assumed to be homosexual, and 'butch' females lesbian, whereas this does not necessarily follow at all. On the other hand, men and women may appear to meet conventional norms of masculinity or femininity and yet may not be heterosexual. Furthermore, heterosexuality is often assumed to be natural while homosexuality, bisexuality or transsexuality is deviant. Yet homosexuality is such a common phenomenon across time and space that it is difficult to deny its 'naturalness'. In some places – ancient Greece being the example most often cited – homosexual and bisexual practices were widespread and considered completely normal. Further, recent research in epigenetics indicates that same-sex attraction may result from biochemical switches, rendering homosexuality just as biologically 'natural' as heterosexuality (see Richards, 2013).

With respect to the institution of patriarchy, while particular forms of the phenomenon may vary according to cultural and/or historical context, it is difficult to deny the prevalence of patriarchy as a social institution across time and space, notwithstanding occasional matrilineal or matrilocal systems or, even more rarely, matriarchical systems. It is one thing, however, to note that patriarchy has been a much more common phenomenon, and another altogether to say that it is therefore a more *natural* kind of social order. We examined the naturalization of power through the construction of hierarchies in the earlier discussion of critical theory, noting that those with power tend to associate it with some natural state of affairs that makes it 'right' and which is also often legitimated by religious authority. The differential status of men and women is no different.

There are also differential statuses within genders inflected by class, ethnicity and other factors which create other forms of hierarchy. One leading author has identified the phenomenon of 'hegemonic masculinity'. Drawing directly on Gramsci's analysis of class relations, and noting that the concept of hegemony 'refers to the cultural dynamic by which a group claims and sustains a leading position in social life', Connell goes on to suggest that a particular form of masculinity tends to be 'culturally exalted' at any given time, thus producing a hegemonic masculinity 'as the configuration of gender practice which embodies the currently accepted answer to the problem of the legitimacy of patriarchy [and] which guarantees ... the domination of men and the subordination of women' (Connell, 2005, p. 77).

The importance to politics of unravelling the complexity of masculinities is because problems such as violence, war and rape, as well as sexism and homophobia, are all associated largely with masculinity. At the same time, masculinity is linked with leadership in government and the military as well as in science, technology, industrialization, economics and the corporate world. A useful way of analysing masculinity in these interwoven contexts, therefore, is to consider it as a form of ideology implicated in the exercise of power and embedded in politics at all levels.

Feminism and Gender in IR

At the beginning of the 1980s, IR in the anglophone world was dominated by neorealism and neoliberalism, especially in the US. In the UK and some other places, the work of the English School provided something of an alternative. Marxist and critical theory approaches had made some impact in the discipline, but constructivist IR had yet to make an appearance. Women were practically invisible either as contributors to the IR canon or as subjects of study. In the mid-1990s, one feminist analyst wrote that IR remained 'one of the most masculinist of disciplines, in its personnel and in its understanding of states, wars and markets' and, not unsurprisingly, had been 'one of the most resistant to feminist scholarship' (Pettman, 1996, p. 2).

In the 'real' world of high politics, female leadership was a rare phenomenon, an interesting exception being the election of Margaret Thatcher (1925–2013) as British prime minister in 1979. Moreover, she led her country into a war with Argentina over the Falkland Islands (Las Malvinas), prompting comparisons with Britain's iconic Iron Age female war leader, Boudicca. But Thatcher was no feminist. She promoted neither the status of women generally nor female-friendly policies, providing 'a clear example of the fact that a successful woman doesn't always mean a step forward for women' (Freeman, 2013).

The second wave of feminism had produced feminist theorizing from at least the 1960s onwards, but it had little impact on the study of politics in either the domestic or the international sphere until the 1980s, partly as a function of the fact that so few women held academic positions in political studies departments and because feminism was not a field to which many male scholars were drawn. In 1989, however, Cynthia Enloe's *Bananas, Beaches and Bases: Making Feminist Sense of International Politics* (Enloe, 2000) marked the irreversible entry of feminism and gender theory into the study of IR. Enloe was among the first to highlight the extent to which discourses of international politics were marked by manliness, as case study 8.1 illustrates.

Another early feminist IR writer, J. Ann Tickner, has argued that both liberalism and Marxism also drew on masculinist constructions; liberalism's focus on the atomistic individual, instrumental rationality and the market economy, she said, was based on male experience, while Marxism's focus on class concealed the gendered division of labour in both public and private spheres. Moreover, all the traditional approaches to IR were linked to the domination and exploitation of nature (Tickner, cited in Griffiths and O'Callaghan, 2002, p. 303). Tickner aimed to 'introduce gender as a category of analysis into the discipline of international relations' while at the same time noting that 'international politics has always been a gendered activity' (Tickner, 1992, p. 5). She pointed out that, because foreign and military policy has been formulated and conducted primarily by men, it should come as no surprise that the discipline that analyses them would be primarily about men and masculinity. Until gender hierarchies are eliminated, she says, the privileging of male characteristics, knowledge and experiences, on the one hand, and the marginalization of women, on the other, will remain a feature of international politics (ibid.).

Enloe and Tickner are often described as representing 'standpoint feminism', an approach that emerged in the 1970s and which sought to

Case Study 8.1 Political Discourses of Manliness in the 'Iran–Contra Affair'

The 'Iran–Contra affair' of the mid-1980s involved certain US foreign policy choices brought about mainly by the Reagan administration's determination to oust the socialist Sandanista government in Nicaragua by funding the right-wing (and US-friendly) Nicaraguan opposition – the 'Contras'. However, a Democrat-controlled Congress had previously legislated against any US funding of the Contras, so a complex, secret arrangement was made to sell arms to Iran – also illegal – and to use a proportion of the profits to support the Contras. The sale of arms and the profits received were channelled through Israel – another interesting twist in itself. The deal with Iran would also involve releasing a number of US hostages held there.

A key figure in the case was Lieutenant-Colonel Oliver North, who in many ways represented the ideal American embodiment of masculinity – a handsome, tough, patriotic Marine often represented as a more refined version of the heroic Hollywood military hero Rambo. To conservatives, it mattered little that North acted illegally and covertly.

Cynthia Enloe examined discourses about this episode, which she found clearly illuminated the 'politics of masculinity' and its role in shaping foreign policy debates. She noted the recurring theme was that 'we live in a dangerous world' in which small risks, not to mention illegalities, were justified to stave off greater risks – such as the risk of socialist expansion and Soviet influence represented by the Sandanistas. 'It was a world in which taking risks was proof of one's manliness and therefore of one's qualification to govern' (Enloe, 2000, p. 12).

This took place in an era when the US defeat in the Vietnam War by communist forces still rankled very deeply among conservatives in particular, a discontent that gave impetus to the New Militia movement. The latter has been analysed as part of an attempt at 'the remasculinization of America' that followed humiliation in Vietnam and provided a mode of identity politics for angry white men. The image of the Vietnam veteran became 'the springboard for a general remasculinization of American culture that is evidenced in the popularity of figures like Ronald Reagan and Oliver North . . .' (Jeffords, quoted in Snyder, 1999, p. 124). At the same time, right-wing critiques of government cast it in negative, feminized terms, especially when associated with civil rights and other such liberal policies (Snyder, 1999, pp. 124–5).

Enloe further noted that the discourse of 'manliness' was not related simply to war. It was also associated with success in managing international financial markets and had found its way into support for deregulation and the kind of robust competitiveness of which the US represented a model for the rest of the world to follow. 'Thus international finance and international diplomacy seem to be converging in their notions of the world and the kind of masculinity required to wield power . . .' (Enloe, 2000, p. 12).

Yet it was not just male figures who displayed such attitudes. Along with former film cowboy Ronald Reagan, Margaret Thatcher had been a champion of deregulation and competition, and her political personality earned her such epithets as 'honorary male' as well as 'iron lady'. These illustrate the ambiguity with which she was regarded. She was an anomaly in the world of politics, but one that could be enveloped within a dominant masculinist discourse.

With respect to Enloe's remarks about risk-taking in foreign affairs being proof of manliness and therefore of fitness to govern in a dangerous world, there is a striking resemblance to another passage from Thucydides dealing with other incidents in the period of warfare which he experienced, and which is quite different from his account of the Melian Dialogue. As events unfolded in the course of the violence of the period, Thucydides reported:

> To fit in with the change of events, words, too, had to change their usual meaning. What used to be described as a thoughtless act of aggression was now regarded as the courage one would expect to find in a party member; to think of the future and wait was merely another way of saying one was a coward; any idea of moderation was just another attempt to disguise one's unmanly character; ability to understand a question meant that one was totally unfitted for action. Fanatical enthusiasm was the mark of a real man . . . (Thucydides, V, 82)

Thucydides rarely makes an appearance in feminist or gender critiques, but he clearly provides a compelling insight into how the terms of discourse shift and change in the circumstances of war and how the concept of 'manliness' underpins justifications for aggression and cruelty.

place women at the centre of analysis (see Sylvester, 2002, p. 242). Indeed, it is committed to articulating the specific experiences and preferences of women and, in the discipline of IR, to challenging realism and neorealism in particular (Steans, 2006, p. 13). Standpoint feminism is based on the primary claim that all knowledge is socially situated and that the knowledge we acquire *as* females *or* males is conditioned by our gender roles. Furthermore, knowledge held by more privileged members of a society may well dominate, but it is also inherently limited by the very fact of that privilege. Those placed differently in a hierarchy, whether this is because of ethnicity, class or gender, have a knowledge of their situation which simply cannot be 'known' by those more privileged. All this challenges the standard conception of objective, value-free social science, as it suggests that men, the primary creators of this body of knowledge, have simply universalized male experience through it. Moreover, men are traditionally seen *as* the norm and thus their standpoint *constitutes* the norm.

Tickner warns, however, that the notion of 'standpoint' does not justify positing a single explanation of women's subordination and therefore a single standpoint from which to deliver a singular, universalist interpretation of the world. She goes on to say that this has been challenged in particular by postmodern feminists, who have objected to a unified representation of women across the lines of race, class and culture. 'Just as feminists more generally have criticized existing knowledge that is grounded in the experiences of white Western males, postmodernists claim that feminists themselves are in danger of essentializing the meaning of women when they draw exclusively on the experiences of white Western women: such an approach runs the additional risk of reproducing the same dualizing distinctions that feminists object to in patriarchal discourse' (Tickner, 1992, p.16). This point of course resonates with postcolonial approaches, the subject of the next chapter.

There is also a distinctive body of *critical* feminism which moves analysis beyond Marxist categories of class and material structures to a critique of the ideas and ideologies that reproduce unequal gender relations (Steans, 2006, p.15). Because critical approaches are concerned with notions of hegemony, and how it is generated and maintained through a particular mode of the social construction of reality, they are well placed to critique the 'hegemonic masculinity' of the discipline of IR itself, as well as the world it both reflects and projects. In the quest for emancipation, however, critical feminist theorists, too, have been cautioned not to assume a single female subjectivity, especially one created by the capitalist world system (see ibid.). But any critical approach that is sensitive to cultural difference must also confront the fact that the sources of the subordination of women are in fact cultural in the first place and that 'culture' is often defined by men, albeit with the acquiescence of compliant women, and is then used to legitimate the continuation of oppressive practices. This accords with Gramscian perspectives on cultural hegemony and the extent to which it persuades people (women in this case) to endorse and participate in the very systems which ensure their own subordination.

Gender, Global Political Economy and Representation

Feminism and gender analysis has highlighted the fact that states and markets – the principal institutions of political and economic power – have historically been dominated by males. In economics, gender is now recognized as a basic organizing principle, shaping the dynamics of production, distribution and consumption both within states and across borders (O'Brien and Williams, 2010, p.281). Historically, wealth, the ability to earn an income, and rights to inheritance, property and assets generally have been held disproportionately by males, creating a significant gender gap in access to financial resources and therefore in economic power. Another issue is that conventional economics does not place a value on women's reproductive or domestic labour (ibid.). It is notable that the original Marxist conception of labour referred only to work in the formal, paid economy, ignoring the fact that domestic, unpaid labour provides essential support to workers in the formal economy (Watson, 2008, p. 47).

While there has been improvement over time in advanced industrial economies, and legal reforms have removed formal barriers in many cases, a gender gap nonetheless persists in the distribution of wealth, assets and income in most of these countries, and much of women's unpaid labour remains unrecognized or undervalued at best. Incidentally, the region that does best as far as gender parity in economic terms is concerned is Scandinavia. As we see shortly, the countries of this region have also achieved the best results in terms of social and political advancement, thus indicating a correlation between economic and political equality.

Women in most developing countries are at an even greater disadvantage vis-à-vis males over a range of social and economic indicators. This is also regarded as a serious impediment to development generally. The World Economic Forum's report on the 'global gender gap' in 2012 noted a strong correlation between the extent of a country's gender gap and national competitiveness and performance. 'Because women account for one-half of a country's potential talent base, a nation's competitiveness in the long term depends significantly on whether and how it educates and utilizes its women' (World Economic Forum, 2012). And a World Bank report has emphasized the fact that promoting gender equality accords with 'smart economics', as it enhances productivity while improving development opportunities for the next generation (World Bank, 2012, p. 2).

The 'feminization of poverty' is yet another issue that has been taken up in global political economy studies. And, again, while there is evidence showing that women in relatively wealthier countries are more likely to experience a life of poverty than males, it is more common in the developing world. This is often linked to social or cultural attitudes. Studies of South Asia, for example, have shown that women are systematically discriminated against within households as males are favoured when it comes to nutrition, education and healthcare, which then impacts negatively on employment prospects and other income-generating activities (O'Brien and Williams, 2010, p. 299). Interestingly, although South Asia has seen women occupy the highest political positions, this does not correlate at all with greater social and economic equality. A survey of gender and political representation in case study 8.2 shows a clear correlation between the economic and political status of women around the world.

Case Study 8.2   Gender and Political Representation in Global Perspective

Despite the extension of voting rights to women around the world over the last hundred years or so, the number of women holding seats in legislatures, let alone high political office, has remained limited. As of September 2013, of 188 countries surveyed by the Inter-Parliamentary Union, only two – Rwanda and Andorra – had 50 per cent or more female members of parliament. Rwanda's achievement was the result of a special quota system introduced in a post-conflict situation which represents a method of 'fast-tracking' a gender balance in politics (Dahlerup, 2013, p. 3). Cuba was placed third on the table, with almost 49 per cent, but only another seven countries had 40 per cent or more. Of the anglophone Western nations, where women might have been expected to be reasonably well represented, New Zealand (the first country in the world to give women the vote) had just over 32 per cent, with Australia, Canada and the UK under 25 per cent. The US had just under 18 per cent.

Sweden, Finland, Iceland, Norway and Denmark ranked in the top thirteen countries along with the Seychelles, Senegal, Nicaragua and Mozambique. Scandinavia was therefore, on average, the best region for female parliamentary representation. The region with the worst record was not the Middle East, as might be expected from the bad press that Muslim majority countries often get on gender issues. Although five Middle Eastern countries – Oman, Yemen, Iran, Lebanon and Qatar – were in the last fifteen, Pacific Island states (all Christian majority states) featured most strongly in this field, with Samoa, Tonga, the Solomon Islands, the Marshall Islands, Papua New Guinea, Micronesia, Palau and Vanuatu leading the race to the bottom (Inter-Parliamentary Union, 2013).

Looking at these figures, it is difficult to escape the conclusion that a gendered division of labour in representative politics runs deep in most parts of the world. It follows that, although women's legal rights have been transformed over the last century, in most cases this has not translated into anything like full political equality. Further, and again despite legal equality, the continuing under-representation of women has negative consequences for equality of actual treatment in the various spheres of life, including employment, the distribution of wealth (and poverty), the delivery of services, access to justice and the division of labour.

A recent UN report found that the lower status of women in many if not most societies is also regarded as a significant factor in the causes and consequences of violence against women and girls. The report highlighted a complex web of social, political, economic and legal factors surrounding the issue:

> Violence against women throughout their life cycle is a manifestation of the historically unequal power relations between women and men. It is perpetuated by traditional and customary practices that accord women lower status in the family, workplace, community and society, and it is exacerbated by social pressures. These include the shame surrounding and hence difficulty of denouncing certain acts against women; women's lack of access to legal information, aid or protection; a dearth of laws that effectively prohibit violence against women; inadequate efforts on the part of public authorities to promote awareness of and enforce existing laws; and the absence of educational and other means to address the causes and consequences of violence. Images in the media of violence against women – especially those that depict rape, sexual slavery or the use of women and girls as sex objects, including pornography – are factors contributing to the continued prevalence of such violence, adversely influencing the community at large . . . (UN, 2010, p. 127)

Gender and War

Traditional approaches to gender, as well as certain feminist approaches, suggest that men make war while women make peace. Most statistics on violence in general, and not just political violence, do show males to be the main perpetrators. Military statistics also show that soldiering, an occupation in which people are trained to kill, is a largely male business. By the beginning of the twenty-first century, one study revealed that about 97 per cent of military personnel in standing armies around the world were male. Of the 3 per cent of women, most were employed as typists and nurses, with only about 1 per cent having a combat role (see Goldstein, 2003, p. 107). But women make up a majority of civilian casualties of war, are the primary targets of sexual violence in war, and constitute the majority (along with children) of refugees (Sjoberg and Via, 2010, p. 10). When it comes to a wartime economy, however, one will often find women heavily involved. In the world wars of the twentieth century, for example, women moved out of their more domestic occupations in significant numbers and into factories serving vital war industries as well as the agricultural sector.

The Fourth World Conference on Women, convened in Beijing in 1995, highlighted the impact of war on women's lives as well as questions of women's agency in both national and international security matters. A UN Security Council resolution adopted five years later observed the relative absence of women from decision-making processes, highlighted the importance of women in preventing and resolving violent conflict, and urged that their role must be increased if sustainable peace was to be achieved in post-conflict situations. It also noted that, during conflict periods, women were more often exposed to physical violence (including sexual assault) in intra-state wars in particular, and that measures should be employed to enhance the protection of women in these circumstances. Such high-level recognition of the special circumstances of women in war, and their potential role in peace-building in post-conflict situations, has been important in at least getting such issues onto the international political agenda (Kuehnast, Oudraat and Hernes, 2011, pp. 1–2).

Some may take all this to imply that women lack agency, that they are simply passive victims of violence perpetrated largely by males, and that this reflects an innate femininity that is naturally pacific and subordinate. However, there are studies showing that, while men do engage more often and more directly in physical violence and that militaries are indeed heavily masculinized, there is little evidence to support assertions that women are innately more peaceful in their attitudes. One leading feminist author, Jean Bethke Elshtain, argues that, the more one studies the issue of gender and war, the less one is inclined to accept simple stereotypes about either men or women, or about their ways of behaving in the context of political violence and military issues generally. She is especially concerned to scrutinize the myth of the peace-loving woman as opposed to the war-mongering male and the notion that a world ruled by women would be more peaceful (see, generally, Elshtain, 1995).

Others note: 'More and more we recognize that claiming inherent differences between men and women contradicts the real life actions of men and women. Simply arguing that men are militarists and women are antimilitarists belies the facts' (Lorentzen and Turpin, 1998, p. xii). For one thing, history has demonstrated that many men resist war through refusal to participate – often through draft evasion – and outright protest. On the other hand, many women have expressed their citizenship, and their nationalism, by proudly sending sons to war, participating in the wartime economy, and serving in the military. This has led some strands of feminist scholarship to abandon the dichotomies endorsed by their predecessors, while still recognizing certain gender differences (ibid.).

Some of these themes receive detailed treatment in Joshua Goldstein's work, including an analysis of how militarized masculinity is constructed. He argues that killing does not come naturally to either men or women, that males have to be heavily socialized into the warrior role in order to kill willingly, and that gender identity is used instrumentally by societies to induce men to fight.

> ### Key Quote   Killing: An Unnatural Act?
>
> Contrary to the idea that war thrills men, expresses innate masculinity . . . all evidence indicates that war is something that societies impose on men, who most often need to be dragged kicking and screaming into it, constantly brainwashed and disciplined once there, and rewarded and honoured afterwards. (Goldstein, 2003, p. 263)

The main point that many contemporary scholars promote in current gender and war debates is that behaviour in wartime is socially conditioned rather than determined by one's biology, including one's gender. Having said that, it must be recognized that humans are biological creatures and that, like any living creature of the plant or animal world, we are hard-wired to seek our own survival. This is the most fundamental principle of evolutionary biology. Sometimes survival may involve killing, and that is almost certainly behind some of the psychology of warfare and the principle of self-defence. However, since species survival is also a key element in evolutionary biology, the same mechanisms may also give rise to an aversion to killing. If one construes the latter as the dominant element, it would support Goldstein's assertion that killing does not come 'naturally' to either males or females. Yet warfare and conflicts in the twentieth century alone killed somewhere between 136 and 149 million people (Leitenberg, 2006, p. 9). This begs the question of why, if killing is 'unnatural', there has been so much of it.

Straightforward killing, however, is just one kind of violence. There is also torture and sexual violence. Here we consider the latter, which is of course a heavily gendered act since it occurs most often in the form of rape of women and girls by men. It is important to note here that rape is not just incidental to war but is used tactically to humiliate and punish the enemy. Although it has been occurring for millennia, it has only recently been recognized as an act of war criminality. This belated recognition is due in part to the impact of feminism and gender studies generally, which for several decades had sought to highlight acts of violence against women in all spheres.

A breakthrough came with the war in the former Yugoslavia in the early 1990s, especially in Bosnia-Herzegovina and Croatia, where well-documented cases of large-scale rape were given extensive publicity. These cases acted as a catalyst for the development of a specific body of international law dealing with sexual assault in war as a form of torture and a crime against humanity. In 1996 eight Bosnian Serb security personnel were indicted by the UN International Criminal Tribunal for war crimes relating specifically to acts of rape (Chanter, 2007, p.150; see also Copelon, 2000). This was a major step forward in gender justice to the extent that rape was now to be considered not just as humiliating, degrading and a stain on the honour of the victim – or her male relatives – but as a serious crime in itself.

Although the focus of sexual violence and abuse, in war and in other situations, has been on women, it would not do to conclude this section without mentioning the fact that men and boys are also often the victims of rape and sexual abuse and that this happens under a variety of conditions. The prevalence of sexual abuse of men in prisons, and of young boys (as well as girls) by institutional carers, clergy and indeed close relatives, is well known (see Stemple, 2009, pp.605–6). Far less attention, however, has been given to sexual violence against males under conditions of war. One harrowing account appeared in a feature story in *The Guardian* in 2011, detailing not only examples of horrendous sexual acts committed against men in conflict situations in East Africa but also the extent to which they suffer social ostracism from their own friends and family. This reflects very rigid and unforgiving conceptions of gender roles. One officer with the Refugee Law Project was reported as saying: 'In Africa no man is allowed to be vulnerable . . . You have to be masculine, strong.' The rape of a man effectively destroys his masculinity (reported in Storr, 2011). Despite widespread knowledge of the practice, very little research appears to have been carried out on the frequency of rape of men in war. The *Guardian* article further noted that one rare survey, published in the *Journal of the American Medical Association* in 2010, found that 22 per cent of men and 30 per cent of women in Eastern Congo reported experiencing sexual violence in conflict-related circumstances (ibid.). While the statistics for women were worse, those for men were certainly significant.

This begs questions about some feminist approaches to the subject. To describe rape as 'an act of violence, power, and domination rather than an act of sex' (Scholz, 2007, p.276) is credible, although contested by some other feminists. Now consider the claim that rape is 'nothing more or less than a conscious process of intimidation by which *all men* keep *all women* in a state of fear' (Susan Brownmiller, quoted ibid.; original emphasis). This claim seems not only grossly indiscriminate in targeting half the human race as morally challenged, to say the least, but it completely ignores male victims of rape. One critic of this view notes that, while gender analysis provides insights on the phenomenon of rape generally, a female-specific approach which excludes all male victims from the analysis of sexual violence is unacceptable (Stemple, 2009, p.606). Whatever we might want to call rape, and other acts of sexual violence or torture, there can be little doubt that it constitutes an act of power with social and political significance for both victims and perpetrators, whether male or female, and constitutes an important dimension of the dynamics of power politics.

Conclusion

The successive waves of feminism discussed here, in all their various permutations, have brought the issue of a particular category of human rights – the rights of women to equal treatment in all spheres of life – squarely onto the political agenda. For, whatever differences there may be between the various strands of feminist theory, it is the basic historic fact of women's inequality and subordination that has underscored each one. Although civil, political and legal rights have been significantly enhanced since the early days of feminist agitation and activism, statistics show that political power is still predominantly in male hands and that women have a long way to go before they achieve substantive equality. This further suggests that any declaration of a 'post-feminist' age is rather premature.

Feminist theory, however, has always been about much more than simply advancing the rights of women in a practical political sense. It has also been about understanding key aspects of the human condition through the lens of gender and in a way that critically interrogates the social construction of a gendered political and social reality. This laid the foundations for the contemporary field of gender studies in which questions of femininity and masculinity as well as sexuality have been analysed in various contexts, and in more nuanced ways.

The implications of gender for politics at both domestic and international levels have been addressed by various theorists, with problems of 'hegemonic masculinity' acknowledged by many observers. However, there is little consensus about what kind of world might emerge should the balance of power between men and women shift to a more even level, or to a (somewhat unlikely) situation in which women predominate. Despite the claims of some feminist approaches, it may not be a more peaceful one. On the other hand, those societies in which greater gender equality has been achieved do show lower levels of violence at the domestic level. They have also been found to be more inclined to pursue peaceful, diplomatic strategies in the international sphere (see

Caprioli and Boyer, 2001). These correlations are indicative of a fruitful research agenda in pursuit of answers to the most basic issue for the study of international relations – the causes of war and the conditions for peace.

Another contribution of feminism and gender theory is the highlighting of aspects of war that have generally been ignored in conventional theoretical approaches, especially in relation to rape and other forms of sexual assault and torture that occur so frequently in the context of political violence. Although sexual violence in conditions of war has a very long history, the phenomenon was largely ignored at the political level until persistent feminist discourses made it impossible to continue to avoid confronting the rape of women in war as a gross violation of human rights, and indeed as a crime against humanity. But it remains an under-acknowledged and under-investigated issue for male victims of rape, who are no less dehumanized and traumatized by the experience. Although these issues are still very far from being dealt with effectively, their presence on the international agenda at all illustrates that intellectual, theoretical reflection combined with advocacy and activism makes a difference.

QUESTIONS FOR DISCUSSION

1 How has liberal thought contributed to the development of feminism?
2 What are the key features of the feminist critique of traditional IR theory?
3 Are conservatism and realism 'anti-female'?
4 Is feminism merely a white, Western, middle-class concern?
5 How is gender socially and politically constructed?
6 What is meant by the term 'hegemonic masculinity'?
7 In what sense is sexual violence a tactic of war?
8 Would a world ruled by women be more peaceful?

FURTHER READING

Ackerley, Brooks A., Maria Stern and Jacqui True (2006) *Feminist Methodologies for International Relations.* Cambridge: Cambridge University Press.
Dudink, Stefan, Karen Hagenamm and John Tosh (eds) (2004) *Masculinities in Politics and War: Gendering Modern History.* Manchester: Manchester University Press.

Hoffman, John (2001) *Gender and Sovereignty: Feminism, the State and International Relations*. Basingstoke: Palgrave.

Parpart, Jane L., and Marysia Zalewski (2008) *Rethinking the Man Question: Sex, Gender and Violence in International Relations*. London: Zed Books.

Shepherd, Laura J. (2010) *Gender Matters in Global Politics: A Feminist Introduction to International Relations*. Abingdon: Routledge.

USEFUL WEBSITES

www.idea.int/gender/ (International Institute for Democracy and Electoral Assistance website on democracy and gender)

www.un.org/womenwatch/ (UN Women Watch)

www.unfpa.org/gender/ (UN Population Fund on gender equality)

www.feminist.org (Feminist Majority Foundation website)

www.xyonline.net (XY – men, masculinities and gender politics)

9

Postcolonialism, Culture and Normative Theory

We have seen in previous chapters that at least some aspects of critical theory, constructivism, the English School and gender approaches are attuned to the diversity produced by cultural difference and varied historical experiences. In postcolonial theory, however, the emphasis on cultural factors, which range from language, religious beliefs, music and the arts to gender relations, economic systems and social and political organization more generally, is much more acute. This emphasis is accompanied by a strong normative orientation to the interpretation of history, especially that of European imperialism and colonialism in the modern period, as well as their ongoing effects. At the ideational level, what is central to virtually all postcolonial approaches, and what tends to give postcolonialism a more distinctive culturalist orientation, is a thoroughgoing critique of Eurocentrism and all that this implies for global relations, both past and present.

The critique of Eurocentrism and its culturalist affinities is evident in particular expressions of postcolonialism which we examine in this chapter, namely, Orientalism and subaltern studies, négritude and Afrocentrism, and the Asian values debate which embodies a form of 'Asianism'. The idea of culture also underpins some important debates in normative IR theory which revolve around the philosophical tensions between universalism and relativism, and which are manifest in two opposing schools of normative thought reflecting these positions – cosmopolitanism and communitarianism respectively. Because postcolonial approaches tend to assert cultural difference in opposition to the universalist premises of much traditional IR theory, as well as to the entity known as 'the West' whose knowledge systems have produced these theories, these approaches appear more attuned to a communitarian ethic. As we shall see, however, some important elements of postcolonial theory also rely on aspects of a universal or cosmopolitan ethic. To examine properly all these issues, and their implications for IR theory, we must look first at the more general formulation of postcolonialism as a response to imperialism and colonialism.

Colonialism and Postcolonialism

Postcolonialism is as complex as any other body of theory examined in this book, with competing strands reflecting disagreements over definitions, concepts, methods, scope and purposes. At the very least, it can be said to denote an approach to the study of imperialism and colonialism which places a particular emphasis on how cultural representations, associated with a self/other binary, underpin power relations. This self/other binary is basic to almost any form of identity construction and identity politics, but, since postcolonialism is concerned primarily with European imperialism and colonialism, the first element in the binary refers to a European, or more generally Western, self which is placed in a dichotomous relation with a non-Western 'other'.

As we saw in the discussion of Derrida's ideas in chapter 7, such binaries are not value-neutral. Rather, they create significant meaning based on the act of valuing one element over the other. These may merge in a series of interconnected binaries which reinforce the valuations. The particular self/other binary identified in postcolonial theory that translates into a West/non-West binary also carries connotations of civilized/barbarian and thus superior/inferior. The strength of this set of binaries reflects the power of the West historically, not just in a material sense but in an ideational sense as well. And it carries over from the colonial past to the postcolonial present. One prominent postcolonial historian notes that political modernity, embodied in the institutions of the state, the bureaucracy and capitalist enterprise and expressed through concepts such as citizenship, the public sphere, human rights, legal equality, the individual, popular sovereignty, social justice, scientific rationality, and so forth, bears 'the burden of European thought and history', and especially that of the European Enlightenment (Chakrabarty, 2008, p. 4).

Postcolonial approaches also seek to show the inherent ethnocentricity of Western knowledge, which, far from being universal, has arisen within its own particular historical experiences and cultural context. The wider epistemological implication of this is that all forms of knowledge are 'situated' in particular cultural/historic contexts and cannot be universalized. This accords with the epistemology of standpoint feminism discussed in the previous chapter, although postcolonialism situates 'the standpoint' itself in a cultural rather than a gendered context.

Both are forms of relativism with strong normative elements, but, while a feminist standpoint approach challenges masculinism, the culturalist/postcolonial approach challenges Western universalism.

Before proceeding further, we should note that, in its attention to historical as well as contemporary issues, postcolonialism is scarcely confined to the literal sense of the term in designating something that simply comes 'after colonialism'. The hyphenated format 'post-colonial' is most commonly used to indicate that temporal dimension, and so we may speak descriptively of the post-colonial sphere as that part of the world which has been formally decolonized. But there is more to the hyphen than this. One commentator notes that, while some see the hyphenated 'post-colonial' as representing a decisive marker in the decolonization process, others hold that the unbroken format is more sensitive to the long history of colonial consequences. Either way, the value of the theory that postcolonialism embodies 'must be judged in terms of its adequacy to conceptualise the complex condition which attends the aftermath of colonial occupation' (Gandhi, 1998, p. 4).

Whatever the fine distinctions between the hyphenated and non-hyphenated versions, there can be no doubt that postcolonial theory is strongly normative, aiming to establish a form of anti-hegemonic discourse targeted not only at the interpretation of colonial history and the binaries which have devalued and oppressed non-Western 'others', in particular, but at any manifestation of neo-colonialism or neo-imperialism in the contemporary period of globalization and neo-liberal ascendancy. The approach is therefore perhaps best described not only as postcolonial but also as *anti*-colonial, constituting a discourse of opposition and resistance to colonial oppression and subordination.

There is also a distinction to be made between the terms 'imperialism' and 'colonialism'. Imperialism is an ideology, or discourse, which seeks to legitimate the control of one nation or country by another using military and/or economic means (McLeod, 2000, p. 7). Because imperialism in the form of economic domination can persist even in the absence of military coercion or formal colonialism, it is regarded as particularly insidious. The act of colonization is a practice involving the physical settlement of people from an original homeland in a new locale, and with the intention on the part of the imperial power (also called 'metropolitan' power) to maintain control. Historically, where large numbers of settlers moved in – a process called 'settler colonialism' – indigenous populations were often displaced and dispossessed. This occurred mainly throughout the Americas and in Australia, New Zealand and parts of Southern Africa, although Europeans (or their descendants) never became a majority population in the African countries. According to contemporary moral standards, imperialism and colonialism are judged to be inherently unjust. At the time, however, they were justified through a variety of moralistic discourses, including those associated with 'civilizing' native races. This often entailed a project of conversion to Christianity and all its alleged virtues, a project which enjoyed various degrees of success. But, whatever moralistic motives attended imperialist/colonial enterprises, violence was almost invariably a key instrument.

One postcolonial IR theorist notes that, while postcolonialism identifies the development of international order with specific forms of violence, this does not imply that the idea of a cosmopolitan global order or society lacks merit. Indeed, 'postcolonial critics find inspirations from a vast community of ecclesiastic, ethical, and moral thinkers worldwide who believed in the idea of a common society of brotherhood but express misgivings about *the methods chosen by Europe to bring it about*' (Grovogui, 2010, p. 240; emphasis added). This comment, however, awards singular agency to a reified entity – 'Europe' – acting on a consciously chosen plan of world domination designed to implement its own particular vision of order.

Such a claim brings to mind the historian Paul Kennedy's observation on the historic rise of the West: 'In the year 1500, the date chosen by numerous scholars to mark the divide between modern and premodern times, it was by no means obvious to the inhabitants of Europe that their continent was poised to dominate much of the rest of the earth' (Kennedy, 1989, p. 3). Kennedy goes on to remark how other centres of power at that time seemed to hold as much if not more potential (ibid., pp. 3–4). What other aspects of postcolonial theory emphasize is the *contingent* nature of history. And if history is indeed a series of contingent events and developments, then there can be no grand plan, let alone a coordinated conspiracy, although there can certainly be grand narratives. These, however, are generally constructed as retrospective explanations or justifications. How Europe, or more especially Western Europe, came to occupy a position of such dominance, and why the West today remains so relatively powerful, is too complex a subject to be explored in detail here, although various explanations have been offered in other literature (see, for example, Diamond, 2005; Watson, 2005).

Orientalism and Subaltern Studies

Previous chapters have shown the extent to which theorizing in IR draws from other disciplines, and postcolonialism is no exception. Literary and cultural studies in fact provided much of the initial impetus for the development of this body of theory, which has contributed much to the critique of global relations. It is a Palestinian-American professor of comparative literature, Edward Said (1935–2003), who is widely regarded as having produced postcolonialism's seminal text, *Orientalism*, first published in 1978. Subtitled 'Western Conceptions of the Orient', Said's work is essentially a critical study of how 'the other' – in this particular case the 'Oriental other' – has been represented in (selected) European literature. In interrogating these representations, however, Said drew on the insights generated through other bodies of European intellectual thought, including critical and postmodern theory and, especially, the works of Gramsci and Foucault.

For Said, Orientalism consists in a discourse, in Foucault's sense, through which Europeans, as imperial authors and scholars claiming 'expert' knowledge, have historically represented the 'Oriental' subject as an essentially inferior 'other' against which contrasting, positive, superior images of the European/Western self have been constructed, thus demonstrating the essential links between power, representation and knowledge. 'The relationship between the Occident and Orient is a relationship of power, of domination, of varying degrees of a complex hegemony . . .' (Said, 1995, p. 5). And it is *cultural* hegemony, in Gramsci's formulation, that Said sees as giving Orientalism its durability and strength, drawing from the very idea of Europe itself as a superior cultural formation in comparison with all non-European others (ibid., p. 7).

While Said's approach claimed to be simply identifying and critiquing an already existing discourse, there is also a sense in which he actually created it by drawing together a selection of literature to support his central arguments. Also, although Said himself warned that the appropriate critical response to his exposure of Orientalism as a hegemonic discourse is not a simplistic 'Occidentalism', his work was readily interpreted in some sectors as implying just that. In an addendum to the 1995 edition of *Orientalism*, Said noted that the conflation of his specific notion of Orientalism with the whole of the West enabled the latter entity to be (wrongly) construed as an enemy of all those once subject to Western colonialism – Arab, Persian, Indian, Chinese, and so on (1995, p.328). But the Orientalist/Occidental dichotomy was to take on a life of its own, as illustrated in the Arab/Islamic world in particular as well as the rise of al-Qaeda and its offshoots, the subject of case study 9.1.

Another distinctive version of postcolonialism was formulated by the Subaltern Studies Project, which began in 1982 as 'an intervention in South Asian historiography' and subsequently developed into a school of postcolonial critique, with contributions from scholars in other parts of the world bridging disciplines from history to anthropology and literary studies (Prakash, 1994, p.1476). The principal challenge of the project was to expose the dominance of narrow elite perspectives in colonial historiography which depicted the play of power and politics as occurring almost exclusively at the elite level of both colonizers and colonized. Absent from most accounts was any acknowledgement of the role of 'subaltern' classes – a term borrowed from Gramsci to indicate any subordinate class, such as peasants, factory workers, and so on, who were usually depicted simply as an inert mass lacking agency or will. In South Asian historiography, this mass was seen as being 'deployed by the dominant elements to serve their own ends according to strategies of their own invention' (Guha, 1997, p.x). In opposition to this kind of historiography, subaltern studies defined itself as 'an attempt to allow the "people" finally to speak within the jealous pages of elitist historiography and, in so doing, to speak for, or sound the muted voices of, the truly oppressed' (Ghandi, 1998, p.2).

The subsequent development of subaltern studies saw a shift from an early focus on Marxist and Gramscian ideas to Foucauldian and post-structural approaches. The latter challenged universalist Enlightenment foundations of critical theory generally as well as those of liberalism. By the late 1980s/early 1990s the term 'postcolonial studies/theory' had become established in the academic lexicon, and subaltern studies, as a specific mode of postcolonial thought, was also having an impact in the Anglo-American intellectual world. It became especially influential in the US, where it joined with a rising tide of postmodernism along with multiculturalist ideas and identity politics, often expressed as the 'politics of difference'. In the US in particular, the influence of literary criticism in subaltern studies saw a shift towards culture, 'conceived in terms of textual and discourse analysis, and away from the economic base as the central zone of power and contestation', thereby accommodating itself to 'the culturalist atmosphere of US humanities departments' (Chaturvedi, 2012, p.xii).

This cultural turn, however, has not gone unchallenged. Critical

Case Study 9.1 Orientalism, Occidentalism and the Rise of al-Qaeda

Within the Arab/Islamic world, Said's work has been taken as demonstrating how that world had been violated by a wicked, predatory West, as well as providing a systematic defence of Arabs and Islam. Said himself protested that this had not been his intention, claiming that his approach was explicitly humanist and anti-essentialist and that he had no interest in defending the virtues of any particular religious/cultural formation (Said, 1995, p. 331). Even so, it is difficult to construct a discourse of Orientalism, as Said did, without inviting or indeed creating a counter-discourse in the form of Occidentalism or anti-Westernism more generally. As one commentator notes, Said's tendency to generalize 'sweepingly and categorically about "the Orientalist" and "Orientalism" . . . appears to mimic the essentializing discourse it attacks' (Clifford, 1988, p. 262). A similar rhetorical strategy has been developed by the fundamentalist Islamist organization al-Qaeda since it emerged in the latter part of the 1980s to become the most infamous Islamist terrorist organization of the contemporary period.

Al-Qaeda (literally, 'the base') emerged during the Soviet war in Afghanistan in the late 1980s as a radical Sunni Muslim organization. It follows the dictates of Sufism – a mystical and puritanical version of Islam – and is strongly fundamentalist in its support for a strict version of sharia law. On the one hand, it is dedicated to global jihad ('struggle') against the corrupting influences of the West in general and the US in particular, but, on the other, it has shown itself to be highly intolerant of other Islamic sects, especially Shia Muslims.

A major grievance of former al-Qaeda leader Osama bin Laden was US support for Israel. He was also opposed strongly to the pro-American Saudi royal family. More generally, he saw the US presence in the Middle East as an imperialist intrusion akin to a modern crusade that was desecrating Islamic homelands. In 1996, bin Laden made a 'Declaration of Jihad' against Americans. Following attacks between 1998 and 2000 on US embassies in East Africa and a US navy ship docked at the Yemeni port of Aden, on 11 September 2001 al-Qaeda used hijacked jets to fly into the twin towers of the World Trade Center in New York and the Pentagon in Washington ('9/11').

Although bin Laden was finally killed in a US raid on his hiding place in Pakistan in 2011, al-Qaeda remains active, and bin Laden stands as an inspirational figure to militant Islamic organizations around the world. These include Boko Haram, which operates in and around northeastern Nigeria and which has been responsible for hundreds of murders and kidnappings. The incident which achieved particular international notoriety was the abduction of over 200 schoolgirls in April 2014 as they were taking exams in the Nigerian village of Chibok. Boko Haram is completely opposed to Western culture and to Western education in particular.

Al-Qaeda is said to have little control over affiliated or imitative organizations, which is also illustrated by the fact that, in the Syrian civil war, al-Qaeda offshoots started fighting each other as well as government forces (see McCormack, 2014). The most notorious offshoot is the Islamic State of Iraq and the Levant (known by the acronym IS) which, as of mid-2014, was in control of significant areas in

Syria and Iraq. It is not affiliated with al-Qaeda but is infused with the same anti-Western ideology.

One commentator on al-Qaeda and their anti-Western jihad notes that, 'In contrast to a Western obsession with Islam as the energizing force behind Al Qaeda, when one focuses on what some of the spokesmen for the group have actually said in various forums, one finds a dogmatic insistence on locating their actions within an historical framework that is recognisably postcolonial, rather than on millenarian ideologies or religious differences.' It is in fact the long history of Western colonialism and resistance to it 'that figures far more prominently in justifications for the actions of a group such as Al Qaeda than does religion' (Krishna, 2009, p. 149). There is certainly much truth in this. At the same time, it is obviously not merely a 'Western obsession' that has linked the actions of al-Qaeda to Islam – al-Qaeda has explicitly invoked Islam at every turn and set it in contrast with the 'decadent West'. This constitutes a form of Occidentalism or the inversion of Orientalism.

theory approaches suggest that the postmodern privileging of identity cast in culturalist terms neglects another particular form of identity – class. This neglect is a direct result of the tendency of postmodern approaches to pour scorn on the tradition of historical materialism, which places class at the centre of analysis. The grounds for doing so are 'that its universalist and objectivist pretensions are really no different to those of liberal modernization theory' (O'Hanlon and Washbrook, 2012, p. 215). The further implications of this move are set out in the following quotation.

Key Quote   Culturalist versus Class Analysis

The true underclasses of the world are only permitted to present themselves as victims of the particularistic kinds of gender, racial and national oppression which they share with preponderantly middle-class American scholars and critics with or in their own voices. What such underclasses are denied is the ability to present themselves as classes: as victims of the universalistic, systemic and material deprivations of capitalism which clearly separate them from their subaltern expositors. In sum, the deeply unfortunate result of these radical postmodernist approaches in the minorities debate is thus to reinforce and to give new credence to the well-known hostility of American political culture to any kind of materialist or class analysis. (Ibid.)

The issue of universalism is also evident in critiques of (Western) feminism, as mentioned in the previous chapter. One prominent postcolonial/subaltern studies critic, Gayatri Spivak, argues that the privileging of the white male as the norm for universal humanity subordinates both the female *and* the racial other in a politically interested manner. The problem with (and for) feminism is that it tends, at the very moment that it exposes the error of the 'masculist [*sic*] truth-claim to universalist or academic objectivity', to perform the lie of 'constituting a truth of global sisterhood where the mesmerizing model remains male and female sparring partners of generalizable or universalizable sexuality who are the chief protagonists in that European contest . . . global sisterhood must receive this articulation even if the sisters in question are Asian, African [or] Arab' (Spivak, 1999, p. 148).

The theoretical concerns of postcolonial feminism are therefore related primarily to issues of representation and location. As Rajan and Park note, postcolonial feminists denounce both the idea of a 'universal woman' and the reification of Third World difference that produces a monolithic 'Third World Woman'. What needs to be recognized, they say, are 'the specificities of race, class, nationality, religion and sexualities that intersect with gender, and the hierarchies, epistemic as well as political, social and economic that exist among women.' This further demands that 'First World feminists' must abandon 'their unexamined ethnocentrism and the reproduction of orientalist categories of thought' while taking up the task of 'uncovering and contesting global power relations, economic, political, military, and cultural-hegemonic' (Rajan and Park, 2005, p. 54). These latter points are not just relevant to a 'reoriented' feminist scholarship but are of direct concern to IR generally.

From Négritude to Afrocentrism

One of the earliest expressions of postcolonialism occurred decades before there was anything literally 'post' about colonialism, and well before the field of postcolonial studies was explicitly conceptualized. It took the form of black African consciousness, emerging among intellectuals from several French colonies in Africa and the Caribbean and whose influence extended from the 1930s through to the 1960s. Its origins are said to lie in the publication between 1931 and 1932, initiated primarily by two sisters from Martinique, of a magazine, *La Revue du Monde Noir* (*Review of the African World*) which circulated among young black intellectuals studying in Paris. These included three men from Martinique, Senegal and French Guyana respectively – Aimé Césaire, Léopold Senghor and Léon-Gontran Damas – who became leading figures in the négritude movement. Senghor went on to become independent

Senegal's first elected president in 1960. The term 'négritude', meaning blackness, is credited to Césaire and is emblematic of a desire to invest the quality of blackness with positivity, in contrast to the negativity emanating from the cultural and intellectual subjugation of Africans by Europeans (see Egar, 2008, pp. 9–11).

An assumption embedded in négritude thought was that culture was racially specific, but that the culture of Africans, rather than being something to be ashamed of, should be celebrated, although this did not mean that French or European culture should be rejected. Rather, both should be appreciated in their different ways (Phillips, 1999). According to Senghor, négritude was needed both as an 'instrument of liberation' and as something which could make a contribution to 'the humanism of the twentieth century' (Senghor, 2010, p. 477). Senghor also spoke of a distinctive 'African personality', which he compared with the idea of a 'black personality' proclaimed by the black movement in the US. He went on to define négritude as 'the sum of the cultural values of the black world; that is, a certain active presence in the world . . . an opening out to the world, contact and participation with others' (ibid.). In writing a preface to a 1948 anthology of négritude literature edited by Senghor, the French philosopher Jean-Paul Sartre, though evincing great sympathy for the movement, signalled a deep problem within it.

Key Quote   Jean-Paul Sartre and the Problem of Négritude

Negritude appears as the minor term of a dialectical progression: The theoretical and practical assertion of the supremacy of the white man is its thesis; the position of negritude as an antithetical value is the moment of negativity. But this negative moment is insufficient by itself, and the Negroes who employ it know this very well; they know that it is intended to prepare the synthesis or realisation of a human society without races. Thus negritude is the root of its own destruction, it is a transition, not a conclusion, a means and not an ultimate end. (Sartre, quoted in Fanon, 1986, p. 133)

Although inspiring innovative critical cultural thought and consciousness and attracting a wide readership through books and journals, négritude declined in the 1960s, coinciding with a period of rapid decolonization. One commentator says that, by this time, the variety and experimental nature of négritude literature had gradually disappeared and that it had declined into 'a nativist cultural ideology concerned with primordial Africanity and a developmentalist political ideology concerned with postcolonial nation building, both of which served to legitimize authoritarian state politics across the continent' (Wilder, 2005, p.299). By the late 1960s a new generation of black Francophiles began to denounce négritude for its disconnections from ordinary people and 'for privileging culture over politics in order to mystify real conditions of social oppression, and for failing to advocate direct action against global capitalism' (ibid.). This is similar to the critique of culturalism by class analysts deploying a critical theory approach.

An important critic of négritude, Frantz Fanon, also from Martinique, set out to 'help the black man free himself of the arsenal of complexes that has been developed by the colonial environment' (Fanon, 1986, p.30). Fanon, however, says that Sartre shattered his illusion in reminding him that his 'blackness was only a minor term' (ibid., p.138). Sartre was also later to write the preface to Fanon's classic work on colonial violence and decolonization, *The Wretched of the Earth*, first published in 1961. But, in this, Fanon rejected all forms of essentialism, as embodied for example in an 'African personality' or even the category of 'the Negro', as well as the notion that an authentic African past, uncontaminated by white influences, could and must be retrieved as part of a project of establishing a black African identity that was equal to a European identity. He was also attuned to issues of class and politics, which he saw as having primacy over culture, while urging education for the masses of illiterate peasants which the elite of the négritude movement had tended to ignore (see Fanon, 1965).

Other critiques of négritude have been delivered by a number of African intellectuals, including the Nobel prize-winning author Wole Soyinka, as well as feminist authors. Again, critiques range from the essentialization of African identity (including in masculinist forms) to the dependence of the discourse on a white/black binary which it was unable to transcend, even as it promoted a form of universal humanism. Even so, négritude must take its place in intellectual history as an important element of colonial and anti-colonial theory and thus a contributor to the postcolonial canon. It is also a significant contributor to a more recent Africanist variant of postcolonial thought – although one barely mentioned in many postcolonial texts – which is contemporary Afrocentrism.

The discourse of Afrocentrism has been promoted mainly in certain African-American intellectual circles, although it is very controversial and is by no means endorsed generally by African-American intellectuals. Indeed, Kwame Anthony Appiah, professor of African-American studies at Harvard University, has been highly critical of it (see Appiah,

1993). But let us consider what its major protagonists claim for it. One leading text in the field says that Afrocentrism is neither a world view nor a theory but, rather, a paradigm that represents 'a revolutionary shift in thinking proposed as a constructural adjustment to black disorientation, decentredness, and lack of agency' (Asante, 2007, p.9). According to this commentator, it is meant to be an assertion not of African superiority but of consciousness, purpose and agency, in which Africans view themselves as subjects and not as objects, as creators of history themselves rather than simply as bit players in a larger European history. In summary, Afrocentrism is '*a consciousness, quality of thought, mode of analysis, and an actionable perspective where Africans seek, from agency, to assert a subject place within the context of African history*' (ibid., p.16; original emphasis).

Similarly, another leading Afrocentric scholar defines it as '*a quality of thought, practice and perspective that perceives Africans as subjects and agents of phenomena acting in their own cultural image and human interest*' (Conyers, 2005, p.1; original emphasis). Afrocentrism is therefore a direct response to the power of Europe and Eurocentrism, which its proponents believe has not merely peripheralized but virtually obliterated African-ness. In its quest to recentre Africans and their very consciousness *as* Africans, the idea of the standpoint once again becomes apparent. The psychological or cultural location, Conyers says, is all important, for Afrocentrism requires 'the ability to view African phenomena from the standpoint of Africans themselves' (ibid., p.3). But in this work we find an implicit endorsement of African moral superiority over Europeans. Conyers says that Africans, unlike Europeans, 'have never dominated another group of people simply because of their biology' and, further, that Europeans (who merge into the more general category of West) are singularly responsible for all the major ills facing human civilization.

Key Quote   The Afrocentric Denunciation of the West

The anti-spiritual and pro-material views of the West have driven the world to the brink of destruction more than once. It is certain that Western technology will not save the world; in fact, it may be that technology will hasten the destruction of the world. The corruption of the earth, from the poisoning of the air and water, to the killing of innocent people as collateral victims of warfare, all attest to the sense of terror that sits at the door of the Western world. . . . We cannot give up the philosophical direction of the earth to those whose patterns of greed and destruction threaten our annihilation. (Conyers, 2005, p.8)

This denunciation is followed almost immediately by a declaration that, from an Afrocentric standpoint, all knowledge must be emancipatory; it must 'break open the prison that hold humans in mental bondage' and critically question injustices and lack of freedom in accord with a 'progress paradigm for liberation' (ibid., p. 9). This is more or less identical to the universalist (Eurocentric) moral position adopted by emancipatory critical theory discussed in chapter 6.

As noted above, Afrocentrism is not without its critics, leading African-American academics among them. Appiah enumerates problems, including the assumption implicit in much Afrocentric scholarship that there is a single, unified body of African culture encompassing everything on the continent, ranging through time and space from the ancient civilizations of the upper Nile to the thousands of language groups of the contemporary period (Appiah, 1993). Another critic, Clarence E. Walker, has focused on a major Afrocentric historical project (which has also been denounced by Appiah) which has sought to show that the philosophical knowledge produced by the ancient Greeks is actually a product of Egyptian civilization *and* that the ancient Egyptians credited as the originators of such esteemed knowledge were in fact black Africans. Moreover, European scholars who have falsely located philosophical wisdom and knowledge in ancient Greece are charged with actually stealing history from black Africans and deliberately erasing them from the historical record. This form of Afrocentric scholarship, however, itself stands accused of producing 'a therapeutic mythology designed to restore the self-esteem of black Americans by creating a past that never was' (Walker, 2002, p. xvii). Another classicist, Mary Lefkowitz, has examined the extensive Afrocentric myth-making surrounding this subject, which includes an assertion that Socrates was a black African (Lefkowitz, 1996, pp. 3–4). Walker, a black American, and Lefkowitz, a white Jewish American, have in turn been accused by defenders of this form of Afrocentric history of self-hatred and racism respectively (see Asante, 2007, pp. 1–8). Such is the politics of identity.

Another highly critical commentator makes an observation that is common to many critiques of postcolonial approaches, and that is the obsession with culture at the expense of class. Afrocentrists in the US, he says, 'have nothing at all to say about the most central problem facing Afro-Americans: the conditions of economic marginality, insecurity and under-privilege under which most of them exist. . . . Economic analysis, and programmes for economic reform, are simply absent, unaddressed'

(Howe, 1998, p. 14). Once again, we can see that the issue of class versus culture is deeply implicated in the critique.

Pan-Asianism as Postcolonial Discourse

A further form of culture-based identity politics which may be analysed in terms of a postcolonial discourse rose to prominence on a tide of rapid economic growth in East and Southeast Asia during the 1980s and most of the 1990s until a major financial crisis struck in the region in 1997. The discourse supported a project of regional identity formation best described as 'new Asianism', distinct from (although comparable to) an older discourse of pan-Asianism which had flourished in the late nineteenth and the first part of the twentieth century, up until the onset of the Second World War, and which had concentrated primarily on the idea of a common struggle against Western imperialism.

The new Asianism emerged some time after the end of colonialism in the region and focused on the assertion of a set of cultural and political values which were not only unique to Asia but superior to those of the West. Interestingly, in the early post-independence period, much of the region (excluding Japan) seemed trapped in a cycle of underdevelopment, and this was often blamed on the legacies of Confucian culture in particular.

When economic growth took off in the 1980s, however, this very same cultural legacy became the explanation, not for backwardness, but for the region's essential dynamism, underpinning the rise of the Asia-Pacific century and all that this promised (Lawson, 2006, pp. 147–8). This discourse was known broadly as the 'Asian values' debate, although the values identified as generally Asian were derived largely from a particular interpretation of Confucian thought which originated in Singapore and which was then projected across the region, mainly by political elites. Case study 9.2 shows how the discourse depended on a stereotypical and over-homogenized version of 'Asia' as well as on an equally stereotypical construction of 'the West', and thus embodied a distinct Orientalist/Occidentalist configuration.

Although the 'new Asianist' discourse was carried along on a tide of economic successes in the region, it was also boosted by the fact that the concept of culture had been taken up in broader intellectual discourses at the time. This followed an intellectual movement in the humanities and social sciences known as the 'cultural turn', a movement concerned to challenge any kind of universal assumption about the political, social

Case Study 9.2   The 'Asian Values' Debate

The 'Asian values debate' was initiated in Singapore under the leadership of Lee Kuan Yew, who, from the early 1980s, began to argue for the superiority of 'Confucian values' over Western values. This resonated in Singapore's domestic context given that the majority of the population are of Chinese descent. 'Confucian values' were later transformed into a general discourse of 'Asian values' which could then be projected over the region more broadly.

The main values of the West were generally described as conflictual, competitive, selfish, individualistic and materialistic, while Asian values were said to embrace harmony, consensus, order, communitarianism and spirituality. These values were then mapped on to particular political models. Western values supported liberal democracy and its underpinnings in civil and political rights, which encouraged conflict and dissent, while Asian values were said to support a model based on harmony and consensus. The Asianist model tended strongly towards authoritarianism, and indeed many of the political elites promoting the debate were clearly concerned to defend authoritarianism through a form of cultural legitimation.

Interestingly, political authoritarianism in Africa in the form of the one-party state had also been defended on precisely the same grounds, namely, that it accorded with traditional African cultural values. In both cases the declared motive for promoting cultural particularism in politics was to serve as a counter to hegemonic Western discourses, especially those supporting liberal democracy and civil and political rights, which were seen as having undermined the legitimacy and value of local culture and tradition. The latter were also held to be more supportive of social, cultural and economic rights.

The Asianist discourse therefore drew on, and fed back into, the broader postcolonial assertion of non-Western values. In most other cases this involved a certain defensiveness, which was partly a product of arguing from a position of relative weakness vis-à-vis Europe or the West, as illustrated by Africanist discourses. Given that it was borne along on a tide of economic dynamism, however, the Asianist standpoint was projected from a much stronger position. Indeed, much of the rhetoric embodied a certain triumphalism. One commentator noted both this facet of the discourse and some of its contradictions:

> Throughout the Inter-Asia region, there is a weird sense of 'triumphalism' directed against the 'West', despite 'internal' antagonisms: the twenty-first century is 'ours'; 'we' are finally centred. Wherever one is geographically positioned, there is an emerging, almost clichéd formula: 'Asia is becoming the centre of the earth' . . .. This is where history comes in. Contrary to the now fashionable claim that we have entered the postcolonial era, the mood of triumphalism as reaction and *reactionary* to colonialism indicates that we still operate within the boundary of colonial history . . . in which all of us are caught up. (Chen, 1998, p. 2)

The new Asianism was much muted in the wake of the major financial crisis which struck the region in 1997, although the idea that various political and

economic dynamics are driven, or even determined, by culture remains a powerful one. A close study of this particular Asianist discourse, however, shows
that the promotion, first, of Confucian culture in Singapore among a population that knew little or nothing about Confucianism at all, and the subsequent
promulgation of a more broadly labelled set of Asian values, was an elite project
with a clear instrumental purpose of delegitimating Western discourses about
democracy and civil and political rights (Lawson, 2006, pp. 153–5).

and economic world and to focus attention instead on the specific cultural contexts within which people are embedded and from which they
acquire a primary intersubjective understanding of the world around
them. The cultural turn had had some impact on the discipline of IR
before the end of the Cold War, mainly through anti-universalist post-
positivist approaches, but it was the sea change brought about by the
collapse of the old bipolar world order that gave an impetus to the search
for fresh approaches. It was in this context that the idea of culture was
taken up as a key explanatory factor for a variety of developments, of
which the rise of Asia, as described above, was a significant one. It also
contributed to a broader debate in international normative theory about
the role of culture in the formulation of human rights, as explained
next.

Culture, Normative Theory and the Communitarian/
Cosmopolitan Divide

Normative theory in IR refers to the moral or ethical dimension of
activities in, and discourses about, the international sphere. The range
of practical issues that come within the purview of normative theory
is enormous, from intervention to distributive justice, from nuclear
issues to environmental matters and all manner of human rights and
wrongs. Normative theory has usually been given little attention by realists, especially when combined with positivist methodology. Since the
1980s there has been a noticeable revival of normative theory, boosted
by increased attention to the role of culture in world politics. One
important debate in normative theory has revolved largely around two
distinct approaches – cosmopolitanism and communitarianism – which
were introduced briefly in chapter 5. This debate has particular implications for human rights, a subject which has become an integral part of
international politics since 1945.

Communitarianism itself comes in two very distinct forms. One is socialist and seeks to oppose the individualism of liberalism when it comes to the distribution of resources in society, urging instead an equitable distribution among members of the community at large. The form of communitarianism with which we are concerned here focuses on the moral status and value of *particular* political communities defined in terms of their culture. This contrasts with the notion of a community of humankind – a *cosmopolis* – that transcends local particularities and cultural norms and possesses a moral status of its own. Cosmopolitan morality therefore involves mutual rights and obligations among all people regardless of their membership of particular communities. The cosmopolitan commitment to human equality also means that certain obligations extend to every human person *regardless* of their religion, gender, age, class, cultural affinity, or any other particularity. This is the essence of universalism (a term often used synonymously with cosmopolitanism) embodied in the notion of human rights.

In contrast, the culturalist view underpinning many communitarian approaches holds that people are first and foremost creatures of a particular community, a defining element of which is *its* culture and which makes its members into particular kinds of people. Moreover, since norms and values – which include notions of rights and duties – are derived primarily from 'culture' and are not inherent in some universal human psyche, it follows that different cultural communities have different notions of right and wrong, good and evil, and so on. Culturalist communitarian critics of cosmopolitan morality argue further that the putative subject of universal human rights – the individual person who stands stripped of his or her cultural or social context – is a fiction, and one that only Western liberals are likely to believe in. Non-Western cultures, they argue, do not have intellectual traditions that view a person apart from his or her community and cannot therefore readily assimilate the notion of individualism, derived largely from liberal thought, that is essential to a theory of universal human rights (see Lawson, 2006, pp. 48–50).

To the extent that culturalist assumptions reject Eurocentrism, they accord with postcolonial approaches. Interestingly, the contrasting positions taken by cosmopolitans and communitarians also reflect the competing streams of thought within the English School (*viz.* pluralists and solidarists) discussed in chapter 7. These have implications, in turn, for humanitarian intervention in the present period in that they map onto the practical dilemma faced by the UN. On the one hand, the UN is founded on the principle of non-intervention in the internal affairs of states, each state being entitled to rule according to its own cultural dictates. On the other, the UN endorses strong principles of humanitarianism as exemplified in the Universal Declaration of Human Rights, which is now taken to imply a duty to intervene in times of crisis in the name of 'human security' and 'the responsibility to protect', both of which rest on universalist premises. However, one postcolonial critic has argued that, far from facilitating progress 'from a world of irrational, tribal, premodern, failed states to one of free, democratic, developing states', humanitarian intervention may be read instead 'as part of a history of global imperialism' (Orford, 2003, p. 47). One implication of this claim is that Western states should therefore refrain from any form of intervention and allow events to take their course even if these involve genocide or mass murder.

It has also been suggested that contemporary IR theory mostly privileges 'a liberal understanding of the growth and dissemination of human rights norms and principles, and its effects in world politics' (Nair, 2002, p. 257). Furthermore, because the discourse of human rights has its origins in Western Enlightenment thought, which also sustained imperialism, colonialism, (white) racism and slavery, not to mention capitalism, it cannot stand apart from these. IR scholarship, it is claimed, 'has been on the whole remarkably silent on these tensions, and on the ways in which knowledge is constructed in the realm of human rights and culture' (ibid., p. 258). Feminist analyses, too, come in for their share of criticism for often failing to consider overlapping hierarchies of race, class, gender and cultural difference in their analysis. It is therefore suggested that, for insights into these issues, one must turn instead to non-IR sources, such as cultural studies and postcolonial theory, 'whose belated inclusion in IR debates is itself noteworthy' (ibid.).

Returning to the more general problem of the universalist/relativist tension in normative theory, and especially the issue of human rights, one solution is to accept elements of both communitarian and cosmopolitan principles. One analyst has argued that the Western, liberal origin of human rights concepts does not render them inapplicable to other contexts, nor does acknowledging the universality of broad human rights principles preclude taking local cultural factors into account. She suggests that this is especially important in African states, whose national communities tend to be highly diverse in cultural terms so that both national and international interpretations need flexibility. The challenge, of course, is how to achieve a balance of values while maintaining standards (Ibhawoh, 2000, p. 838). Ibhawoh's analysis highlights the fact that, although we do indeed live in a world in which cultural pluralism features at many different levels, this does not preclude either the establishment of cosmopolitan standards, on the one hand, or the denial of cultural difference, on the other.

Postcolonial IR

Writing towards the end of the twentieth century, Phillip Darby observed that postcolonialism had made little impact on international relations to that time (Darby, 1997, p. 5). However, it clearly has particular resonance for those IR scholars concerned with Third World–First World or North–South relations – terms which, despite their problems, remain indispensable to 'situational positioning' in the process of critique. But what a postcolonial perspective in IR has to offer is a different way of conceptualizing relations between these categories, one that breaks with established ways of analysing the Third World as fixed in, and indeed defined by, a subordinate position vis-à-vis the First World and which inhibit strategies for change in the international engagement between these spheres (ibid., pp. 2–3).

For students of IR, postcolonial approaches provide critical insights into how European colonialism and imperialism, as historic practices, have shaped the contemporary international system and configured relations within that system. While Europeans are scarcely the only ones who have engaged in imperialism and colonialism (indeed, empires have been the most common form of international system in world history, existing on every continent except Australia), the European empires changed the entire world in ways that other forms of imperialism and colonialism did not, providing, among other things, the basis for contemporary globalization. This, at least, is the view of those in IR who take an interest in long-term historical developments, including the early English School theorists:

Key Quote   The English School and Eurocentric History

The present international political structure of the world – founded upon the division of mankind and of the earth into separate states, their acceptance of one another's sovereignty, of principles of law regulating their coexistence and co-operation, and of diplomatic conventions facilitating their intercourse – is, at least in its most basic features, the legacy of Europe's now vanquished ascendancy. Because it was in fact Europe and not America, Asia, or Africa that first dominated and, in doing so, unified the world, it is not our perspective but the historical record itself that can be called Eurocentric. (Bull and Watson, quoted in Seth, 2011, p. 171)

To state the case simply in the terms set by Bull might seem to downplay the agency and influence of the non-European world in international affairs generally. As Sanjay Seth argues, any plausible account of the emergence of the modern international system cannot simply chart how a system that developed in Europe radiated outwards and enveloped others but must also explore the various ways in which international society has been shaped by the interactions between Europe and those it colonized (Seth, 2011, p.174). The implication is that the latter were always active rather than passive; they were not merely *acted upon* but *interacted with* Europeans, who were in turn changed by the experience.

A further implication is that histories of international relations therefore need to move beyond what Europe (or the West) has enacted on the rest of the world and acknowledge the agency of forces emanating from other cultural formations. Thus, as the authors of a critique of the Eurocentricity of mainstream security studies point out, the taken-for-granted approach of the latter misrepresents the role of the Global South in security relations, as well as that of Europe and the West more generally. An adequate understanding of security relations, both past and present, requires 'acknowledging the mutual constitution of Europe and the non-European world and their joint role in making history' (Barkawi and Laffey, 2006, p.330). But there is also a strong moralistic edge to this argument: Eurocentric security studies, they say, sides with the rulers, with the powerful and with the imperialists – not with the weak and the oppressed (ibid., p.344). The implication is that a postcolonial approach does indeed champion the cause of the weak.

Recent work in postcolonial IR scholarship has therefore been concerned not only with ongoing manifestations of imperialist projects in the present but also with how IR itself is largely a product of European, or more generally Western, knowledge practices and the normative implications of this. Whether this makes IR itself a form of Orientalism, at least when it deals with non-Western subjects, is a moot point. Certainly, all of its principal theoretical strands appear to have emerged historically in Europe and North America, including the most critical strands. Thus virtually all IR theory may be regarded as ethnocentric, and this includes the very theories that critique Eurocentrism! Marxist and post-Marxist theories, postmodernism and poststructuralism – these are the theories from which critiques of Eurocentrism and the knowledge/power nexus have been drawn by postcolonial authors. Yet they are themselves theories situated squarely in the intellectual milieu of the Western academy.

One significant question raised by this is: why has no discernible body of IR theory emerged from a non-Western location? This question has been addressed by a group of scholars whose interests lie primarily in the Asia-Pacific region, a region which is suitable as a starting point for the project because it has a very long history of international relations distinct from the West and a set of very rich traditions of political philosophy. These, along with the specific political experiences of the region, may provide some of the basic tools for IR theory-building, but they are yet to be deployed systematically to provide distinctive theoretical frameworks. To date, much of the theoretical work carried out by scholars of or from the Asian region has been concerned with testing (Western) IR theory in Asian national or regional settings rather than using ideas and practices that have arisen within the region as a starting point (Acharya and Buzan, 2010, p. 15).

Another question raised by the foregoing is whether postcolonial theory can itself lay a claim to being non-Western or indigenous in some sense. While many of its leading proponents bear names which may identify them as non-Western, they are nonetheless products of a Western education system and, indeed, write mainly from privileged positions in Western universities, using arguments and critical forms of analysis developed within that system. So, although Edward Said cast himself as the 'Oriental subject', this self-representation was somewhat disingenuous for, as Aijaz Ahmad notes, not only was Said's 'own cultural apparatus ... so overwhelmingly European', but he also commanded 'such an authoritative position in the American university' (Ahmad, 1994, p. 171).

Another problem is that, because postcolonialism is constructed very explicitly as an anti-Orientalist, anti-Eurocentric discourse, it cannot stand apart as an autonomous body of theory but exists only as a mode of critique which is connected directly to the object of critique. Arif Dirlik argues that the very language of postcolonial discourse is the language of First World poststructuralism, 'as postcolonial critics readily concede, although they do not dwell long on its implications' (Dirlik, 1994, p. 341). Dirlik goes on to criticize the tendency of postcolonial approaches to focus on issues of culture at the expense of those emanating from capitalism, which is, after all, the foundation of European power and the motive force of its globalization. Without it, Eurocentrism would have been just another ethnocentrism alongside any other form.

> **Key Quote   Arif Dirlik on Cultural Mystification**
>
> An exclusive focus on Eurocentrism as a cultural or ideological problem that blurs the power of the relationships that dynamized it and endowed it with hegemonic persuasiveness fails to explain why, in contrast to regional or local ethnocentrisms, this particular ethnocentrism was able to define modern global history and itself as the universal aspiration and end of that history. By throwing the cover of culture over material relationships . . . such a focus diverts criticism of capitalism to the criticism of Eurocentric ideology, which not only helps postcolonialism disguise its own ideological limitation but also, ironically, provides an alibi for inequality, exploitation, and oppression in their modern guises under capitalist relationships. The postcolonialist argument projects upon the past the same mystification of the relationship between power and culture that is characteristic of the ideology of global capitalism of which it is a product. (Dirlik, 1994, pp. 346–7)

Despite these criticisms, the insights of postcolonial theory are invaluable to a discipline which, while purporting to explain the world, has clearly been viewing it from a limited, Eurocentric set of perspectives. Whether it is possible simply to abandon all Eurocentric assumptions about how the world works, as Barkawi and Laffey (2006, p. 333) suggest, is another matter, for implicit in this suggestion is a belief that ethnocentricity of any kind really can be transcended. This actually cuts against the culturalist logic on which many postcolonial approaches are based – a logic that insists that, because all knowledge is attuned to and shaped by the particularities of time, place and circumstance, it is simply not possible to transcend any form of ethnocentricity, whether it is Eurocentric, Indocentric, Sinocentric or Afrocentric or embodies some other 'centrism'.

Conclusion

Postcolonial theory is a broad, interdisciplinary enterprise which has performed a valuable service in exposing many taken-for-granted assumptions about the world to critical scrutiny. It has foregrounded in particular the problem of Eurocentrism and the reaction against it, as is evident in the various postcolonial approaches examined here, from Orientalism and subaltern studies to négritude, Afrocentrism and the 'Asian values' debate. When its analytical insights are focused on IR, postcolonial theory seeks to highlight the fact that virtually all theorizing within the discipline, although purporting to be universally applicable, has in fact been highly Eurocentric. One question this raises is: how could it have been otherwise? This introduces in turn the more general problem of establishing neutral ground for theorizing in an irredeemably pluralistic world. Is it possible to transcend all or any 'centricity' in critique and analysis, or are we always to be trapped in the particularities of our own place and culture? For, if that is the case, there may be little point in accusing 'Western' theorists of Eurocentricity as if it were something that could and should have been avoided.

A more nuanced postcolonial approach suggests that the problem of Eurocentricity (or any other centricity) may be assuaged by a more committed effort at cross-cultural understanding and an appreciation of the fact that one's own interpretation of the world is just that – an interpretation – and not an established 'fact' that can be universalized. Cross-cultural dialogue and recognition of the 'other' on equal terms, and not the assertion of a dogmatic universalism underpinned by a superior sense of self, is therefore key to establishing positive relations in a world of cultural difference. But a nuanced postcolonialism and a dynamic form of cross-cultural dialogue must also reject an attitude of dogmatic relativism that imprisons people within cultural silos and forever determines that they hold just one culturally particular view of the world. At the same time, it would do well to acknowledge that 'culture' is not the only relevant concept for a theory that purports to be attuned to social injustices, and that issues of class, not to mention gender, are equally if not more important when it comes to the burdens of everyday life.

QUESTIONS FOR REVISION

1 In what sense is postcolonialism a form of identity politics?
2 What are the implications of the claim that all forms of knowledge are situated in particular cultural/historic contexts?
3 Does 'Orientalism' necessarily give rise to an equally problematic 'Occidentalism'?
4 How does the analysis of al-Qaeda (and affiliated organizations) fit within the postcolonial paradigm?
5 What are the implications of the shift to culturalist themes evident in subaltern studies and négritude?
6 Is Afrocentrism an inverted form of racism?
7 To what extent does the 'Asian values' debate represent a political rather than a cultural standpoint.
8 What value do postcolonial perspectives add to the theorizing of world politics?

FURTHER READING

Donaldson, Laura E., and Pui-Lan Kwok (2002) *Postcolonialism, Feminism and Religious Discourse*. London: Routledge.

Huggan, Graham, and Ian Law (2009) *Racism Postcolonialism Europe*. Liverpool: Liverpool University Press.

Jones, Branwen Gruffydd (ed.) (2006) *Decolonizing International Relations*. Lanham, MD: Rowman & Littlefield.

King, C. Richard (ed.) (2000) *Postcolonial America*. Champaign: University of Illinois Press.

Persram, Nalini (ed.) (2007) *Postcolonialism and Political Theory*. Lanham, MD: Rowman & Littlefield.

USEFUL WEBSITES

http://ipcs.org.au/ (Institute of Postcolonial Studies website)
http://postcolonialist.com (*The Postcolonialist*)
http://postcolonialnetworks.com (Postcolonial Networks website)
www.youtube.com/watch?v=JncXpQQoZAo (Edward Said, lecture on Orientalism)
www.youtube.com/watch?v=TeD1hPr8zJI (Kishore Mahbubani, 'What Are Asian Values?')

10

Green Theory

Green theory is the product of the rise of environmentalism as a political, social and intellectual movement over the last fifty years or so, prompted in turn by various crises associated with the effects of industrialization on the physical or natural world. The profile of the field has strengthened further in recent years, with growing concerns in particular about climate change, which, according to most scientific studies, is driven by excessive emissions of carbon dioxide and other greenhouse gases and is likely to devastate the global environment if not checked. This has been reinforced by a perception that extreme weather events are increasing in frequency, intensity and duration, from superstorms and floods at one end of the spectrum to devastating bushfires and droughts at the other. Other aspects of the anthropogenic impact on the earth's systems, such as mining, agricultural production, deforestation, and the damming of river systems, have produced significant changes in the element and water cycles which are fundamental to life on earth. All these changes are now said to be driving the sixth major extinction event in the earth's history. And, as the human population has grown to more than 7 billion – and predictions point to an increase to 9 billion by the middle of the century – consuming ever more resources and generating the waste to match, concern and indeed alarm over the future of life on the planet is now firmly on the agenda for international politics.

Of particular importance for IR scholars are regimes of environmental governance at both local and global levels, a variety of issues in international political economy, including development and economic growth, the nature of security, the role of state sovereignty and, at the most basic level, how the problems and challenges generated by environmental degradation are to be conceptualized and theorized. The initial sections of this chapter look at the advent of environmentalism as a form of social and political consciousness, the emergence of green political theory generally and, more specifically, the idea of a green theory of value. We then go on to examine a variety of approaches which come under the general rubric of ecologism. The final section considers the 'greening of IR', with specific attention to some of the issues noted above as well as the role of that most central of political institutions, the sovereign state. Once again, this chapter will illustrate the strongly normative dimensions of theorizing. Green theory is also the body of theory that brings ideas of 'nature' most strongly to the fore – hardly surprising given the subject matter around which it revolves.

The Emergence of Environmentalism

Human activity has been generating environmental problems since the advent of cities and agriculture some thousands of years ago, from water and air pollution to land degradation. However, it was only when the environmental consequences of the Industrial Revolution began to make a significant impact from around the middle of the nineteenth century that 'environmental consciousness' started to emerge. This was the starting point for green politics, although it would be a long time before such terminology came into vogue. In fact it was only in the 1960s that 'the environment' emerged as a concept in politics or policy discourses at all (Young, 1992, p. 10; Dryzek, 1997, p. 4). But, as Marx and Engels noted in the mid-nineteenth century, the development of industrial society to that point in time had given rise to unprecedented forces in both the social and the natural sphere.

Key Quote **Marx and Engels on the Subjection of Nature's Forces**

The bourgeoisie, during its rule of scarce one hundred years, has created more massive and more colossal productive forces than have all preceding generations together. Subjection of Nature's forces to man, machinery, application of chemistry to industry and agriculture, steam-navigation, railways, electric telegraphs, clearing of whole continents for cultivation, canalisation of rivers, whole populations conjured out of the ground – what earlier century had even a presentiment that such productive forces slumbered in the lap of social labour? (Marx and Engels, 1969, p. 16)

While these developments were seen as a great triumph for capitalist industrialization, the 'subjection of nature's forces to man' produced a whole array of problems which in turn prompted philosophical and theoretical speculation on such categories as 'nature' and 'the environment'.

The first environmental protectionist groups were formed in Britain in the 1860s, while, in the US, concerns over wilderness preservation and resource conservation saw a nascent movement emerge by the turn of the century (McCormick, 1991, p. vii). The German biologist Ernst Haeckel had coined the term 'ecology' in 1866, and by the end of the century the word 'biosphere' had made its appearance in *The Oxford English Dictionary*. But a systematic mode of thought about the environment combining scientific and philosophic elements had yet to emerge (Crosby, 1995, p. 1182). The first half of the twentieth century saw a continuing development of environmental consciousness and some policy action, but the period from 1945 onwards, and especially from the 1960s, has seen an exponential growth in all aspects of environmentalism and green politics, much of it in response to the fallout from vastly increased economic and industrial activity as well as very significant world population growth.

Probably the most significant work produced at this time was *Silent Spring*, by the biologist Rachel Carson, first published in 1962. It not only emphasized the by now obvious fact that humankind had acquired the capacity, through nuclear technology, to obliterate humankind along with most other living things on the planet but that, even if this did not occur, the biosphere was being poisoned by the massively increasing release of toxic substances. This, Carson noted, was partly a product of research into chemical warfare conducted during the Second World War, which had produced a plethora of toxic synthetic chemicals subsequently deployed as insecticides on a large scale by agricultural industries. But they did not simply kill crop-destroying insects. Because of their bioaccumulative properties, they found their way, through earth and water cycles, into every living species (Carson, 1963, pp. 18–20). One of the best known of the organochlorine chemicals is dichloro-diphenyl-trichloroethane, otherwise known as DDT, used in enormous quantities in the postwar period along with even more toxic hydrocarbons – dieldron, aldrin and endrin – all of which resulted in a significant destruction of wildlife as well as numerous illnesses and deaths among humans exposed to it (ibid., pp. 23–6).

This work had a very significant impact in two very different ways. First, it increased public awareness of the dangers of such pollutants as well as of environmental issues more generally, leading eventually to political action in the form of environmental controls on the use of chemicals and other pollutants. The US Environmental Protection Authority (EPA) was established in 1970, the same year in which the first Earth Day was celebrated. The EPA's website today specifically credits Carson with these achievements:

[handwritten margin note: First significant work on environmentalism]

> **Key Quote   The US Environmental Protection Agency on Rachel Carson**
>
> In the process of transforming ecology from dispassionate science to activist creed, Carson unwittingly launched the modern idea of environmentalism: a political movement which demanded the state not only preserve the earth, but act to regulate and punish those who polluted it. (EPA, 1992)

DDT was banned in the US in 1972, the same year that the UN Environment Programme was established, the UN Conference on the Human Environment was convened in Stockholm, the first Earth Summit was held in Rio de Janeiro, Greenpeace was founded in Vancouver, Canada, the Norwegian philosopher Arne Næss coined the term 'deep ecology', and the first Green political parties were founded in New Zealand and Australia. The period also saw the emergence of 'survivalist' themes in a number of important publications, which were met in turn with a 'Promethean' viewpoint. These perspectives provide an excellent example of how the same problems can generate opposite viewpoints concerning solutions.

Among the first studies in the survivalist genre was Garrett Hardin's influential essay 'The Tragedy of the Commons' (Hardin, 1968). Hardin mounted a strong critique of the then popular notion that, whatever problems might emerge, a technical solution could be found, and that this would therefore require little or nothing in the way of changes in human values. One human value that came in for particular attention was the relentless pursuit of self-interest, which, while rational at an individual level, spelt disaster for the future of humans (and other life forms) in the longer term, for the rate at which individual humans were consuming the resources of the 'global commons' – water, soil, air, earth, etc. – was simply unsustainable.

Hardin, echoing the concerns of Thomas Malthus (see chapter 4), identified population growth as a particular problem and highlighted the fact that a finite world with finite resources can carry only a finite population. He pointed out that there was no technical fix for overpopulation, the only solution being 'relinquishing the freedom to breed'. And this move would require a considerable rethink on a number of moral positions (Hardin, 1968, p.1248). Another leading author, Paul Ehrlich, writing in the same year as Hardin, noted that there are only two solutions to the population problem, as the next key quote shows.

> **Key Quote   Paul Ehrlich's Solutions to the Population Problem**
>
> One is a 'birth rate solution', in which we find ways to <u>lower the birth rate</u>. The other is the '<u>death rate solution</u>', in which ways to <u>raise the death rate</u> – war, famine, pestilence – *find us*. (Ehrlich, 1968, p. 17; original emphasis)

The year 1968 also saw the formation of a group of scientists, business people and politicians concerned with lack of government (and inter-government) action on looming long-term dilemmas concerning the cluster of problems surrounding population growth, the depletion of non-renewable resources, widespread malnutrition and environmental degradation. Called the 'Club of Rome', the group commissioned what was to become another highly influential book, *The Limits to Growth*, first published in 1972, which was based on an elaborate modelling of trends around these issues and reiterated the survivalist theme. There were two choices: continue as usual and face the consequences in terms of a sudden and uncontrollable decline in both population and industrial capacity from the mid- to late twenty-first century; or start planning immediately for ecological and economic stability to achieve a state of global equilibrium sufficient to meet the basic material needs of all people (Meadows, Randers and Meadows, 2004, pp. 21–4).

The problem of population growth and resources depletion remains. When the earth emerged from the last ice age and entered the era we call the Holocene – an era of relatively congenial climatic conditions suitable for human thriving – the total world population is estimated to have stood at around 5 million. By the late eighteenth century it was about 1 billion. In 2011 it passed 7 billion, at which time the UN predicted a further increase to over 9 billion before the middle of this century (UN News Centre, 2011). In the meantime, a more recent report noted that 'short-term political and economic strategies are driving consumerism and debt, which, together with a growing global population . . . is sub-jecting the natural environment to growing stress.' Predictions were that, by 2030, 'the world will need at least <u>50 per cent more food</u>, <u>45 per cent more energy</u>, and <u>30 per cent more water</u> – all at a time when environmental limits are threatening supply' (UNEP, 2012, p. xii).

The survivalist theme, also dubbed the 'gloom and doom' approach, stands in contrast to a 'Promethean' viewpoint (named for the mythical Greek Titan, who stole fire from Zeus), as discussed in case study 10.1. Prometheanism promotes confidence in human abilities and technolog-ical skills to overcome all manner of problems, including environmental

Case Study 10.1   Survivalism versus Prometheanism in the Climate Change Debate

The UN's Intergovernmental Panel on Climate Change, established in 1988 to review and assess scientific data in relation to climate change and its environmental and socio-economic impacts, released its fifth assessment report in 2013. It confirmed that anthropogenic change is occurring across the planet, as evidenced by numerous observations of the atmosphere, land, oceans and cryosphere (frozen or iced regions). Climate change is in large measure the result of increased atmospheric concentrations of greenhouse gases such as carbon dioxide, methane and nitrous oxide. These gases occur naturally in lesser concentrations, absorbing solar radiation and providing a sufficiently warm atmosphere for life to flourish.

The consumption of fossil fuels and the clearing of land for agriculture, however, has seen atmospheric and sea temperatures rise above their normal level, resulting in large-scale melting of ice, rising sea levels and extreme weather events such as floods, droughts, heat waves, cyclones and storm surges (IPCC, 2014a). In addition, increasing ocean acidification will have significant impacts on marine ecosystems.

Apart from the immediate hazards associated with extreme weather events, and the fact that periods of more intense heat and cold can kill thousands of people in a single region, climate change will certainly have a serious impact on food and water security in the longer term (NRS, 2011). Population growth and economic growth are the main drivers of carbon dioxide emissions from fossil fuel combustion, and their increase has far outpaced attempts at emissions reduction to date (IPCC, 2014b). And the longer it takes to implement effective emissions reduction, the more costly the measures will be.

The response has so far concentrated on limiting emissions to keep the average increase in global average temperature to less than 2 degrees Celsius. A major emphasis is on less carbon-intensive energy production together with a significant increase in renewable energy – solar, wind, etc. Hydroelectricity is carbon neutral but has deleterious effects on waterways. More controversial is a proposed increase in nuclear energy, which is also carbon neutral but has long been opposed by the green lobby. Much more efficient energy use is also part of the solution.

In the economic sphere, carbon taxes and/or emissions trading schemes have been implemented in a number of countries. In addition to such measures, a broad-based survivalist response would emphasize essential changes in attitudes and behaviour, new economic models not predicated on endless growth, and a concerted effort to limit population growth. In many countries, this last entails changes in attitudes towards women to allow them more control over reproduction.

Despite the significantly increased attention to the dangers of climate change, little has been achieved in the way of effective emissions reduction, and the earth seems still to be heading towards a much warmer and consequently more dangerous future. A Promethean response would endorse all the practical measures outlined above, including a switch to efficient new-generation nuclear energy, but would look to measures in the emerging field of geoengineering as well. The two main techniques are carbon capture, which aims to remove and store excess atmospheric carbon, and solar-radiation management, which would offset the warming effect of increased greenhouse gases by releasing sulphur particles into the stratosphere (see Peters, 2012).

Carbon capture and storage involves certain technology-driven methods – for example, by capturing emissions at source (e.g., from industrial plants or coal-powered stations), compressing it, and storing it underground. This can also be partly achieved by 'natural' methods in the form of large-scale afforestation and reforestation projects – scarcely objectionable from a green perspective. Solar-radiation management would deploy much more controversial technologies. It leaves greenhouse gases in the atmosphere but counters their warming effects by reflecting heat back into space. Proposals for achieving this include the use of stratospheric sulfate aerosols to achieve an effect similar to that provided by large-scale volcanic eruptions – a comparison that provides a 'natural analogue'. The difference with the geoengineering technique is that the sulfates would be continuously replenished (Rasch et al., 2008).

Options in geoengineering technology were examined for the first time by the IPCC in their 2013 report. Although these are not recommended as a desirable solution, the IPCC has been accused of effectively 'normalizing' extreme technical measures even by including them as possible adjuncts to other measures (Watson, 2013). More specifically, it has been pointed out that the 'lure of the techno-fix' creates a number of ethical dilemmas concerning consent, governance, legal mechanisms, the involvement of commercial interests, and the 'moral hazard' of encouraging irresponsible behaviour in continuing patterns of consumption and energy use (Preston, 2012, pp. 4–5).

ones – a confidence that Hardin, among others, considered a highly dangerous approach. Prometheanism is often accompanied by 'cornucopianism' – a belief that there are virtually 'unlimited natural resources, unlimited ability of natural systems to absorb pollutants, and unlimited corrective capacity in natural systems' (Dryzek, 1997, p. 45). This viewpoint resonates with the neoliberal belief in the self-correcting capacity of markets discussed in chapter 5, and indeed Prometheanism has a strong following among neoliberal economists, as it promises to deal with climate change without disrupting current economic models premised on continuing growth.

Towards the end of the 1960s it seemed that the human capacity for producing technological marvels was indeed unlimited, with the Apollo missions culminating in the triumphal moon landing in 1969. But the same Apollo missions also brought us the famous image of 'earthrise', showing a beautiful but fragile and vulnerable planet enclosed in a thin layer of protective atmosphere floating in infinite space. With this and other developments discussed above, a multifaceted environmental movement was on the way to making a significant impact on political developments, from the local through to the global level, as well as on political thought about the environment.

Carson's work and various moves to protect the environment, however, also triggered a backlash from those commercial interests which stood to lose from adverse publicity and bans on the use of many of their products. Carson herself was depicted as emotional and hysterical – thus sexism and personal attacks became additional weapons. Beyond that, she was accused of fanaticism and environmental mysticism and of using science illegitimately to further a political cause (Mooney, 2005, p. 31). This was the beginning of a period in which commercial interests more generally began to resist or deny scientific findings that might compromise profitability. One of the most infamous was the tobacco lobby, which, when faced with mounting evidence of links between smoking and a range of diseases, including cancer, that had been produced by researchers working independently of commercial interests, proceeded to employ their own scientists to try and cast doubt on this evidence (Oreskes and Conway, 2010, p. 10), an endeavour in which they ultimately failed.

At the same time, a number of politically conservative think-tanks and foundations, located mainly in the US, began to fund research in various areas, from acid rain and stratospheric ozone depletion to global warming, that once again attempted to cast doubt on the considerable scientific evidence pointing to the industrial sources of these problems and the dangers they presented (Oreskes and Conway, 2010, pp. 1–9). The link between politically conservative (or right-wing) politics, Promethean/cornucopian views and general environmental scepticism – and the science that supports it – remains a strong one, especially in the US (see Mooney, 2005, esp. pp. 33–4; Jacques, Dunlap and Freeman, 2008).

Environmental politics is not, however, simply a matter of conservative or right-wing, pro-industrial, pro-capitalist ideologues opposing left-wing, anti-industrial, anti-capitalist, pro-environmental protection ideologues. There are various positions along a complex spectrum of beliefs and values that shift and change as new problems or issues emerge, as scientific studies produce new knowledge or perspectives, and as technologies proliferate. The environmental movement itself is just as varied. In 1970, *New Republic* magazine described the movement in the US as 'the biggest assortment of ill-matched allies since the Crusades – young and old, radicals of left and right, liberals and conservatives, humanists and scientists, atheists and deists' (quoted in McCormick, 1991, p.ix). And, as Robert Goodin put it in introducing the first issue of the journal *Environmental Politics*, 'there are many different shades of green', demonstrating the significant range of approaches taken on environmental issues, from mild reformism through to calls for a radical reordering of society and political relations (Goodin, 1992a, p.7). These are reflected in the varieties of environmental or green political theory that we consider next.

Green Political Theory

With the rise of so much activity and discussion focused on environmental issues, environmentalism became established as a broad term encompassing social movements with a political orientation moved both by a set of ideas about the natural world and the human relationship with it and a range of prescriptions for the future of the planet. This made it inevitable that various philosophical approaches reflecting different strands within the movement would develop, eventually giving rise to what is now commonly called 'green theory'. However, as with other broad bodies of theory discussed in this book, there is no singular, uncontested body of thought encompassed by this term; rather there is a plurality of approaches. Green theory as such can therefore be described only minimally, as 'a form of normative theory that has, as a central and defining focus, a concern for the protection of the natural environment' (Humphrey, 2010a, p.573).

The term 'environment' is also difficult to define with any precision, as there is an infinitely overlapping series of environments, from that of the cow pat in which a dung beetle thrives, to the field in which the cow grazes, to the valley in which the field is situated, and so on. Yet there is an overwhelming belief that there is, after all is said and done, one all-encompassing global environment (Attfield, 1999, p.9). This is reinforced by the fact that pollution, especially atmospheric and water pollution, cannot be prevented from crossing borders and is therefore scarcely amenable to 'border security' measures.

Green political theory has been conceptualized as falling within two main categories – 'environmentalism' and 'ecologism'. Proponents of the latter tend to distinguish themselves from those of the former by arguing for a radical approach to politics and society which goes well beyond a mere problem-solving environmental managerialism assuming that environmental problems can be solved without radical changes to patterns of production and consumption, let alone basic values and attitudes. Thus ecologism asserts that 'a sustainable and fulfilling existence presupposes radical changes in our relationship with the non-human natural world, and in our mode of social and political life' (Dobson, 2007, pp. 2–3). Environmentalism as a managerialist approach is also associated with anthropocentrism, 'a view that the interests of humans are of higher priority than those of nonhumans' (Buell, 2005, p. 134). Anthropocentrism is therefore used as an antonym for ecocentrism or biocentrism, approaches which constrain the interests of any particular species, placing the ecosphere or biosphere at the centre of their ethic of value (ibid., pp. 134, 137).

Ecologism is based on ideas about 'ecology' and 'ecosystems', which have reasonably precise scientific definitions. 'Ecosystem' refers to the sum of organisms in a particular region, the environment in which they live, and the relationships and energy flows between all the various elements, including non-organic matter such as water, soil and air, which together constitute an interactive system that is relatively self-contained. Ecology refers primarily to the study of ecosystems with a focus on the relationships between the various elements. There is also the term 'ecosphere', which goes beyond the particularities of discrete ecosystems and sets up a global category, producing a 'planetary ecosystem'. The notion of a whole, interdependent planetary system is embodied in the 'Gaia hypothesis', a somewhat mystical approach which departs from mainstream ecologism. Originating in the mid-1970s in the work of James Lovelock, a scientist, inventor and one-time NASA consultant, the hypothesis holds that the earth, taken as a whole, is a self-regulating entity. Implicit in this is the idea that Gaia also constitutes a self-correcting mechanism – a view which Lovelock later acknowledged as problematic given the magnitude of environmental problems evident in the twenty-first century (Lovelock, 2000, pp. i–x).

What is distinctive about ecologism is that it takes a holistic view, considering particular environmental problems not as isolated or self-contained, and therefore treatable on that basis, but rather as part of a more general pattern which requires an all-encompassing approach. It therefore attends not just to the parts of a system but to the whole system (in this case a planetary or whole earth system) and demonstrates the links between social, political, cultural, economic, geographic, biological, and any other relevant factors which together form an extensive and highly complex pattern of global interdependence. The scale of this version of interdependence goes far beyond the form of 'complex interdependence' recognized by liberal theory, which is, in comparison, very limited.

Another more recent approach is 'bright green environmentalism', a term coined by the journalist Alex Steffen to distinguish it from the pragmatic reformism of light greens and the radical ecocentrism of dark greens. It is based on ideas derived from 'ecological modernization theory', which originated as a form of social theory in the 1980s and which challenged the idea that we needed to deindustrialize as well as fundamentally reorder the core institutions of modern society to ensure a sustainable future (see Mol and Spaargaren, 2000). Bright green environmentalism is broadly anthropocentric but promotes a need for radical economic and social change in order to protect the environment, and therefore goes beyond light green reformism (Bloor, 2010, p. 247). It also embraces elements of Prometheanism, although, in light of its call for radical social and economic change, it rejects a business as usual approach. It therefore contrasts with anti-modernist and anti-industrial approaches, instead possessing an 'emphasis on design, technology, innovation, entrepreneurialism, and consumption practices' (Newman, 2011, p.39). Economic prosperity and growth are not antithetical to environmental sustainability, nor do they necessitate social exploitation. Indeed, bright green environmentalism commends 'green social engineering' to achieve a variety of positive environmental and social outcomes (ibid.). In summary, bright green discourse advocates a move away from the gloom and doom, survivalist and 'eco-tragic' perspectives to more optimist, positive framings of future possibilities (McGrail, 2011, p. 123).

Bright green environmentalism aside, the distinction between light green and dark green approaches remains a common or standard way of distinguishing between *environmental* political thought and *green* political thought, with some reserving the latter for ecologism. This division mirrors other labels – the former being associated with shallow ecology, humanism and anthropocentrism, while the latter denotes deep ecology and ecocentric or biocentric approaches (Eckersley, 1992, p. 8). Another approach, however, considers green political theory to be a 'broad category encompassing all forms of political thought that have as a high priority the conservation or preservation of the natural environment' (Humphrey, 2010b, p.182). This chapter adopts the same approach and so does not reserve the term 'green theory' for just the more radical approaches. For present purposes, the latter will be referred to as ecologism or ecocentric theory, which we now examine in a little more detail, noting that even within this category there is considerable variation.

Ecologism and the Green Theory of Value

It has been suggested that there are two distinct aspects to ecologism – one political and the other philosophical. The political aspect is based on the belief that the relentless pursuit of Western-style industrialization has precipitated a global environmental crisis which now threatens not just the future of humanity but all life on earth, and that the remedy is to be found in deindustrialization and a thoroughgoing transformation in social, political and economic life. Linked to these positions is a philosophical theory of value which is said to challenge the entire basis of Western political thought. While the latter is essentially anthropocentric, ecologism (not surprisingly) is avowedly ecocentric, assigning primacy of value to the natural world or ecosphere as a whole (see Humphrey, 2010a, pp. 573–4).

A green theory of value provides 'the unified moral vision' underpinning green politics. It tells us what is to be valued and why (Goodin, 1992b, p. 15). The entity to be valued is 'nature', not just as something which has been made available to humans 'for the support and comfort of their being', as the early liberal theorist John Locke (quoted in Eckersley, 1992, p. 23) wrote in an explicitly instrumentalist vein, but as something that has intrinsic value in and of itself. In other words, 'nature' possesses a value that exists independently of humanity (Goodin, 1992b, p. 45). These contrasting theories of value are commonly known as axiological and instrumental: the former denotes an approach in which the object – in this case nature – possesses intrinsic value while the latter refers to the value of the object insofar as it serves human needs and purposes.

One point to be noted regarding the antithetical notion that nature exists for the benefit of humans is that it is not just liberals who have taken, and extended, this view. Marxist approaches have often been no better when it comes to valuing nature: 'while social relations between humans are theoretically different under capitalism and socialism, the relationship between humans and the rest of nature appears to be essentially the same' (Eckersley, 1992, p. 22). This is because both of them support and indeed urge the pursuit of what may be called the 'material good life' that industrialism appears to deliver and which calls for the mastery of nature and its utilization for the advancement of human interests. Of course, the preservation or conservation of nature is not incompatible with this pursuit. But the point remains that, in conventional liberal and Marxist thought, nature remains valued for the benefits it brings to humankind, not for its own sake. Both are therefore profoundly anthropocentric. This, however, does not necessarily hold for later versions of post-Marxist critical theory (see ibid.).

Another general point that derives from valuing nature is that it gives rise to various conceptualizations of 'the natural'. What is natural, and therefore to be valued, is often understood in contrast to that which is 'artificial', in the sense of being made or constructed in one way or another by human hands – that is, 'manufactured' in the most literal sense of the Latin word from which the term is derived. That which is natural is good; the artificial is either *not* good, or at least not as good as the 'real thing'. To call something ersatz, faux, fake, etc., is dismissive if not contemptuous. And, as we have seen in a previous chapter, to call something 'unnatural' is often to condemn it on some moral ground, while that which is 'natural' is seen as right and good.

There is also the question of whether humans are to be regarded as part of nature, for if they are fully assimilated *with* nature, at least theoretically, then everything they do is by extension 'natural'. Some religious positions, however, may assert that humans are somewhat above the rest of nature – that we are an especially special part of a phenomenon that owes its existence to a grand hierarchical design. Even without adopting such a position, human reflection on nature as an entity defined apart from human activity or agency, and possessing intrinsic value, implies a distinction between 'humanity', on the one hand, and the 'natural world', on the other, even if we then want to dismiss the distinction as an artificial one.

But let us consider again the notion that the value that nature possesses exists independently of humanity, and that such value is, in the final analysis, a form of moral value. This raises the question of how, without humans to attribute such value to the entity nature, it could be valued in any moral sense at all. This brings us straight back to the anthropocentric position that the very idea of moral value is humanly constructed rather than constructed by non-human animals, let alone by vegetation or rocks which have no cognitive capacity at all. In other words, how can moral value exist in the absence of humans and their apparently unique capacity to engage in the kind of complex, abstract thought that produces moral value? Even if some believe that the ultimate source of morality is a deity of one kind or another, it is humans who are enjoined to contemplate and enact morality.

Religious beliefs aside, if we follow the logic of the social construction of reality, we come to the point where we must conceptualize 'nature' not as a reality that exists 'out there', as an independent entity, but as a social construct – a product of the human imagination as situated in specific historical and/or cultural contexts and which may therefore vary quite radically according to these contexts. This is, perhaps, the ultimate in anthropocentric thought for, while it purports to pluralize, relativize and in some sense democratize human thought, it privileges the human mind and the actions that follow from human thought above all else. This suggests that there is no escape from some form of anthropocentrism in the formulation of any moral values, including those which regard humans as *the* central *moral* problem in a thoroughgoing ecocentric theory of the ultimate value of a pristine natural world untouched by humans.

Another aspect of a green theory of value and morality is the extension of the boundary of the moral community to include not just all humans, as traditional cosmopolitan theory does, but all life on the planet and possibly even the planet itself (Dobson and Lucardie, 1993, p.x). This poses some difficult problems for conventional theories of justice and morality, which may regard nature as an object of moral discourse but not as a subject. It follows that nature is not a moral agent and cannot itself distribute justice (see Wissenburg, 1993). Such problems, however, have not deterred those fully committed to ecocentrism, a position best represented by 'deep ecology' and certain variations on this theme, which addresses a number of the issues raised above.

Deep Ecology, Bioregionalism and Biocentrism

As mentioned earlier, the concept of deep ecology was pioneered in the early 1970s by the Norwegian philosopher Arne Næss (1912–2009). He also promoted the idea of 'ecosophy', a normative world view which joins the study of interrelationships in the natural world with the study of wisdom, and was the first to distinguish between the anthropocentric, humans-first value system of 'shallow' environmentalism and that of deep ecology, which emphasizes the intrinsic worth of all beings, from microbes to elephants, as well as respect for cultural diversity, social justice and advocacy of non-violence in all spheres, both natural and cultural (Drengsen, 2008, p.27). Næss was concerned to distinguish between scientific approaches, which dealt only with the facts, and an evaluative approach which sought to articulate values. This is why he distinguished the mere science of ecology, concerned only with value-free investigations of fact, from 'deep' ecology, characterized by an explicitly normative stance.

Key Quote   Arne Næss and Normative Ecology

Chemistry, physics, and the science of ecology acknowledge only change, not valued change. But . . . a change in the bio-conditions of a river or ocean which excluded most forms of life contends that it would constitute a devastation of diversity. The inability of the science of ecology to denounce such processes . . . suggests that we need another approach which involves the inescapable role of announcing values, not only 'facts'. (Næss, 1989, p. 47)

There is also a strong spiritual element in deep ecology that encourages respect for all beings and a commitment to living in harmony in both the natural and the cultural world. This indicates not a subordination of humanity to nature (as is sometimes assumed by critics of the movement) but the harmonious integration of human lifestyles with the natural world. This also means that ecocentrism does not contemplate humans as separate from the ecosphere but as much a part of it as any other organism. It does, however, seek to decentre them. But it is obviously humans who have created the serious environmental problems of late modernity, and so it is a deep-seated change in human thought and behaviour that is required. Deep ecology therefore seeks to treat not just the symptoms but the essential causes.

A set of ideas which can be described as the political organizational side of deep ecology is bioregionalism. It seeks to address some of the key problems identified by deep ecologists with respect to both the social and environmental problems generated by modern industrial society through a return to community-based living, close to the land in decentralized, naturally defined areas, with the aim of establishing economic self-sufficiency within that area or region. Along with minimizing human impact on the environment through organic farming, the use of alternative medicines and treatments, and localized marketing, it promotes communitarianism, nature-based wisdom, spirituality, mutual aid, participatory politics and 'speciate humility' (Sale, 2000, p. xix). There are, of course, criticisms of this approach. In such small communities – which are ideally only around 10,000 people – there may well arise problems of cultural and intellectual impoverishment leading to lack of innovation, including innovation in environmentally friendly technologies. Another is that cooperation and coordination of larger-scale environmental measures may be more difficult. And, on the social side, it has been suggested that, far from encouraging more democratic outcomes, social control mechanisms may well become oppressive (Carter, 2008, p. 59).

We saw earlier that some critiques of deep ecology had been made by ecofeminists. However, according to one ecofeminist author, most ecofeminists endorse the insights of deep ecology 'into our human identity with nature and the ethic of care that stems from this' (Salleh, 2000, p. 110). But Salleh also refers to the ongoing failure of deep ecology to attend adequately to the insights of gender perspectives supplied by ecofeminists and to consider their implications for identity and difference. The latter relate not just to gender but to indigenous identity and difference as well, thus raising the issue of Eurocentrism, which many deep ecologists – as well as liberals and socialists – stand accused of ignoring. According to the ecofeminist perspective, one of the lessons that indigenous societies afford is that they had learned to live well within their means. This does not mean that we should somehow attempt a return to the past, but that we (where 'we' refers to persons immersed in Western industrial culture) should at least question 'ingrained habits of thought and [be] more fully conscious of what we are about' (ibid., p. 121).

An alternative to the broad ecocentrism of deep ecology and its variants is biocentrism. This approach also holds that value is not to be understood simply in terms of human interests but, rather, resides in all living entities. But this also means that ecosystems (which include non-living elements such as minerals and water) are not the repositories of value except insofar as they support life (Humphrey, 2010a, p. 574). A further implication is that they are not moral subjects, and so 'the purely physical conditions of a natural environment must, from a moral point of view, be sharply separated from the animals and plants that depend on those conditions for their survival' (Taylor, 2011, p. 18). This life-centred approach raises a series of questions for environmental ethics:

- Is human conduct in relation to natural ecosystems properly subject to moral constraints, or are they applicable only to the ways humans treat each other?
- If the answer is yes, what particular moral constraints are involved, and how are they different from those governing our actions towards other humans?
- How would the standards and rules arising from those constraints be rationally justified?

- Assuming we have moral duties towards the natural world, how are these to be weighed against human values and interests?' (Ibid., p. 10)

The general answer given by this particular author, formulated as a biocentric theory of environmental ethics, is that we do have a moral duty to the natural world which is quite independent of the duties owed to fellow humans. This contrasts clearly with an anthropocentric environmental ethic, which holds that all duties to the natural world derive ultimately from the duties we owe to other humans, including future generations. In this formulation, even the responsibility to protect endangered species is linked directly to human values (ibid., p. 11).

Whether one agrees with it or not, this approach to biocentrism is a serious intellectual attempt at establishing the basis for a form of environmental ethics or normative theory. In the populist literature, however, a very different kind of biocentrism has been advanced and, along with it, some fairly extravagant claims. The principal text in this particular genre, entitled *Biocentrism: How Life and Consciousness are the Keys to Understanding the True Nature of the Universe* (Lanza and Berman, 2009), begins with the assertion that our current theories of the physical world, trapped as they are in 'the cages in which Western science has unwittingly managed to confine itself', simply do not account for 'life and consciousness' (ibid., pp. 1–2). The idea of consciousness emphasized in this particular text purports to reveal a startling truth, and that is that 'the animal observer creates reality and not the other way around' (ibid., p. 15). Biocentrism therefore 'arrives at a very different view of reality than that which has generally been embraced for the last several centuries' (ibid., p. 17).

What these authors believe to be a revolutionary insight is in fact derived from a style of centuries-old idealist philosophy (different from the political idealism with which political realism is contrasted in IR theory), which holds that reality can only ever reside in human consciousness. Although there are some overlaps, this differs from theories based on the sociology of knowledge in which facts about the material world, as discussed in chapter 7, are seen as mediated by social or cultural institutions and experienced but not actually created by them. This view leaves space for an external, independent, non-social reality such as 'nature', even though it may be subject to many different interpretations (see Bloor, 1996). The main point to note, however, is that the almost mystical form of biocentrism described here as a variation on idealist philosophy (and which has in fact been endorsed by the freelance mystic Deepak Chopra) has little to do with the biocentric environmental ethic formulated by Taylor, which belongs squarely within a tradition of green theory with serious philosophical credentials.

Eco-authoritarianism and Eco-anarchism

Two other forms of ecologism that must be mentioned here are eco-authoritarianism to eco-anarchism. As the terms suggest, they occupy antithetical political/ideological positions. Eco-authoritarianism had its heyday in the 1970s but still attracts adherents. It is underpinned by a Hobbesian/Malthusian survivalist perspective and is associated with 'doom and gloom' prophets such as Garrett Hardin. One of eco-authoritarianism's chief proponents, William Ophus, has promoted the idea that liberal democracy is ill-suited to resolving the myriad problems of the environment and resource scarcity confronting contemporary society, and indeed has actually been responsible for creating them. In the face of an impending crisis, what is needed is a 'green Leviathan' with the knowledge and power to make prudent, enforceable ecological decisions (see Barry, 1999, p. 196; Keulartz, 1998, p. 3).

At the opposite end of the political spectrum to eco-authoritarianism is eco-anarchism, sometimes called social ecology. Its best-known proponent, Murray Bookchin (1921–2006), started from the premise that the domination of nature by man stems from the very real domination of human by human (Bookchin, 2005, p. 1). Bookchin, echoing some of the views of the nineteenth-century anarchist theorist Peter Kropotkin, promoted a benign view of nature, seeing it as essentially interdependent and egalitarian and certainly without hierarchies. Humans, who are assumed to be naturally cooperative, flourish best in the realm of nature, living under egalitarian social arrangements in which none dominate either their fellow humans *or* nature. Such was life in the pre-literate, organic communities of earlier human societies, which were subsequently transformed by the rise of social hierarchies characterized by divisions based on gender, age, class, religion and race and driven by the dynamics of competition and conflict rather than cooperation for mutual benefit (Carter, 2008, p. 75), or so Bookchin imagined.

Bookchin was also at odds with aspects of deep ecology, which he described as 'mystical eco-la-la'. He dismissed the idea that positive change emerges from 'a transformation of individual world-views stimulated by better spiritual connections with nature' and accused the movement of harbouring misanthropic views, detecting in their ideas 'support for coercive forms of population control, immigration and aid policy' (2005, p. 76). Indeed, some deep ecologists have advocated 'letting nature take its course', thereby allowing 'natural' disasters such as famine and disease to play their part in depopulating the earth (Chase, 1991, p. 20). Bookchin would have found this view morally repugnant. Despite these differences, deep ecology and eco-anarchism share some common ground, including a certain hostility to the state, which they see as inimical to their ecological and social values (Carter, 2008, p. 76). They also share a commitment to radical ecologism, whatever form that might take, in opposition to mere environmental reformism. The latter fails to challenge the basis of modern capitalist industrial society, which has, in the final analysis, wrought the social and environmental damage that ecologism seeks to address at the most basic level.

The Greening of IR

This chapter has shown the extent to which concerns about environmental degradation have prompted individuals and groups not only to engage in social and political action but also to formulate more abstract, philosophical ideas about the human relationship with the environment with a view to informing that action. And since at least the 1970s, both thought and action have been on a global scale. As we have seen, 1972 was a big year for environmental action generally, with the founding of Greenpeace and the first green parties as well as with the UN setting up its Environment Programme, convening the Stockholm conference and organizing the first Earth Summit in Rio de Janeiro. These latter have been hailed as watershed events in establishing environmental issues firmly on the agenda of world politics and providing an initial framework for global environmental governance (Elliott, 2004, p. 7). We have also seen that the early writers in this period were mainly scientists – Rachel Carson, Paul Ehrlich and Garrett Hardin, among others – followed then by philosophers and political theorists, who have developed varying normative approaches to the environment under the general rubric of green political theory. Green IR theory does not really stand apart from the more general field of green political theory, but there are some issues that are of special concern to IR. These include international political economy and the development agenda, the changing nature of security, and the role of the sovereign state.

As the environmental movement was gathering momentum and environmental issues began to occupy a prominent place on the global agenda in the 1970s, international political economy also started developing as a specialist field within IR. As it did so, it was required to grapple with the twin issues of economic development and environmental protection, issues which the UN recognized were inextricably entwined. One thing that became clear very quickly was that, if the underdeveloped countries of the South were simply to replicate the economic and industrial strategies of the developed world, the consequences for the environment would be disastrous. But to do nothing to assist in mitigating poverty and disease and raising living standards was simply not an option given the UN's social justice commitments.

In 1983 the UN established the World Commission on Environment and Development, otherwise known as the Brundtland Commission, which focused on three interlocking themes: economic development, environmental protection and social equality. Its report, entitled *Our Common Future* (WCED, 1987), introduced into the vocabulary of international politics the term 'sustainable development' – defined in terms of meeting the needs of the present generation without compromising the resources available to future generations. In addition to noting numerous environmental disasters, which included severe weather events as well as horrendous industrial accidents around the world, the report highlighted the fact that many countries spent a far greater proportion of their GDP on the military than on protecting the environmental resources that actually keep their people alive on a daily basis (ibid., para. 22). It was clear that acid rain, ozone depletion, global warming, species loss and desertification were as much, if not more, of a concern for national security as the threat of an invading military force. These concerns were reinforced in 1992 by the UN Conference on Environment and Development (UNCED), otherwise known as the Rio Earth Summit, the largest ever gathering of world leaders to that time, which concluded with the Rio Declaration setting out guiding principles for environmental conservation, preservation and restoration (see UN, 1992).

The link between development, the environment and security was made more explicit in the UN's *Human Security Report* of 1994, which introduced the term 'human security' – a term which shifted the focus of security to 'people rather than territories, with development rather than arms' thereby promoting 'a new paradigm of sustainable human development' (UNDP, 1994a). Human security was defined as multifaceted, with environmental security being listed as one dimension of security along with economic security, food security, health security, personal security, community security and political security (UNDP, 1994b, pp.24–5). Although all are important, the theme that has garnered the most consistent national and international attention is environmental security, especially to the extent that it underpins several of the other dimensions of security – food and health being the most obvious. Other dimensions not specifically mentioned here are energy and water security but, again, both are closely linked to environmental security. The environment is now also seen as a possible source of traditional security threats. As one commentator notes, there is a growing potential for violence and warfare over access to resources that are directly related to environmental problems and which are therefore now part and parcel 'of the calculus of international politics' and an extended security agenda (Dalby, 2002, p. xix).

This raises the question of just how adequate our political institutions, both national and international, are in addressing these interlocking dimensions of security. One commentator suggests that our institutions of politics and governance have been primarily responsible for failures of environmental security, pointing to the need for the environment to be securitized more robustly at a political institutional level (Barnett, 2001, p. 10). This is borne out by the fact that, although many noble principles and intentions have been enunciated in numerous UN and other fora, serious sustained action has rarely followed. Others, however, have argued that the major institutions of global economic governance – the World Bank, the IMF and the WTO – have in fact internalized norms of sustainable development and integrated ideas about environmental protection within a liberal economic world order over the last two decades or so (O'Neill, 2009, p. 161). There have also been some moves in this direction by multinational corporations conscious of their brand name and public image, as well as the need to 'minimize risks and uncertainties associated with multiple and shifting governmental and inter-governmental rules' (ibid., p. 171).

All this, however, suggests a reformist approach which is moving at snail's pace within the existing framework of modern industrial capitalism and its neoliberal economic framework, which would scarcely satisfy those promoting a deeper green or more critical approach and who therefore seek a much more radical challenge to that entire framework. This has been expressed, at one level, through the 'anti-globalization' movement, which has made its presence felt at high-level meetings of various organizations. The first major occasion for a mass demonstration was a 1999 WTO meeting in Seattle, which drew around 30,000 activists from different groups around the world 'unified by trenchant critiques of neoliberal globalization and a commitment to ecological and social justice' (O'Neill, 2009, p. 162). 'Global protest' groups have continued their activities at major international gatherings, from the WTO and the IMF to the G8 and the Asia-Pacific Economic Cooperation forum, all of which have become major security events as a result.

Whatever the legitimacy of the various claims made by the anti-globalization movement, there can be little doubt that international cooperation through robust global institutions is essential to mitigation of environmental damage. This is a liberal institutionalist approach and accords with what appears to be a commonsense position, namely, that when it comes to threats posed by environmental degradation – of which climate change is possibly the most significant at the present time – individual states cannot simply go it alone. Here it is interesting to note the idea, commonplace in the 1970s, that state sovereignty is actually a fundamental obstacle to dealing with transnational or global environmental problems. This encouraged the further idea that a world government would be the only truly effective institution capable of tackling something on the scale of the environmental crisis, an idea that attracted much criticism for its alleged authoritarian implications. Such ideas were subsequently challenged by liberal regime theory, which highlighted the extent to which cooperation across borders was in fact taking place, especially with respect to increasing regulation concerning environmental problems, a development seen in some quarters as eroding state sovereignty (see Paterson, 1999, pp. 798–9).

A significant intervention in the sovereignty/global environmental debate appeared in the late 1990s with the questioning of conventional understandings of sovereignty in the context of the challenges presented by global environmental concerns. Karen Litfin, in her preface to an edited collection on this theme, first noted the apparent incongruity between the territorial boundaries delineating the political world, on the one hand, and the natural world of interconnected ecosystems, on the other, and the assumption that there is therefore an essential incompatibility between sovereignty and ecology. 'Yet the proliferation of international environmental agreements and transnational activism over the last three decades raises the possibility that existing political institutions, including the prevailing norms of sovereignty, can be altered in ways that permit and even foster ecologically benign practices' (Litfin, 1998, p. xi). She went on to describe this in terms of a transformation of sovereignty.

> ### Key Quote   The Greening of Sovereignty
>
> Sovereignty has proven itself to be an enduring and malleable set of norms, with its locus shifting from the absolute monarchs of the early modern period to the 'people' in contemporary democracies. Thus, it is not surprising that we find the norms of sovereignty shifting once again in the face of attempts to cope with ecological destruction. [We] refer to this phenomenon as *the greening of sovereignty*. (Ibid.; original emphasis)

Also notable is the extent to which 'constitutive discourses of sovereignty [had] begun to absorb ecological arguments' and that global discourses around the themes of development, security and intervention had 'begun' to 'shift shared understanding of legitimate state conduct in a greener direction' (Litfin, 1998, p. 203). Similarly, it has been pointed out that the role of the state in the global politics of the environment is by no means fixed, for, although the state may be perceived as an interested self-maximizer or an agent of elite economic interests, and thus aligned with enemies of the environment, 'the state is also the vehicle by which these corporate interests can be challenged' (Elliott, 2004, p. 111). This has been reinforced by other proponents of the efficacy of state sovereignty from a critical theory perspective, who, without discounting the important role of non-state actors as well as trends in green consumerism and investment, highlight the fact that states remain the primary institutions of governance and that democratic states still have the greatest capacity as well as the legitimacy to regulate both corporate activities and those of other social agents along ecologically sustainable lines. Thus Barry and Eckersley argue that the democratic state emerges 'as the preeminent (although not necessarily exclusive) institution to assume the role of protecting public environmental goods such as human health, ecosystem integrity, biodiversity, and the global commons' (2005, p. xii). They further suggest that this notion reflects the Hegelian formulation of the state as embodying both public reason and ethics – a formulation which is very different from 'the liberal idea of the state as neutral umpire, the anarchist idea of the state as an inherently oppressive institution, or the orthodox Marxist idea of the state as an instrument of the ruling class' (ibid.)

In practical terms, there has been a considerable increase in the extent to which states are held responsible for environmental matters. It is no longer acceptable for states to exploit natural resources in any way they see fit, especially when this has a negative impact on other states. Thus sovereignty, 'like the processes of modernization, has become reflexive in adapting to global environmental change' (Eckersley, 2004, p.209). The key to grasping how these shifts have occurred lies in understanding the interaction of changing norms and perceptions of state identities and interests. This points to the utility of constructivism rather than to realist and liberal approaches in assessing, from a theoretical perspective, how and why change occurs and how even such apparently rock-like concepts as sovereignty may be transformed and adapted in evolving political contexts. Some of these issues are reflected in case study 10.2.

Case Study 10.2   Sovereignty and World Heritage Protection

In October 1972, UNESCO formulated the Convention Concerning the Protection of the World Cultural and Natural Heritage, declaring that this heritage was 'increasingly threatened with destruction not only by the traditional causes of decay, but also by changing social and economic conditions which aggravate the situation with even more formidable phenomena of damage or destruction' (UNESCO, 1972). UNESCO went on to state that loss of heritage is a global concern; that heritage protection at the national level often remained incomplete due, among other things, to insufficient resources; that cultural or natural heritage of outstanding interest needs to be preserved as part of the world heritage of [humankind] as a whole; that, in view of new dangers threatening them, it is incumbent on the international community to promote protection of heritage of outstanding universal value by complementing the activities of states; and that this 'requires new provisions in the form of a convention establishing an effective system of collective protection of the cultural and natural heritage of outstanding universal value, organized on a permanent basis and in accordance with modern scientific methods' (ibid.).

Article 6 of the Convention states that, while 'fully respecting the sovereignty of the States on whose territory the cultural and natural heritage . . . is situated, and without prejudice to property right provided by national legislation, the States Parties to this Convention recognize that such heritage constitutes a world heritage for whose protection it is the duty of the international community as a whole to co-operate.'

Article 7 says that international protection 'shall be understood to mean the establishment of a system of international co-operation and assistance designed to support States Parties to the Convention in their efforts to conserve and identify that heritage.' Article 11 goes on to request State Parties to the Convention to submit an inventory of heritage property – not to be considered exhaustive – and notes that heritage listing requires the consent of the state. The World Heritage Committee (WHC) set up under the Convention is to define the criteria for listing and may decline requests for listing if they are considered inappropriate.

One of the first countries to ratify the convention was Australia, which currently has forty-one listed sites. These include a number of convict sites (the earliest European settlements, indigenous sites, rainforests, the Great Barrier Reef, Sydney Opera House and the Tasmanian wilderness (Australian Government, 2014)). In June 2014, the conservative Liberal–National coalition government of Australia, led by Prime Minister Tony Abbott, applied to the UN to have 74,000 hectares of forest in Tasmania's World Heritage Area removed from World Heritage listing to allow logging. It was part of an area of 170,000 hectares that had been added only the year before by the previous Labor government. It had been subject to the normal procedures of investigation and confirmation by the WHC (which does not list just any area submitted for consideration).

The basis for the Abbott government's request was that the forest had previously been logged, was therefore already degraded, and should therefore be unlocked for further logging. Opponents of the move said that only a small proportion had been logged and the remainder was still pristine old-growth rainforest. The 'fact check' provided by the Australian Broadcasting Corporation reported expert analysis findings that more than 85 per cent of the area had not been logged, and that UNESCO does not, in any case, require an area to be 'pristine' to be listed. The WHC described the Abbott government's case to have the area delisted as 'feeble' and declined the application (Australian Broadcasting Corporation, 2014a).

The general issue of a global or international body such as UNESCO, ruling on a matter that appears to lie wholly within the sovereign territory of a state, raises a number of points for debate. Does this case illustrate the 'loss of sovereignty' to a global regime? Several issues need to be considered in approaching the question. On the one hand, a democratically elected national government of a sovereign state was prevented from acting on a matter entirely within its own borders. On the other hand, Australia, under a different government, was in fact responsible for having it listed as a World Heritage site in the first place, and it was well known that delisting rarely occurs – there have only been two cases since 1972. States – or rather their governments – have the power to enter into international treaties, or not, as the case may be. But, once entered into, they become binding (if not enforceable) in international law. This may be a compromise on sovereignty, but it is a voluntary one. One could argue that sovereignty is not an absolute principle, and that it is best moderated in practice, especially when it comes to matters concerning environmental protection, as well as human rights.

One commentator has noted the various ways in which local opposition to World Heritage listing has previously been couched – 'as a surrender of Tasmanian sovereignty to "the communist dictatorships that control the United Nations", or, perhaps more commonly, as "a political ploy" by a cynical federal government to curry electoral favour with green-tinged voters in key marginal electorates in the large (non-Tasmanian) cities of Sydney and Melbourne' (Hay, 1994, p. 1). Another (conservative) politician was reported as saying that 'he finds it offensive that the state has to appeal to an international body to make use of its own land' (Australian Broadcasting Corporation, 2014b).

It has been suggested that what really drives the conflict is actually 'a fundamental disagreement over the appropriate relationship between species *homo i sapiens* and the earth's wild places' (Hay, 1994, p. 1). This brings some of the deeper normative theoretical issues back into play, entangling them with the equally normative questions concerning state sovereignty vis-à-vis the 'international community', which is itself a product of the agency of the states who agreed to create such a community in the first place.

Conclusion

It has been noted that global environmental politics is a relatively new field of study and that, as in all other fields, its proponents – or at least some of them – have engaged in concerted attempts to construct grand theory (Princen, 2008, p. 1). That no single theory of this kind has emerged is scarcely surprising, given the diversity of viewpoints on even the most basic concepts such as 'nature' and 'the environment', the tensions between anthropocentrism and ecocentrism (or biocentrism) and the relationship between the local and the global, as well as the nature of IR's most basic concept – sovereignty. In this respect, green theorizing is little different from any other body of theory discussed in this book, all of which have produced endless variations on certain central themes.

Some may argue that the stakes are rather higher when it comes to the continuing degradation and possible destruction of the global environment, on which humanity as well as all other species depend for their very lives. Although the threat of annihilation through even a limited nuclear war is still very much with us as a traditional military security issue, it is worth noting that this threat is still largely an environmental or ecological one. This is because, although millions would die as a direct result of a nuclear strike on a specific part of the earth's surface, life on the planet as a whole may not survive the consequences of the 'nuclear winter' that is likely to ensue (see Schell, 2000). For the time being, however, it is not the possibility of global cooling that appears to be the greatest threat but, rather, the opposite prospect of an overheated earth, with all the implications that this carries for security at every possible level, and which therefore appears more urgent for political theory and political action.

QUESTIONS FOR REVISION

1 What is the difference between 'environmentalism' and 'ecologism'?
2 What is the key issue in the debate between 'survivalism' and 'Prometheanism'?

3 To what extent can Marxist and liberal/capitalist approaches be distinguished when it comes to the exploitation of the environment and its resources?
4 How are conceptualizations of 'nature' and 'the natural' reflected in the various strands of green theory?
5 How does the biocentric approach outlined by Taylor set out moral rules for humans to follow?
6 Can the concept of state sovereignty be reinterpreted to encompass and address the challenges posed by green theory in the twenty-first century?
7 Are contemporary institutions of global governance adequate to the task of addressing major problems such as climate change?
8 How does the historical development of environmentalism generally illustrate the links between theory and practice?

FURTHER READING

Bernstein, Steven F. (2001) *The Compromise of Liberal Environmentalism*. New York: Columbia University Press.
Coupe, Laurence (2000) *The Green Studies Reader: From Romanticism to Ecocriticism*. London: Routledge.
Curry, Patrick (2011) *Ecological Ethics*. Cambridge: Polity.
Fitzpatrick, Tony (2011) *Understanding Environmental and Social Policy*. Bristol: Policy Press.
LaFreniere, Gilbert F. (2008) *The Decline of Nature: Environmental History and the Western Worldview*. Bethesda, MD: Academia Press.

USEFUL WEBSITES

www.gov.uk (UK Environment Agency)
http://ec.europa.eu/environment/index_en.htm (European Commission – Environment)
www.unep.org (United Nations Environment Programme)
www.epa.gov (United States Environmental Protection Agency)
http://wwf.panda.org (Worldwide Fund for Nature)

11

Conclusion

When IR was established as a formal academic discipline almost a century ago, it sought first and foremost to analyse the causes of war and the conditions for peace in an international sphere which had been ravaged by a war unprecedented in its scope and violence, bringing with it enormous human suffering. It was therefore very practical in its initial orientation, and it has remained that way as the scope of its subject matter and the number of issues presenting themselves for attention has expanded. It is also evident that a practical orientation does not mean an absence of theoretical speculation or imagination. Indeed, theoretical development in the discipline of IR has proceeded apace, especially in the latter part of the twentieth century. As this book has shown, IR theory has moved well beyond debates between realism and liberalism to embrace a range of theoretical approaches, each presenting distinctive views of the world, the range of problems confronting it and possible solutions.

The examination of each of the main IR theories in this book has also shown that they are largely derivative, taking their cue from political theory more generally, with elements of social theory and economic theory adding additional insights. It is clear that the forms of realism developed in IR draw on the more basic theory of political realism in its classical form, while neorealism derived in part from microeconomics. Liberalism in IR is founded, rather obviously, on liberal political philosophy. Marxism is an amalgam of political and economic theory, while post-Marxist critical theory and World-Systems Theory both draw on social theory as well. Constructivism, postmodernism/poststructuralism, postcolonialism, feminism and gender theory, and green theory have also taken their cue from social and cultural theory more generally, mediated by political theory and then formulated as specimens of IR theory.

IR theory has therefore been very much influenced by developments in other disciplines, including sociology, anthropology, philosophy, literary studies, history, law and economics. It is almost always the case that a particular theoretical development arrives in IR theory after it has become established in political or social theory, as most chapters have in fact shown through sketching the history of ideas behind each of them. But it has not been a one-way flow. Once taken up in IR, the discipline has added an important international or global dimension to concepts and ideas which were once theorized almost exclusively within the bounds of the nation-state, with comparisons of similarities and differences between states being made in the sub-discipline of comparative politics.

This also raises the question of whether IR really is a discipline in its own right, or whether it is more of a sub-discipline of politics, as comparative politics is. There are obviously different views on this. My own opinion is that, although I do refer to the 'IR discipline' for the sake of simplicity, it is indeed a species of political studies. But, because it is attuned to the international or global sphere, it offers a distinctive approach to the theory and practice of politics that transcends the boundaries of the state, thereby widening the scope of political studies, which has, traditionally, been very much state bound. The extent to which IR has drawn on other disciplines also makes it a very dynamic field of political study rather than one which is 'merely' derivative. It is certainly in little danger of becoming static and stale.

IR theory is also strongly normative in ways that relate directly to its practical, problem-solving orientation. Indeed, it is the element of normativity that gives most of the theories discussed in this book their ideological aspect. Even realism, which purports to eschew normative theorizing, is attuned to themes of tragedy in political affairs, thereby indicating a clear normative sensitivity. Many of its proponents have explored the ways and means by which the level of human suffering wrought by political violence under conditions of anarchy can be minimized. While often dismissing the efficacy of international institutions, realists are nonetheless forced to acknowledge that mechanisms such as balance of power cannot be relied on to keep the peace indefinitely and that the only real solution to international anarchy and the violence and injustice it generates is a form of world government, which in turn means a world state. Arguably, this is the logical end point of realist theorizing. Yet, not only do realists see very little chance of this developing in the foreseeable future, it is not necessarily seen as an unmitigated 'good' in any case. A world state may well be authoritarian and perpetrate many injustices in the name of a politically united humanity. Realists therefore have normative reasons to be wary of any such development.

Liberalism is of course more explicitly normative as well as more optimistic about the prospects for building stable political order in an anarchic international sphere through law and institutions, although for most liberals these stop well short of a world government and its possibly undesirable consequences. Indeed, for many liberals, who see more virtue in individual freedom and the free market, the less government the better. In international affairs, as in domestic affairs, however, there is a certain tension between cooperation and competition which needs to be kept in balance lest there is a slide into conflict. An international sphere of which the constituent members are mainly democracies would, according to the liberal vision, be inherently peaceful. This would make it unnecessary for a world state to keep order. Other elements of liberal theory – individualism in particular – have provided the essential basis for theories of human rights and cosmopolitan normative theory more generally. As we have seen, however, cosmopolitanism has been opposed by communitarian theory, which rejects the normative priority awarded to the individual and locates morality in the groups in which individuals are inevitably enmeshed and which are possessed of varying cultural norms and values.

These opposing approaches to international normative theory are reflected in the different positions taken by English School theorists on issues of intervention versus state sovereignty, with solidarists favouring a cosmopolitan approach and pluralists a communitarian approach. Beyond that, scholars of the English School introduced elements of social theory to IR at an early stage in conceptualizing 'international society' as constituted by norms and values as well as power and interests, while also developing notions about the relationship between order and justice. English School theory, however, does not represent a radical departure from either realism or liberalism in its problem-solving approach. It takes the sovereign state to be the foundational unit of the international system, with anarchy as its primary characteristic as well as the main problem to be overcome, while capitalism is accepted as the appropriate economic engine of the system.

In contrast, Marxist and post-Marxist critical theory see hierarchy and hegemony rather than anarchy as the main problem. These are perpetuated by the capitalist system and the class divisions on which capitalism is based. The principal aim of both classical Marxism and post-Marxist critical theory is strongly normative in calling for the emancipation of people both from the unfair social and economic conditions that blight their lives and from the hegemonic ideologies that often mask their own true interests and make their subordination appear 'natural'.

World-System Theory is specifically concerned with the global division of wealth and poverty and with exposing the mechanisms through which it is maintained. A principal message of all of the variants that come under the rubric of Marxism and critical theory is that people cannot be truly free until and unless they achieve a certain level of economic security and equality. Further, their point is not simply to understand the world but to change it. Therein lies both a very practical and a normative purpose.

Constructivism is not explicitly normative (or ideological); it does not provide an account of how the world is and how it ought to be. Its insights, however, are applicable to normatively attuned theorizing. As we have seen, constructivism has contributed a highly insightful methodological approach to the concept of 'reality'. We know, more or less intuitively, that people do see the world in different ways and that what one person regards as very 'real' may not be so regarded by others. Rather, perceptions of reality are due largely to one's social location. Constructivism is especially useful in revealing that what people often regard as 'natural', and therefore right and good, is a socially constructed version of reality that does not hold for all times and in all places. In other words, it is neither universal nor naturally occurring. In addition, constructivist thought has drawn attention to the relationship between the ideational and the material and the role of human agency in the construction of concepts such as anarchy and sovereignty. While there is no essential normative position underpinning constructivism as a methodological tool, its proponents do adopt a problem-solving approach to such questions as, for example, how we might move from the law of the jungle to the rule of law in the international sphere.

Postmodern/poststructural approaches take social constructivism to another level altogether, challenging notions of 'reality' in a much more profound way and linking it very closely to the exercise of power. In other words, what poses as objective knowledge, truth and justice is very likely to be what those with power project and what accords with their own interests. Grand narratives, regimes of truth, value-laden binary oppositions and modern science itself – all convey messages seeking to entrench as 'natural' and legitimate some particular interpretation of the world which is, in the final analysis, no more than an expression of deeply subjective interests. From this perspective, there is no such thing as a set of objective truths about the world. Postmodern/poststructural approaches therefore provide theoretical tools for social and political critique. However, the critique of power, and everything that goes with it, does have normative implications, and indeed it sometimes has very moralistic overtones. But, given that postmodern/poststructural approaches reject all foundations for knowledge, including moral knowledge, it is difficult to extract any positive normative theoretical conclusions or positions from the genre. The most that can be said from this perspective is that morality is not given by nature but emerges from highly contingent social contexts.

Feminism and gender theory draw on many of the insights of social constructivism, with feminism's normative purpose focused clearly on the inequities, and iniquities, that women have faced in the past and which are still very much in evidence today. As with other critical approaches, feminism and gender theory challenge conventional notions of what is 'natural', and therefore what is 'right', when it comes to roles and power relations within and between the genders. As a practical project, feminism has achieved much in the areas of women's rights, although there is still a long way to go in many places. Applied to the sphere of international politics, feminism and gender theory have highlighted important aspects of the social construction of reality in masculinist terms. In relation to practical issues such as rape in war, it is certainly because of the women's movement and feminist political activism that it has become recognized as a war crime – a development that has implications for male victims of sexual violence in war as well. All this points to a measure of 'moral progress' even if it is painstakingly slow and partial.

Postcolonialism is founded on a very explicit moral conviction that the injustices of imperialism and colonialism, and their residues around the world, are a reflection of the abuse of power on the part of certain major powers, historically located mainly in the West. It also draws attention to the fact that the discipline of IR – and virtually all other disciplines, for that matter – and the views of the world they present as forms of 'knowledge' are profoundly Eurocentric. Postcolonial theory has taken various forms, but all have aimed to establish an anti-hegemonic or counter-hegemonic discourse and, to that extent, share something in common with post-Marxist critical theory, although they also use some of the tools supplied by postmodern/poststructural approaches. Some postcolonial discourses, however, focus primarily on cultural issues at the expense of class-related ones, and, although these are related, the consequences of socio-economic class are still the most pressing when it comes to everyday survival. If there is a socio-economic divide in world politics, it runs along 'North–South' lines, and it is this particular form of hierarchy that more critical approaches see as requiring normative attention in the study of IR.

Most versions of green theory are at once profoundly normative and profoundly action-oriented. Indeed, the whole point of much green theorizing has been to inspire sustained political action aimed squarely not just at human survival but the survival of all other life forms on the planet. As we have seen, some forms of green theory have awarded moral value to the entity 'nature' while others have a more restricted notion of where moral value lies, locating it essentially within humanity itself. These have been expressed in ecocentric and biocentric approaches, on the one hand, and anthropocentric approaches, on the other. But, wherever moral value may lie, moral agency can logically be exercised only by humans. Moreover, at a practical level, it is humans who are responsible for damage to the environment, and the obligation is on humans to repair it. Positive action on environmental rehabilitation may be applauded on a variety of grounds, including those that award intrinsic moral value to nature itself, however that entity is conceptualized. But there is a strong sense in which green theory highlights the fact that the current generation of humans has a moral obligation to future generations of humans, an obligation that therefore transcends the boundaries of space and time.

The idea of nature is obviously central to green theory, but the issue of nature and what is natural has underscored a variety of theoretical perspectives in politics and IR and has therefore been a theme throughout the book. 'Nature, red in tooth and claw' – the famous line of Alfred Lord Tennyson's – evokes the pitiless, anarchic state of nature envisaged by Hobbes which reflects an underlying reality about the human condition. Nature is therefore what needs to be overcome by the institution of sovereignty in order to live the good life free from the constant dangers posed by the state of nature and in which the worst aspects of human nature are unconstrained. Those who have experienced the conditions of war – civil or interstate – may well endorse this view. Others have painted a far less dismal scenario, emphasizing the cooperative side of human nature and repudiating the brutal, amoral condition of 'natural man'. This is what makes it possible to ameliorate the conditions of human suffering, both with respect to war and in the provision of the basic necessities of life which relies on cooperative social and political mechanisms.

At a different level we have also seen that nature has often been taken to provide a normative standard for what is right and good, at least in some of the more conservative theoretical approaches. This resonates with certain religious ideas which, in taking God as the author of nature, assume that it does indeed provide moral guidance and that established hierarchies are simply a reflection of the natural order of things. But more critical approaches have taken issue with all such assumptions, arguing that they serve only to legitimate those in power while delegitimating others on the basis of their gender, race or socio-economic class. Critical approaches therefore seek to expose the 'realities' supposedly given by nature as nothing more than a social construction serving the interests of the privileged.

The issue of 'reality' has also loomed large in this book. From classical realism through to postmodern/poststructural approaches, we have observed the extent to which reality is a contested concept. Efforts to deliver scientifically objective statements of fact about the world through the empirical methodologies characteristic of positivism have found much favour in the US, but less so elsewhere. Many would argue that such approaches fail to capture anything more than some useful correlations. Constructivist approaches have at the very least served to highlight that there is more to reality than sets of facts, and that facts of any kind are always subject to interpretation and mediation in social contexts. Thus 'reality' may be seen to consist of a combination of brute facts about the material world overlain by ideational subjectivities which are an inescapable aspect of human consciousness.

And so we return to our starting point. The brute facts of large-scale interstate warfare, accompanied by a normative (and therefore ideational) concern to prevent such episodes, underscored the original purpose of the discipline of IR. Identifying the causes of war and exploring the conditions for peace and security has been pursued in many different ways at the level of both theory and practice, and this book has been concerned to illustrate the very dynamic relationship between theory and practice – between the world of ideas and the world of action – neither of which can be isolated from the other. Whether this interaction has produced much real progress over the last century is, of course, a matter of debate. But few would suggest that the effort should be abandoned and that we should simply give in to the notion that there is a fixed reality that cannot be improved on.

References

Acharya, Amitav, and Barry Buzan (2010) 'Why is There No Non-Western International Relations Theory? An Introduction', in Barry Buzan and Amitav Acharya, *Non-Western International Relations Theory: Perspectives On and Beyond Asia*. Abingdon: Routledge.

Acton, H. B. (1972) *The Illusion of the Epoch: Marxism–Leninism as a Philosophical Creed*. London: Routledge & Kegan Paul.

Adler, Emanuel (1997) 'Seizing the Middle Ground: Constructivism in World Politics', *European Journal of International Relations*, 3(3): 291–318.

Agger, Ben (1991) 'Critical Theory, Poststructuralism, Postmodernism: Their Sociological Relevance', *Annual Review of Sociology*, 17: 105–31.

Ahmad, Aijaz (1994) *In Theory: Classes, Nations, Literatures*. London: Verso.

Amin, Samir (2011) *Global History: A View from the South*. Capetown: Pambazuk Press.

Anagol, Padma (2005) *The Emergence of Feminism in India, 1850–1920*. Aldershot: Ashgate.

Anderson, Perry (1998) *The Origins of Postmodernity*. London: Verso.

Appiah, Kwame Anthony (1993) 'Fallacies of Eurocentrism and Afrocentrism', Lecture delivered at the American Enterprise Institute, 10 May, www.aei. org/article/society-and-culture/citizenship/fallacies-of-eurocentrism-and-afrocentrism/.

Archer, Margaret (2000) *Being Human: The Problem of Agency*. Cambridge: Cambridge University Press.

Archer, Margaret (2003) *Structure, Agency and the Internal Conversation*. Cambridge: Cambridge University Press.

Aron, Raymond (2003) *Peace and War: A Theory of International Relations*. New Brunswick, NJ: Transaction.

Arrighi, Giovanni (1994) *The Long Twentieth Century: Money, Power, and the Origins of Our Times*. London: Verso.

Asante, Molefi Kete (2007) *An Afrocentric Manifesto: Toward an African Renaissance*. Cambridge: Polity.

Ashcroft, Bill, Gareth Griffiths and Helen Tiffin (2000) *Postcolonial Studies: The Key Concepts*. London: Routledge.

Ashley, Richard K. (1984) 'The Poverty of Neorealism', *International Organization*, 38(2): 225–86.

Ashley, Richard K., and R. B. J. Walker (1990) 'Speaking the Language of Exile: Dissident Thought in International Studies', *International Studies Quarterly*, 34(3): 259–68.

Attfield, Robin (1999) *The Ethics of the Global Environment*. Edinburgh: Edinburgh University Press.

Australian Broadcasting Corporation (2014a) 'Tony Abbott's Tasmanian Wilderness Claim Doesn't Check Out', 24 June, www.abc.net.au/news/2014-03-26/tony-abbott-tasmanian-wilderness-claim-does-not-check-out/5345072.

Australian Broadcasting Corporation (2014b) 'No Economic Cost Associated with World Heritage Extension', 19 June, www.abc.net.au/news/2014-06-19/tch-harriss-fiat/5534814.

Australian Government (2014) 'Australia's World Heritage', www.environment.gov.au/topics/heritage/about-australias-heritage/world-heritage.

Aylesworth, Gary (2013) 'Postmodernism', in *The Stanford Encyclopedia of Philosophy*, ed. Edward N. Zalta, http://plato.stanford.edu/archives/sum2013/entries/postmodernism/.

Balibar, Etienne (1998) *Spinoza and Politics*. London: Verso.

Barkawi, Tarak, and Mark Laffey (2006) 'The Postcolonial Moment in Security Studies', *Review of International Studies*, 32(2): 329–52.

Barker, Philip (2003) *Foucault: An Introduction*. Edinburgh: Edinburgh University Press.

Barnett, Jon (2001) *The Meaning of Environmental Security: Ecological Politics and Policy in the New Security Era*. London: Zed Books.

Barry, John (1999) *Rethinking Green Politics: Nature, Virtue and Progress*. London: Sage.

Barry, John, and Robyn Eckersley (2005) 'An Introduction to Reinstating the State', in John Barry and Robyn Eckersley (eds), *The State and the Global Ecological Crisis*. Cambridge, MA: MIT Press.

Baudrillard, Jean (1994) *Simulacra and Simulation*, trans. Sheila Faria Glaser. Ann Arbor: University of Michigan Press.

Baudrillard, Jean (1995) *The Gulf War Did Not Take Place*, trans. Paul Patton. Bloomington: Indiana University Press.

BBC (2003a) 'US Names "Coalition of the Willing"', 18 March, http://news.bbc.co.uk/2/hi/americas/2862343.stm.

BBC (2003b) 'Rum Remark Wins Rumsfeld an Award', 2 December, http://news.bbc.co.uk/2/hi/3254852.stm.

de Beauvoir, Simone (2010) *The Second Sex*. London: Vintage.

Bell, Duncan (2010) 'Political Realism and the Limits of Ethics', in Duncan Bell (ed.), *Ethics and World Politics*. Oxford: Oxford University Press.

Bellamy, Alex J. (2003) 'Humanitarian Intervention and the Three Traditions', *Global Society*, 17(1): 3–20.

Bellamy, Alex J. (2004) 'Introduction: International Society and the English

School', in Alex J. Bellamy (ed.), *International Society and its Critics*. Oxford: Oxford University Press.

Bellamy, Alex J. (2010) 'The Responsibilty to Protect – Five Years On', *Ethics and International Affairs*, 24(2): 143–69.

Bellamy, Richard (1987) 'Hegel and Liberalism', *History of European Ideas*, 8(6): 693–708.

Bellamy, Richard (1994) 'Introduction', in Richard Bellamy (ed.), *Gramsci: Pre-Prison Writings*. Cambridge: Cambridge University Press.

Berger, Peter L., and Thomas Luckmann (1991) *The Social Construction of Reality: Treatise in the Sociology of Knowledge*. London: Penguin.

Best, Geoffrey (1999) 'Peace Conferences and the Century of Total War: The 1899 Hague Conference and What Came After', *International Affairs*, 75(3): 619–34.

Bhaskar, Roy (2008) *A Realist Theory of Science*. Abingdon: Routledge.

Blackburn, Simon (2005) *Truth: A Guide*. Oxford: Oxford University Press.

Bloor, David (1996) 'Idealism and the Sociology of Knowledge', *Social Studies of Science*, 26(4): 839–56.

Bloor, Kevin (2010) *The Definitive Guide to Political Ideologies*. Milton Keynes: AuthorHouse.

Blumer, Herbert (1986) *Symbolic Interactionism: Perspective and Method*. Berkeley: University of California Press.

Bookchin, Murray (2005) *The Ecology of Freedom: The Emergence and Dissolution of Hierarchy*. Edinburgh: AK Press.

Booth, Ken (2011) 'Realism Redux: Contexts, Concepts, Contests', in Ken Booth (ed.), *Realism and World Politics*. Abingdon: Routledge.

Brown, Chris (1991) 'Hegel and International Ethics', *Ethics and International Affairs*, 5: 73–86.

Brown, Chris (2007) 'Situating Critical Realism', *Millennium: Journal of International Studies*, 32(2): 409–416.

Budd, Adrian (2011) *Robert Cox and Neo-Gramscian International Relations*. London: Routledge.

Buell, Lawrence (2005) *The Future of Environmental Criticism: Environmental Crisis and Literary Imagination*. Oxford: Blackwell.

Bull, Hedley (1977) *The Anarchical Society: A Study of Order in World Politics*. London: Macmillan.

Buzan, Barry (2004) *From International to World Society? English School Theory and the Social Structure of Globalisation*. Cambridge: Cambridge University Press.

Buzan, Barry, and George Lawson (2013) 'The Global Transformation: The Nineteenth Century and the Making of Modern International Relations', *International Studies Quarterly*, 57(3): 620–34.

Campbell, David (2010) 'Poststructuralism', in Tim Dunne, Milja Kurki and Steve Smith (eds), *International Relations Theory: Discipline and Diversity*. 2nd edn, Oxford: Oxford University Press.

Caprioli, Mary, and Mark A. Boyer (2001) 'Gender, Violence and International Crisis', *Journal of Conflict Resolution*, 45(4): 503–18.

Carlsnaes, Walter, Thomas Risse and Beth A. Simmons (eds) (2012) *Handbook of International Relations*. 2nd edn, London: Sage.

Carr, E. H. (2001) *The Twenty Years' Crisis 1919–1939: An Introduction to the Study of International Relations*. Basingstoke: Palgrave.

Carson, Rachel (1962) *Silent Spring*. Robbinsdale, MN: Fawcett Crest.

Carter, Neil (2008) *The Politics of the Environment: Ideas, Activism, Policy*. 2nd edn, Cambridge: Cambridge University Press.

Cassells, Alan (1996) *Ideology and International Relations in the Modern World*. London: Routledge.

Caverley, Jonathan D. (2010) 'Power and Democratic Weakness: Neoconservatism and Neoclassical Realism', *Millennium: Journal of International Studies*, 38(3): 593–614.

Chakrabarty, Dipesh (2008) *Provincializing Europe: Postcolonial Thought and Historical Difference*. New edn, Princeton, NJ: Princeton University Press.

Chanter, Tina (2007) *Gender: Key Concepts in Philosophy*. London: Continuum.

Chase, Steve (1991) 'Introduction: Whither the Radical Ecology Movement?', in Steve Chase (ed.), *Defending the Earth: A Dialogue Between Murray Bookchin and Dave Foreman*. Cambridge, MA: South End Press.

Chaturvedi, Vinayak (2012) 'Introduction', in Vinayak Chaturvedi (ed.), *Mapping Subaltern Studies and the Postcolonial*. London: Verso.

Checkel, Jeffrey T. (1998) 'The Constructivist Turn in International Relations Theory', *World Politics*, 50(2): 324–48.

Chen, Kuang-Hsing (1998) 'The Decolonization Question', in Kuang-Hsing Chen (ed.), *Trajectories: Inter-Asia Cultural Studies*. London: Routledge.

Chernoff, Fred (2002) 'Scientific Realism as a Meta-Theory of International Relations', *International Studies Quarterly*, 46(2): 189–207.

Childs, Peter, and Roger Fowler (eds) (2006) *The Routledge Dictionary of Literary Terms*. Abingdon: Routledge.

Chu, Yun-Han (2013) 'Sources of Regime Legitimacy and the Debate over the Chinese Model', *China Review*, 13(1): 1–42.

Claeys, Gregory (ed.) (2005) *Encyclopedia of Nineteenth Century Thought*. Abingdon: Routledge.

Clapham, Andrew (2012) *Brierley's Law of Nations: An Introduction to the Role of International Law*. Oxford: Oxford University Press.

Clausewitz, Carl von (1989) *On War*, ed. and trans. Michael Howard and Peter Paret. Princeton, NJ: Princeton University Press.

Clifford, James (1988) *The Predicament of Culture: Twentieth-Century Ethnography, Literature, and Art*. Cambridge, MA: Harvard University Press.

Cohen, Arthur A. (1965) 'Maoism', in Milorad M. Drachkovitch, *Marxism in the Modern World*. Stanford, CA: Stanford University Press.

Connell, R. W. (2005) *Masculinities*. 2nd edn, Cambridge: Polity.

Connell, Raewyn (2009) *Gender*. 2nd edn, Cambridge: Polity.

Conyers, James L., Jr (2005) 'Afrocentricity: Notes on a Disciplinary Position', in James L. Conyers, Jr. (ed.), *Afrocentric Traditions*. New Brunswick, NJ: Transaction.

Cooper, Danny (2011) *Neoconservatism and American Foreign Policy: A Critical Analysis*. Abingdon: Routledge.

Copelon, Rhonda (2000) 'Gender Crimes as War Crimes: Integrating Crimes against Women into International Criminal Law', *McGill Law Journal*, 46(1): 217–40.

Cott, Nancy F. (1987) *The Grounding of Modern Feminism*. New Haven, CT: Yale University Press.

Cox, Robert (1981) 'Social Forces, States and World Orders: Beyond International Relations Theory', *Millennium: Journal of International Studies*, 10(2): 126–55.

Cox, Robert (1983) 'Gramsci, Hegemony and International Relations: An Essay in Method', *Millennium: Journal of International Studies*, 12(2): 162–75.

Cozette, Murielle (2008) *Raymond Aron and the Morality of Realism*, Working Paper 2008/5, Canberra, Department of International Relations, Australian National University.

Craig, Campbell (2007) 'Hans Morgenthau and the World State Revisited', in Michael C. Williams (ed.), *Realism Reconsidered: The Legacy of Hans J. Morgenthau in International Relations*. Oxford: Oxford University Press.

Crosby, Alfred W. (1995) 'The Past and Present of Environmental History', *American Historical Review*, 100(4): 1177–89.

Crouch, Colin (2011) *The Strange Non-Death of Neo-Liberalism*. Cambridge: Polity.

Dahlerup, Drude (2013) 'Introduction', in Drude Dahlerup (ed.), *Women, Quotas and Politics*. Abingdon: Routledge.

Dalby, Simon (2002) *Environmental Security*. Minneapolis: University of Minnesota Press.

Darby, Phillip (1997) 'Introduction', in Phillip Darby (ed.), *At the Edge of International Relations: Postcolonialism, Gender and Dependency*. London: Continuum.

Darwin, Charles (1985) *The Origin of Species: Or the Preservation of Favoured Species in the Struggle for Life*. London: Penguin.

Delanty, Gerard, and Engin F. Isin (eds) (2003) *Handbook of Historical Sociology*. London: Sage.

Derrida, Jacques (2004) *Dissemination*, trans. Barbara Johnson. London: Continuum.

Diamond, Jared (2005) *Guns, Germs and Steel: A Short History of Everybody for the Last 13,000 Years*. London: Vintage.

Dikötter, Frank (2010) *Mao's Great Famine: The History of China's Most Devastating Catastrophe, 1958–1962*. London: Bloomsbury.

Dirlik, Arif (1994) 'The Postcolonial Aura: Third World Criticism in the Age of Global Capitalism', *Critical Inquiry*, 20(2): 328–56.

Dirlik, Arif (2005) *Marxism in the Chinese Revolution*. Lanham, MD: Rowman & Littlefield.

Dobson, Andrew (2007) *Green Political Thought*. 4th edn, Abingdon: Routledge.

Dobson, Andrew, and Paul Lucardie (1993) 'Introduction', in Andrew Dobson and Paul Lucardie (eds), *The Politics of Nature: Explorations in Green Theory*. London: Routledge.

Donaldson, Thomas (1992) 'Kant's Global Rationalism', in Terry Nardin and David R. Mapel (eds), *Traditions of International Ethics*. Cambridge: Cambridge University Press.

Donnelly, Jack (1992) 'Twentieth Century Realism', in Terry Nardin and David R. Mapel (eds), *Traditions of International Ethics*. Cambridge: Cambridge University Press.

Doyle, Michael W. (1986) 'Liberalism and World Politics', *American Political Science Review*, 80(4): 1151–69.

Drengsen, Alan (2008) 'Introduction: The Life and Work of Arne Naess: An Appreciative Overview', in Alan Drengsen and Bill Devall (eds), *The Ecology of Wisdom: Writings by Arne Naess*. Berkeley, CA: Counterpoint.

Dryzek, John (1997) *The Politics of the Earth: Environmental Discourses*. Oxford: Oxford University Press.

Dunne, Tim (1998) *Inventing International Society: A History of the English School*. London: Macmillan.

Ebenstein, William, and Ebenstein, Alan O. (1991) *Great Political Thinkers: Plato to the Present*. 5th edn, Fort Worth, TX: Harcourt, Brace, Jovanovich.

Eccleshall, Robert (2003) 'Liberalism', in Robert Eccleshall, Alan Finlayson, Vincent Geoghegan et al., *Political Ideologies: An Introduction*. 3rd edn, London: Routledge.

Eckersley, Robyn (1992) *Environmentalism and Political Theory: Towards an Ecocentric Approach*. Albany: State University of New York Press.

Eckersley, Robyn (2004) *The Green State: Rethinking Democracy and Sovereignty*. Cambridge, MA: MIT Press.

Edgar, Andrew, and Peter Sedgwick (eds) (1999) *Key Concepts in Cultural Theory*. London: Routledge.

Egar, Emanuel Edame (2008) *The Crisis of Négritude: A Study of the Black Movement against Intellectual Oppression in the Early Twentieth Century*. Boca Raton, FL: Brown Walker Press.

Ehrlich, Paul (1968) *The Population Bomb*. New York: Ballantyne.

Elliott, Lorraine (2004) *The Global Politics of the Environment*. Basingstoke: Palgrave Macmillan.

Elshtain, Jean Bethke (1995) *Women and War*. Chicago: University of Chicago Press.

Emerson, Rupert (1971) 'Self-Determination', *American Journal of International Law*, 65(3): 459–75.

Enloe, Cynthia (2000) *Bananas, Beaches and Bases: Making Feminist Sense of International Politics*. Berkeley: University of California Press.

EPA (Environmental Protection Authority) (1992) 'The Guardian: Origins of the EPA', www2.epa.gov/aboutepa/guardian-origins-epa.

Fairweather, A. M. (2006) *Aquinas on Nature and Grace: Selections from the Summa Theologica*. Louisville, KY: Westminster John Knox Press.

Fanon, Frantz (1965) *The Wretched of the Earth*, trans. Constance Farrington. New York: Grove Press.

Fanon, Frantz (1986) *Black Skin: White Masks*. London: Pluto Press.

Fassbender, Bardo (2009) *The United Nations Charter as the Constitution of the International Community*. Leiden: Martinus Nijhoff.

Finnemore, Martha (2003) *The Purpose of Intervention: Changing Beliefs about the Use of Force*. Ithaca, NY: Cornell University Press.

Ford, Lynne E. (2008) *Encyclopedia of Women and American Politics*. New York: Infobase.

Forde, Steven (1992) 'Classical Realism', in Terry Nardin and David R. Mapel (eds), *Traditions of International Ethics*. Cambridge: Cambridge University Press.

Foucault, Michel (2011) 'Nietzsche, Genealogy, History', in Imre Szeman and Timothy Kaposy (eds), *Cultural Theory: An Anthology*. Chichester: Wiley-Blackwell.

Frank, Andre Gunder, and Barry Gills (1993) 'The 5,000-Year World System: An Interdisciplinary Introduction', in Andre Gunder Frank and Barry K. Gills (eds), *The World System: Five Hundred Years or Five Thousand?* London: Routledge.

Freeman, Hadley (2013a) 'Margaret Thatcher Was No Feminist', *The Guardian*, 9 April, www.theguardian.com/commentisfree/2013/apr/09/margaret-thatcher-no-feminist.

Freeman, Hadley (2013b) 'Margaret Thatcher Left a Dark Legacy that Has Still Not Disappeared', *The Guardian*, 11 April, www.theguardian.com/politics/interactive/2013/apr/11/margaret-thatcher-legacy-best-writing#hugo-young.

Friedan, Jeffry A., and David A. Lake (2005) 'International Relations as a Social Science: Rigor and Relevance', *Annals of the American Academy of Political and Social Science*, 600(1): 136–56.

Fukuyama, Francis (1989) 'The End of History', *National Interest*, 16: 3–18.

Gamble, Sarah (2006) 'Postfeminism', in Sarah Gamble (ed.), *The Routledge Companion to Feminism and Postfeminism*. London: Routledge.

Gandhi, Leela (1998) *Postcolonial Theory: A Critical Introduction*. Crows Nest, NSW: Allen & Unwin.

Garner, John, Peter Ferdinand and Stephanie Lawson (2012) *Introduction to Politics*. 2nd edn, Oxford: Oxford University Press.

Gay, Peter (1977) *The Enlightenment: The Rise of Modern Paganism*. New York: W. W. Norton.

Gelb, Leslie H., with Richard K. Betts (1979) *The Irony of Vietnam: The System Worked*. Washington, DC: Brookings Institution.

George, Jim (1994) *Discourses of Global Politics: A Critical (Re)Introduction to International Relations*. Boulder, CO: Lynne Rienner.

Giddens, Anthony (1984) *The Constitution of Society: Outline of the Theory of Structuration*. Berkeley: University of California Press.

Giddens, Anthony (1985) *The Nation-State and Violence*. Berkeley: University of California Press.

Giddens, Anthony (1993) *New Rules of Sociological Method*. 2nd edn, Stanford, CA: Stanford University Press.

Gill, Stephen (2003) *Power and Resistance in the New World Order*. New York: Palgrave Macmillan.

Goldstein, Joshua S. (2003) 'War and Gender', in Carol R. Ember and Melvin Ember, *Encyclopedia of Sex and Gender*, Vol. 2: *Men and Women in the World's Cultures*. New York: Kluwer Academic/Plenum.

Gombrich, E. H. (2001) 'The Renaissance – Period or Movement?', in Robert Black (ed.), *The Renaissance: A Reader*. London: Routledge.

Goodin, Robert E. (1992a) 'The High Ground is Green', *Environmental Politics*, 1(1): 1–8.

Goodin, Robert E. (1992b) *Green Political Theory*. Cambridge: Polity.

Gower, Barry (1997) *Scientific Method: An Historical and Philosophical Introduction*. London: Routledge.

Gramsci, Antonio (1975) *Prison Notebooks*, Vol. 1, ed. Joseph A. Buttigieg. New York: Columbia University Press.

Griffiths, Martin, and Terry O'Callaghan (2002) *International Relations: The Key Concepts*. London: Routledge.

Grotius, Hugo (2004) *On the Law of War and Peace*. Whitefish, MT: Kessinger.

Grovogui, Siba N. (2010) 'Postcolonialism', in Tim Dunne, Milja Kurki and Steve Smith (eds), *International Relations Theory: Discipline and Diversity*. 2nd edn, Oxford: Oxford University Press.

Guha, Ranajit (1997) *Dominance without Hegemony: History and Power in Colonial India*. Cambridge, MA: Harvard University Press.

Gutmann, Myron B. (1988) 'The Origins of the Thirty Years' War', *Journal of Interdisciplinary History*, 18(4): 749–70.

Guzzini, Stefano (1998) *Realism in International Relations and International Political Economy: The Continuing Story of a Death Untold*. London: Routledge.

Habermas, Jürgen (1981) 'Modernity versus Postmodernity', *New German Critique*, 22(winter): 3–14.

Habermas, Jürgen (1982) 'The Entwinement of Myth and Enlightenment: Re-Reading Dialectic of Enlightenment', *New German Critique*, 26(spring-summer): 13–30.

Habermas, Jürgen (2001) *On the Pragmatics of Social Interaction: Preliminary Studies in the Theory of Communicative Action*, trans. Barbara Fultner. Cambridge, MA: MIT Press.

Hall, Thomas D. (1999) 'World Systems and Evolution: An Appraisal', in P. Nick Kardulias (ed.), *World-Systems Theory in Practice and Exchange*. Lanham, MD: Rowman & Littlefield.

Hardin, Garrett (1968) 'The Tragedy of the Commons', *Science*, 162: 1243–8.

Harrington, Austin (2005) 'Introduction', in Austin Harrington (ed.), *Modern Social Theory: An Introduction*. Oxford: Oxford University Press.

Hay, P. R. (1994) 'The Politics of Tasmania's World Heritage Area: Contesting the Democratic Subject', *Environmental Politics*, 3(1): 1–21.

Hay, Peter (2002) *Main Currents in Western Environmental Thought*. Bloomington: Indiana University Press.

Herz, John H. (1950) 'Idealist Internationalism and the Security Dilemma', *World Politics*, 2(2): 157–80.

Heywood, Andrew (2004) *Political Theory: An Introduction*. 3rd edn, Basingstoke: Palgrave Macmillan.

Higgins, Alexander Pearce (2010) *The Hague Peace Conferences and Other International Conferences Concerning the Laws and Usages of Wars: Texts and Conventions with Commentaries*. New York: Cosimo.

Hobbes, Thomas (1985) *Leviathan*. London: Penguin.

Hobden, Stephen (1998) *International Relations and Historical Sociology*. London: Routledge.

Hobsbawm, Eric (2011) *How to Change the World: Reflections on Marx and Marxism*. New Haven, CT: Yale University Press.

Hodgson-Wright, Stephanie (2006) 'Early Feminism', in Sarah Gamble (ed.), *The Routledge Companion to Feminism and Postmodernism*. London: Routledge.

Hoffman, John (2007) *A Glossary of Political Theory*. Stanford, CA: Stanford University Press.

Hoffman, John, and Paul Graham (2006) *Introduction to Political Ideologies*. Harlow: Pearson Education.

Hoffman, Stanley (1977) 'An American Social Science: International Relations', *Daedalus*, 106(3): 41–60.

Hoffman, Stanley (1985) 'Raymond Aron and the Theory of International Relations', *International Studies Quarterly*, 29(1): 13–27.

Hohendahl, Peter U. (1985) 'The Dialectic of Enlightenment Revisited: Habermas' Critique of the Frankfurt School', *New German Critique*, 35(spring–summer): 3–26.

Holsti, K. J. (1987) *The Dividing Discipline: Hegemony and Diversity in International Theory*. Boston: Allen & Unwin.

Honneth, Axel (1992a) 'Preface', in Axel Honneth, Thomas McCarthy, Claus Offe and Albrecht Wellmer (eds), *Cultural-Political Interventions in the Unfinished Project of the Enlightenment*. Cambridge, MA: MIT Press.

Honneth, Axel (1992b) 'Integrity and Disrespect: Principles of a Conception of Morality Based on a Theory of Recognition', *Political Theory*, 20(2): 187–201.

Horkheimer, Max (1972) *Critical Theory: Selected Essays*. New York: Seabury Press.

Horkheimer, Max, and Theodore Adorno (2002) *Dialectic of Enlightenment: Philosophical Fragments*, ed. Gunzelin Schmid Noerr, trans. Edmund Jephcott. Stanford, CA: Stanford University Press.

Howe, Stephen (1998) *Afrocentrism: Mythical Pasts and Imagined Homes*. London: Verso.

Hume, David (2007) *A Treatise on Human Nature*, Vol. 2. Rockville, MD: Wildside Press.

Humphrey, Mathew (2010a) 'Green Political Theory', in Mark Bevir (ed.), *Encyclopedia of Political Theory*, Vol. 1, London: Sage.

Humphrey, Mathew (2010b) 'Green Political Theory', in Daniel Bell (ed.), *Ethics and World Politics*. Oxford: Oxford University Press.

Hurrell, Andrew (2007) *On Global Order: Power, Values, and the Constitution of International Society*. Oxford: Oxford University Press.

Ibhawoh, Bonny (2000) 'Between Culture and Constitution: Evaluating the Cultural Legitimacy of Human Rights in the African State', *Human Rights Quarterly*, 22(3): 838–60.

Inter-Parliamentary Union (2013) 'Women in National Parliaments', www.ipu.org/wmn-e/classif.htm.

IPCC (Intergovernmental Panel on Climate Change) (2014a) 'Introduction', *Fifth Assessment Report*, www.climatechange2013.org/images/report/WG1AR5_Chapter01_FINAL.pdf.

IPCC (2014b) 'Summary for Policymakers', *Fifth Assessment Report*, http://report.mitigation2014.org/spm/ipcc_wg3_ar5_summary-for-policymakers_approved.pdf.

Jacques, Peter J., Riley E. Dunlap and Mark Freeman (2008) 'The Organization of Denial: Conservative Think Tanks and Environmental Skepticism', *Environmental Politics*, 17(3): 349–85.

James, Patrick (1993) 'Neorealism as a Research Enterprise: Toward Elaborated Structural Realism', *International Political Science Review*, 14(2): 123–48.

Jay, Martin (1996) *The Dialectical Imagination: A History of the Frankfurt School and the Institute of Social Research, 1923–1950*. Berkeley: University of California Press.

Jones, Daniel Stedman (2012) *Masters of the Universe: Hayek, Friedman and the Birth of Neoliberal Politics*. Princeton, NJ: Princeton University Press.

Kant, Immanuel (1994) *Ethical Philosophy*, trans. James W. Ellington. 2nd edn, Indianapolis: Hackett.

Kant, Immanuel (2003) *Observations on the Feeling of the Beautiful and the Sublime*. Berkeley: University of California Press.

Kant, Immanuel (2007) *Perpetual Peace*. Minneapolis: Filiquarian.

Kaplan, Robert (2012) 'Why John J. Mearsheimer is Right (about Some Things)', *The Atlantic*, Jan/Feb, www.theatlantic.com/magazine/archive/2012/01/why-john-j-mearsheimer-is-right-about-some-things/308839/3/.

Keene, Edward (2002) *Beyond the Anarchical Society: Grotius, Colonialism and Order in World Politics*. Cambridge: Cambridge University Press.

Kennedy, Paul (1989) *The Rise and Fall of the Great Powers: Economic Change and Military Conflict from 1500 to 2000*. London: Fontana.

Kenny, Charles (2013) 'Guns Don't Kill People, Gun Culture Does', *Businessweek*, 13 January, www.businessweek.com/articles/2013-01-13/guns-dont-kill-people-gun-culture-does.

Keohane, Robert O. (1984) *After Hegemony: Cooperation and Discord in the World Political Economy*. Princeton, NJ: Princeton University Press.

Keohane, Robert O. (1986) 'Realism, Neorealism and the Study of World Politics', in Robert O. Keohane (ed.), *Neorealism and its Critics*. New York: Columbia University Press.

Keohane, Robert O., and Joseph S. Nye, Jr. (1973) 'Power and Interdependence', *Survival: Global Politics and Strategy*, 15(4): 158–65.

Keulartz, Jozet (1998) *The Struggle for Nature: A Critique of Environmental Philosophy*. London: Routledge.

Kharbe, Ambreen Safre (2009) *English Language and Literary Criticism*. New Delhi: Discovery.

King, Preston (1999) *The Ideology of Order: A Comparative Analysis of Jean Bodin and Thomas Hobbes*. London: Frank Cass.

Kingsbury, Benedict (1997–8) 'A Grotian Tradition of Theory and Practice?: Grotius, Law, and Moral Skepticism in the Thought of Hedley Bull', *QLR*, 17(3): 3–33.

Knutsen, Torbjørn L. (1997) *A History of International Relations Theory*. 2nd edn, Manchester: Manchester University Press.

Koslowski, Rey, and Friedrich Kratochwil (1994) 'Understanding Change in International Politics: The Soviet Empire's Demise and the International System', *International Organization*, 48(2): 215–47.

Kosso, Peter (2011) *A Summary of Scientific Method*. Dordrecht: Springer.

Krasner, Stephen D. (1983) 'Preface', in Stephen D. Krasner (ed.), *International Regimes*. Ithaca, NY: Cornell University Press.

Krisch, Nico (2010) 'The Security Council and the Great Powers', in Vaughan Lowe, Adam Roberts, Jennifer Welsh and Dominik Zaum (eds), *The United Nations Security Council and War: The Evolution of Thought and Practice Since 1945*. Oxford: Oxford University Press.

Krishna, Sankaran (2009) *Globalization and Postcolonialism: Hegemony and Resistance in the Twentieth Century*. Lanham, MD: Rowman & Littlefield.

Kuehnast, Kathleen R., Chantal de Jong Oudraat and Helga Hernes (eds) (2011) 'Introduction', in Kathleen R. Kuehnast, Chantal de Jong Oudraat and Helga Hernes (eds), *Women and War: Power and Protection in the 21st Century*. Washington, DC: United States Institute of Peace.

Kurki, Milja (2007) 'Critical Realism and Causal Analysis in International Relations', *Millennium: Journal of International Studies*, 35(2): 361–78.

Lane, Ruth (1996) 'Positivism, Scientific Realism and Political Science: Recent Developments in the Philosophy of Science', *Journal of Theoretical Politics*, 8(3): 361–82.

Lanza, Robert, with Robert Berman (2009) *Biocentrism: How Life and Consciousness are the Keys to Understanding the True Nature of the Universe*. Dallas, TX: BenBella Books.

Lapid, Yosef (1989) 'The Third Debate: On the Prospects of International Theory in a Post-Positivist Era', *International Studies Quarterly*, 33(3): 235–54.

Lawson, Stephanie (2006) *Culture and Context in World Politics*. Basingstoke: Palgrave Macmillan.

Lawson, Stephanie (2008) 'Political Studies and the Contextual Turn', *Political Studies*, 56(3): 584–603.

Lawson, Stephanie (2012) *International Relations*. 2nd edn, Cambridge: Polity.

Lebow, Richard Ned (2003) *The Tragic Vision of Politics: Ethics, Interests and Orders*. Cambridge: Cambridge University Press.

Lefkowitz, Mary R. (1996) 'Ancient History, Modern Myths', in Mary R. Lefkowitz and Guy Maclean Rogers (eds), *Black Athena Revisited*. Durham: University of North Carolina Press.

Legro, Jeffrey W., and Andrew Moravcsik (1999) 'Is Anybody Still a Realist', *International Security*, 24(2): 5–55.

Leitenberg, Milton (2006) *Deaths in Wars and Conflicts in the 20th Century*, Occasional Paper #29. 3rd edn, Ithaca, NY: Cornell University Peace Studies Program, www.cissm.umd.edu/papers/files/deathswarscon-flictsjune52006.pdf.

Lenin, Vladimir (2010) *Imperialism: The Highest Stage of Capitalism*. London: Penguin.

Lin Biao (1996) 'Why a Cultural Revolution?', in Michael Schoenhals (ed.), *China's Cultural Revolution 1966–1969: Not a Dinner Party*. New York: M. E. Sharpe.

Linklater, Andrew (1998) *The Transformation of Political Community*. Cambridge: Polity.

Linklater, Andrew (2011) *The Problem of Harm in World Politics: Theoretical Investigations*. Cambridge: Cambridge University Press.

Linklater, Andrew, and Hidemi Suganami (2006) *The English School of International Relations: A Contemporary Reassessment*. Cambridge: Cambridge University Press.

Litfin, Karen T. (ed.) (1998) *The Greening of Sovereignty in World Politics*. Cambridge, MA: MIT Press.

Little, Richard (1996) 'The Growing Relevance of Pluralism?', in Steve Smith, Ken Booth and Marysia Zalewksi (eds), *International Theory: Positivism and Beyond*. Cambridge: Cambridge University Press.

Locke, John (2008) *Of Civil Government: The Second Treatise*. Rockville, MD: Wildside Press.

Long, David, and Peter Wilson (1995) *Thinkers of the Twenty Years' Crisis: Inter-War Idealism Reassessed*. Oxford: Oxford University Press.

Lorentzen, Lois Ann, and Jennifer Turpin (1998) 'Preface', in Lois Ann Lorentzen and Jennifer Turpin (eds), *The Women and War Reader*. New York: New York University Press.

Lose, Lars G. (2001) 'Communicative Action and the World of Diplomacy', in Karin Fierke and Knud Erik Jørgensen (eds), *Constructing International Relations: The Next Generation*. Armonk, NY: M. E. Sharpe.

Lovelock, James (2000) *Gaia: A New Look at Life on Earth*. Oxford: Oxford University Press.

Lovin, Robin W. (1995) *Reinhold Niebuhr and Christian Realism*. Cambridge: Cambridge University Press.

Lyotard, Jean-François (1993) 'The Postmodern Condition', excerpt in Joseph Natoli and Linda Hutcheon (eds), *A Postmodern Reader*. Albany: State University of New York Press.

McCormack, T. Y. (2014) 'Al Qaeda Core: A Short History', *Foreign Policy*, 17 March, www.foreignpolicy.com/articles/2014/03/17/al_qaeda_core_a_short_history.

McCormick, John (1991) *Reclaiming Paradise: The Global Environmental Movement*. Bloomington: Indiana University Press.

McGrail, Stephen (2011) 'Environment in Transition? Emerging Perspectives, Issues and Future Practices in Contemporary Environmentalism', *Journal of Futures Studies*, 15(3): 117–44.

Machiavelli, Niccolò (2009) *The Prince*, trans. W. K. Marriott, ed. Randy Dillon. Plano, TX: Veroglyphic.

McLeod, John (2000) *Beginning Postcolonialism*. Manchester: Manchester University Press.

Mahoney, Daniel J. (1992) *The Liberal Political Science of Raymond Aron: A Critical Introduction*. Lanham, MD: Rowman & Littlefield.

Malpas, Simon (2005) *The Postmodern*. Abingdon: Routledge.

Mannheim, Karl (1954) *Ideology and Utopia: An Introduction to the Sociology of Knowledge*. New York: Harcourt.

Mao Tse Tung (1972) *Quotations from Chairman Mao Tse Tung*. San Francisco: China Books.

Marx, Karl (1950) 'Preface' to *A Contribution to the Critique of Political Economy*, in Karl Marx and Frederick Engels, *Selected Works*, Vol 1. Moscow: Foreign Languages Publishing House; https://www.marxists.org/archive/marx/works/1859/critique-pol-economy/preface.htm.

Marx, Karl, and Friedrich Engels (1969) *The Communist Manifesto*, in Karl Marx and Frederick Engels, *Selected Works*, Vol 1. Moscow: Progress.

May, Ernest R., Richard Rosecrance and Zara Steiner (eds) (2010) *History and Neorealism*. Cambridge: Cambridge University Press.

Meadows, Donella H., Jørgen Randers and Dennis L. Meadows (2004) *The Limits to Growth: The 30-Year Update*. New York: Universe Books.

Mearsheimer, John J. (2001) *The Tragedy of Great Power Politics*. New York: W. W. Norton.

Mearsheimer, John J. (2010) 'Structural Realism', in Tim Dunne (ed.), *International Relations Theory: Discipline and Diversity*. Oxford: Oxford University Press.

Mearsheimer, John J. (2014) 'Getting Ukraine Wrong', *New York Times*, 13 March, www.nytimes.com/2014/03/14/opinion/getting-ukraine-wrong. html?_r=0.

Melzer, Arthur (1983) 'Rousseau's Moral Realism: Replacing Natural Law with the General Will', *American Political Science Review*, 77(3): 633–51.

Merton, Robert K. (1937) 'The Sociology of Knowledge', *Isis*, 27(3): 493–503.

Mill, John Stuart (1869) *The Subjection of Women*. London: Longmans, Green, Reader and Dyer.

Mol, Arthur P. J., and Gert Spaargaren (2000) 'Ecological Modernisation Theory in Debate: A Review', *Environmental Politics*, 9(1): 17–49.

Monahan, Arthur P. (2007) *The Circle of Rights Expands: Modern Political Thought after the Reformation, 1521 (Luther) to 1762 (Rousseau)*. Montreal: McGill-Queen's University Press.

Mooney, Chris (2005) *The Republican War on Science*. New York: Basic Books.

Morefield, Jeanne (2005) *Covenants without Swords: Idealist Liberalism and the Spirit of Empire*. Princeton, NJ: Princeton University Press.

Morgenthau, Hans J. (1970) *Truth and Power: Essays of a Decade, 1960–1970*. London: Pall Mall Press.

Morgenthau, Hans J. (1978) *Politics among Nations: The Struggle for Power and Peace*. 5th rev. edn, New York: Alfred A. Knopf.

Muggli, Monique E., Jean L. Forster, Richard D. Hurt, and James L. Repace (2001) 'The Smoke You Don't See: Uncovering Tobacco Industry Scientific Strategies Aimed against Environmental Tobacco Smoke Policies', *American Journal of Public Health*, 91(9): 1419–23.

Murphy, Cornelius (1982) 'The Grotian Vision of World Order', *American Journal of International Law*, 76(3): 477–98.

Murray, Alastair J. H. (1997) *Reconstructing Realism: Between Power Politics and Cosmopolitan Ethics*. Edinburgh: Keele University Press.

Næss, Arne (1989) *Ecology, Community and Lifestyle: Outline of an Ecosophy*, trans. and ed. David Rothenberg. Cambridge: Cambridge University Press.

Nair, Sheila (2002) 'Human Rights and Postcoloniality: Representing Burma', in Geeta Chowdhry and Sheila Nair (eds), *Power, Postcolonialism and International Relations: Reading Race, Gender and Class*. London: Routledge.

Newman, Julie (ed.) (2011) *Green Ethics and Philosophy: An A–Z Guide*. Thousand Oaks, CA: Sage.

Niebuhr, Reinhold (1947) *Moral Man and Immoral Society: A Study in Ethics and Politics*. New York: Charles Scribner's Sons.

Nietzsche, Friedrich (2010) *On Truth and Untruth: Selected Writings*, trans. and ed. Taylor Carman. New York: HarperCollins.

Norris, Christopher (1992) *Uncritical Theory: Postmodernism, Intellectuals, and the Gulf War*. London: Lawrence & Wishart.

NRS (National Research Council) (2011) *Warming World: Impacts by Degree*, http://dels.nas.edu/resources/static-assets/materials-based-on-reports/booklets/warming_world_final.pdf.

Nye, Joseph S. (1990) 'Soft Power', *Foreign Policy*, 80: 153–71.

Nye, Joseph S. (2004) *Soft Power: The Means to Success in World Politics*. New York: Public Affairs Books.

O'Brien, Robert, and Marc Williams (2010) *Global Political Economy*. 3rd edn, Basingstoke: Palgrave Macmillan.

O'Hanlon, Rosalind, and David Washbrook (2012) 'After Orientalism: Culture, Criticism and Politics in the Third World', in Vinayak Chaturvedi (ed.), *Mapping Subaltern Studies and the Postcolonial*. London: Verso.

O'Neill, Kate (2009) *The Environment and International Relations*. Cambridge: Cambridge University Press.

Onuf, Nicholas (2013) *World of our Making: Rules and Rule in Social Theory and International Relations*. Columbia, SC: University of South Carolina Press.

Onuf, Nicholas, and Frank F. Klink (1989) 'Anarchy, Authority, Rule', *International Studies Quarterly*, 33(2): 149–73.

Orakhelashvili, Alexander (ed.) (2011) *Research Handbook on the Theory and History of International Law*. Cheltenham: Edward Elgar.

Oreskes, Naomi, and Erik M. Conway (2010) *Merchants of Doubt: How a Handful of Scientists Obscured the Truth on Issues from Tobacco Smoke to Global Warming*. New York: Bloomsbury Press.

Orford, Anne (2003) *Reading Humanitarian Intervention: Human Rights and the Use of Force in International Law*. Cambridge: Cambridge University Press.

Paret, Peter (1985) *Clausewitz and the State*. Rev. edn, Princeton, NJ: Princeton University Press.

Paterson, Matthew (1999) 'Interpreting Trends in Global Environmental Governance', *International Affairs*, 75(4): 793–802.

Peters, Chris (2012) 'When it Comes to Geoengineering, Are You a Promethean?', 6 June, www.carbonbrief.org/blog/2012/06/geoengineering-promethean-soterian/.

Petras, James (1981) 'Dependency and World System Theory: A Critique and New Directions', *Latin American Perspectives*, 8(3/4): 148–55.

Pettman, Jan Jindy (1996) *Worlding Women: A Feminist International Politics*. St Leonards, NSW: Allen & Unwin.

Phillips, Caryl (1999) 'Truth and Reconciliation', *New York Times*, 17 January, www.nytimes.com/books/99/01/17/reviews/990117.17phillit.html.

Piirimäe, Eva (2002) 'Spinoza on Freedom', *Trames: Journal of the Humanities and Social Sciences*, 4(6): 355–73.

Pogge, Thomas, and Michele Kosch (2007) *John Rawls: His Life and Theory of Justice*. New York: Oxford University Press.

Poole, Steven (2007) 'Obituary: Jean Baudrillard', *The Guardian*, 7 March, www.theguardian.com/news/2007/mar/07/guardianobituaries.france.

Portmann, Roland (2010) *Legal Personality in International Law*. Cambridge: Cambridge University Press.

Prakash, Gyan (1994) 'Subaltern Studies as Postcolonial Criticism', *American Historical Review*, 99(5): 1475–90.

Preston, Christopher J. (2012) 'The Extraordinary Ethics of Solar Radiation Management', in Christopher J. Preston (ed.), *Engineering the Climate: The Ethics of Solar Radiation Management*. Lanham, MD: Lexington Books.

Price, Matthew C. (2007) *The Wilsonian Persuasion in American Foreign Policy*. New York: Cambria Press.

Primoratz, Igor, and Aleksandar Pavković (2007) *Patriotism: Philosophical and Political Perspectives*. Aldershot: Ashgate.

Princen, Thomas (2008) 'Notes on the Theorizing of Global Environmental Politics', *Global Environmental Politics*, 8(1): 1–5.

Project for the New American Century (1997) 'Statement of Principles', http://cf.linnbenton.edu/artcom/social_science/clarkd/upload/PNAC–statement%20of%20principles.pdf.

Pufendorf, Samuel (1698) *Of the Nature and Qualification of Religion: In Reference to Civil Society*. London: A. Roper.

Pugh, Michael (2012) *Liberal Internationalism: The Interwar Movement for Peace in Britain*. Basingstoke: Palgrave Macmillan.

Rahman, Momin, and Stevi Jackson (2010) *Gender and Sexuality: Sociological Approaches*. Cambridge: Polity.

Rajan, Rajeswari Sunder, and You-me Park (2005) 'Postcolonial Feminism/ Postcolonialism and Feminism', in Henry Schwartz and Sangeeta Ray (eds), *A Companion to Postcolonial Studies*. Oxford: Blackwell.

Rasch, Philip J., Simon Tilmes, Richard P. Turco et al. (2008) 'An Overview of Geoengineering of Climate Using Stratospheric Sulphate Aerosols', *Philosophical Transactions of the Royal Society*, 336: 4007–37, http://rsta.royal-societypublishing.org/content/366/1882/4007.full.

Rathbun, Brian (2008) 'A Rose by Any Other Name: Neoclassical Realism as the Logical and Necessary Extension of Structural Realism', *Security Studies*, 17(2): 294–321.

Reynolds, P. A. (1975) 'International Studies: Retrospect and Prospect', *British Journal of International Studies*, 1(1): 1–19.

Rich, Paul (2002) 'Reinventing Peace: David Davies, Alfred Zimmern and Liberal Internationalism in Interwar Britain', *International Relations*, 16(1): 117–33.

Richards, Sabrina (2013) 'Can Epigenetics Explain Homosexuality?', *The Scientist*, 1 January, www.the-scientist.com/?articles.view/articleNo/33773/title/Can-Epigenetics-Explain-Homosexuality-/.

Richardson, James L. (2001) *Contending Liberalisms in World Politics: Ideology and Power*. Boulder, CO: Lynne Rienner.

Rose, Gideon (1998) 'Neoclassical Realism and Theories of Foreign Policy', *World Politics*, 51(1): 144–72.

Rosenthal, Joel (1991) *Righteous Realists: Political Realism, Responsible Power and American Culture in the Nuclear Age*. Baton Rouge: State University of Louisiana Press.

Rossides, Daniel W. (1998) *Social Theory: Its Origins, History and Contemporary Relevance*. Dix Hills, NY: General Hall.

Rousseau, Jean-Jacques (1992) *Discourse on the Origin of Inequality*, trans. Donald A. Cress. Indianapolis: Hackett.

Ruggie, John Gerard (1982) 'International Regimes, Transactions and Change: Embedded Liberalism in the Postwar Economic Order', *International Organization*, 36(2): 379–415.

Ruggie, John Gerard (1998) *Constructing the World Polity: Essays on International Institutionalization*. London: Routledge.

Ruggie, John Gerard (2008) 'Introduction: Embedding Global Markets', in John Gerard Ruggie (ed.), *Embedding Global Markets*. Aldershot: Ashgate.

Rummell, Rudolph J. (1994) *Death by Government*. New Brunswick, NJ: Transaction.

Russell, Bertrand (1979) *History of Western Philosophy*. London: Unwin.

Russett, Bruce (2005) 'Bushwacking the Democratic Peace', *International Studies Perspectives*, 6(4): 395–408.

Russett, Bruce, John R. Oneal and David R. Davis (1998) 'The Third Leg of the Kantian Tripod for Peace: International Organizations and Militarized Disputes, 1950–85', *International Organization*, 52(3): 441–67.

Sabine, George H. (1948) *A History of Political Theory*. 3rd edn, London: Harrap.

Said, Edward (1995) *Orientalism: Western Conceptions of the Orient*. London: Penguin.

Sale, Kirkpatrick (2000) *Dwellers in the Land: The Bioregional Vision*. 2nd edn, Athens: University of Georgia Press.

Salleh, Ariel (2000) 'In Defense of Deep Ecology: An Ecofeminist Response to a Liberal Critique', in Eric Katz, Andrew Light and Andrew Rothenberg (eds), *Beneath the Surface: Critical Essays in the Philosophy of Deep Ecology*. Cambridge, MA: MIT Press.

Schell, Jonathan (2000) *The Fate of the Earth: And, the Abolition*. Stanford, CA: Stanford University Press.

Scholz, Sally J. (2007) 'War Rape's Challenge to Just War Theory', in Steven P. Lee (ed.), *Intervention, Terrorism and Torture: Contemporary Challenges to Just War Theory*. Dordrecht: Springer.

Schweller, Randall L. (2006) *Unanswered Threats: Political Constraints on the Balance of Power*. Princeton, NJ: Princeton University Press.

Senghor, Léopold (2010) 'Négritude: A Humanism of the Twentieth Century', in Roy Richard Grinker, Stephen C. Lubkemann and Christopher B. Steiner (eds), *Perspectives on Africa: A Reader in Culture, History and Representation*. 2nd edn, Chichester: Wiley-Blackwell.

Sessions, Robert (1991) 'Deep Ecology versus Ecofeminism: Healthy Differences or Incompatible Philosophies?', *Hypatia*, 6(1): 90–107.

Seth, Sanjay (2011) 'Postcolonial Theory and the Critique of International Relations', *Millennium: Journal of International Studies*, 40(1): 167–83.

Shukla, Bhaskar A. (2007) *Feminism: From Mary Wollstonecraft to Betty Friedan*. New Delhi: Sarup & Sons.

Simon, Lawrence H. (ed.) (1994) *Karl Marx: Selected Writings*. Indianapolis: Hackett.

Sjoberg, Laura, and Sandra Via (2010) *Gender, War and Militarism: Feminist Perspectives*. Santa Barbara, CA: Praeger/ABC-Clio.

Slattery, Martin (2003) *Key Ideas in Sociology*. Cheltenham: Nelson Thomas.

Slaughter, Anne-Marie (1995) 'International Law in a World of Liberal States', *European Journal of International Law*, 6(1): 503–38.

Smith, Adam (2009) *The Wealth of Nations*. Lawrence, KS: Digireads.com.

Smith, James (2008) *Terry Eagleton*. Cambridge: Polity.

Smith, Michael Joseph (1992) 'Liberalism and International Reform', in Terry Nardin and David R. Mapel (eds), *Traditions of International Ethics*. Cambridge: Cambridge University Press.

Smith, Steve (2000) 'The Discipline of International Relations: Still an American Social Science', *British Journal of Politics and International Relations*, 2(3): 374–402.

Snyder, Claire R. (1999) *Citizen-Soldiers and Manly Warriors: Military Service and Gender in the Civic Republican Tradition*. Lanham, MD: Rowman & Littlefield.

Soros, George (2010) 'Anatomy of a Crisis', 9 April, http://ineteconomics. org/sites/inet.civicactions.net/files/INET%20C@K%20Paper%20Session%20 1%20-%20Soros_0.pdf.

Spencer, Herbert (1902) *Notes and Comments*. New York: D. Appleton.

Spivak, Gayatri Chakravorty (1999) *A Critique of Postcolonial Reason: Toward a History of the Vanishing Present*. Cambridge, MA: Harvard University Press.

Steans, Jill (2006) *Gender and International Relations: Issues, Debates and Future Directions*. Cambridge: Polity.

Stemple, Lara (2009) 'Male Rape and Human Rights', *Hastings Law Journal*, 60(February): 605–47.

Stephanson, Anders (2005) *Manifest Destiny: American Expansion and the Empire of Right*. New York: Hill & Wang.

Storr, Will (2011) 'The Rape of Men: The Darkest Secret of War', *The Observer*, 17 July, www.theguardian.com/society/2011/jul/17/the-rape-of-men.

Suchting, W. A. (1983) *Marx: An Introduction*. Brighton: Harvester Press.

Suganami, Hidemi (1978) 'A Note on the Origin of the Word "International"', *British Journal of International Studies*, 4(3): 226–32.

Swift, Adam (2011) *Political Philosophy*. Cambridge: Polity.

Sylvest, Casper (2004) 'Interwar Internationalism, the British Labour Party, and the Historiography of International Relations', *International Studies Quarterly*, 48(2): 409–32.

Sylvest, Casper (2005) 'Continuity and Change in British Liberal Internationalism c. 1900–1930', *Review of International Studies*, 31(2): 263–83.

Sylvester, Christine (2002) *Feminist International Relations: An Unfinished Journey*. Cambridge: Cambridge University Press.

Taylor, Paul W. (2011) *Respect for Nature: A Theory of Environmental Ethics*. Princeton, NJ: Princeton University Press.

Teddie, Charles, and Abbas Tashakkori (2011) 'Mixed Methods Research: Contemporary Issues in an Emerging Field', in Norman K. Denzin and Yvonna S. Lincoln (eds), *The Sage Handbook of Qualitative Research*. 4th edn, London: Sage.

Tesón, Fernando R. (2001) *The Liberal Case for Humanitarian Intervention*. Public Law and Legal Theory Working Paper no. 39, Florida State University College of Law.

Thomas, Peter D. (2009) *The Gramscian Moment: Philosophy, Hegemony and Marxism*. Leiden: Brill.

Thornham, Sue (2006) 'Second Wave Feminism', in Sarah Gamble (ed.), *The Routledge Companion to Feminism and Postmodernism*. London: Routledge.

Thucydides (1972) *History of the Peloponnesian War*, trans. Rex Warner. London: Penguin.

Tickner, J. Ann (1992) *Gender in International Relations: Feminist Perspectives on Achieving Global Security*. New York: Columbia University Press.

Toft, Peter (2005) 'John J. Mearsheimer: An Offensive Realist between Geopolitics and Power', *Journal of International Relations and Development*, 8(4): 381–408.

Tucker, Spencer C. (2011) *The Encyclopedia of the Vietnam War: A Political, Social, and Military History*. 2nd edn, Santa Barbara, CA: ABC-Clio.

UN (1948) Convention on the Prevention and Punishment of the Crime of Genocide, 9 December, www.ohchr.org/EN/ProfessionalInterest/Pages/CrimeOfGenocide.aspx.

UN (1992) UN Conference on Environment and Development, www.un.org/geninfo/bp/enviro.html.

UN (2010) *The World's Women 2010: Trends and Statistics*, http://unstats.un.org/unsd/demographic/products/Worldswomen/WW2010pub.htm.

UN News Centre (2011) 'As World Passes 7 Billion Milestone, UN Urges Challenges to Meet Key Challenges', www.un.org/apps/news/story.asp?NewsID=40257#.U6yrR_2gG9g.

UNDP (1994a) *Human Development Report*, http://hdr.undp.org/en/reports/global/hdr1994/.

UNDP (1994b) http://hdr.undp.org/en/media/hdr_1994_en_chap2.pdf.

UNEP (2012) *Inclusive Wealth Report 2012: Measuring Progress Towards Sustainability*. Cambridge: Cambridge University Press; www.unep.org/pdf/IWR_2012.pdf.

UNESCO (1972) Convention Concerning the Protection of the World Cultural and Natural Heritage, 17 October, http://whc.unesco.org/en/convention-text/.

Vasquez, John A. (1998) *The Power of Power Politics: From Classical Realism to Neotraditionalism*. Cambridge: Cambridge University Press.

Wæver, Ole (1998) 'The Sociology of a Not So International Discipline: American and European Developments in International Relations', *International Organization*, 53(4): 687–727.

Walker, Clarence (2002) *We Can't Go Home Again: An Argument about Afrocentrism*. New York: Oxford University Press.

Wallerstein, Immanuel (1979) *The Capitalist World-Economy*. Cambridge: Cambridge University Press.

Wallerstein, Immanuel (2004) *World-Systems Analysis: An Introduction*. Durham, NC: Duke University Press.

Waltz, Kenneth N. (1979) *Theory of International Politics*. Boston: McGraw-Hill.

Waltz, Kenneth N. (2000) 'Structural Realism after the Cold War', *International Security*, 25(1): 5–41.

Waltz, Kenneth N. (2001) *Man, the State and War: A Theoretical Analysis*. New York: Columbia University Press.

Warren, Karen J. (1997) 'Introduction', in Karen J. Warren (ed.), *Ecofeminism: Women, Culture, Nature*. Bloomington: Indiana University Press.

Watson, Matthew (2008) 'The Historical Roots of Theoretical Traditions in Global Political Economy', in John Ravenhill (ed.), *Global Political Economy*. 3rd edn, Oxford: Oxford University Press.

Watson, Matthew (2013) 'Why We'd Be Mad to Rule Out Climate Engineering', *The Guardian*, 8 October, www.theguardian.com/environment/2013/oct/08/climate-engineering-geoengineering-climate-change.

Watson, Peter (2005) *Ideas: A History from Fire to Freud*. London: Phoenix.

WCED (World Commission on Environment and Development) (1987) *Our*

Common Future, http://conspect.nl/pdf/Our_Common_Future-Brundtland_Report_1987.pdf.

Weber, Cynthia (2009) *International Relations: A Critical Introduction*. 3rd edn, Abingdon: Routledge.

Weber, Max (2005) 'Politics as a Vocation', in Michael L. Morgan (ed.), *Classics of Moral and Political Theory*. 4th edn, Indianapolis: Hackett.

Wendt, Alexander (1992) 'Anarchy is What States Make of It: The Social Construction of Power Politics', *International Organization*, 26(2): 391–425.

Wendt, Alexander (1996) 'Identity and Structural Change in International Politics', in Yosef Lapid and Friedrich Kratochwil (eds), *The Return of Culture and Identity in IR Theory*. Boulder, CO: Lynne Rienner.

Wendt, Alexander (1999) *Social Theory of International Politics*. Cambridge: Cambridge University Press.

WHO (World Health Organization) (2001) 'Smallpox', www.who.int/topics/smallpox/en/.

Wight, Colin (2002) 'Philosophy of Social Science and International Relations', in Walter Carlsnaes, Thomas Risse and Beth A. Simmons (eds), *Handbook of International Relations*. London: Sage.

Wight, Martin (2000) 'Why is There No International Theory?', in Andrew Linklater (ed.), *International Relations: Critical Concepts in Political Science*, Vol. 1. London: Routledge.

Wilder, Gary (2005) *The French Imperial Nation-State: Négritude and Colonial Humanism*. Chicago: University of Chicago Press.

Williams, Andrew, Amelia Hadfield and J. Simon Rofe (2012) *International History and International Relations*. Abingdon: Routledge.

Williams, Gareth (2011) *Angel of Death: The Story of Smallpox*. New York: Palgrave Macmillan.

Willis, Ellen (1989) 'Foreword', in Alice Echols, *Daring to be Bad: Radical Feminism in America, 1967–1975*. Minneapolis: University of Minnesota Press.

Wilson, Ernest J. (2008) 'Hard Power, Soft Power, Smart Power', *Annals of the American Academy of Political and Social Science*, 616(1): 110–24.

Wilson, Woodrow (2005) *Woodrow Wilson: The Essential Political Writings*. Lanham, MD: Lexington Books.

Wissenburg, Marcel (1993) 'The Idea of Nature and the Nature of Distributive Justice', in Andrew Dobson and Paul Lucardie (eds), *The Politics of Nature: Explorations in Green Theory*. London: Routledge.

Wollstonecraft, Mary (1891) *A Vindication of the Rights of Woman: With Strictures on Political and Moral Subjects*. London: T. F. Unwin.

World Bank (2012) *World Development Report 2012: Gender Equality and Development*. Washington, DC: International Bank for Reconstruction and Development.

World Economic Forum (2012) *The Global Gender Gap Report 2012*, www.weforum.org/issues/global-gender-gap.

Worsley, Peter (1980) 'One World or Three: A Critique of the World-System Theory of Immanuel Wallerstein', *Socialist Register*, 17: 298–338.

Yang Su (2011) *Collective Killings in Rural China during the Cultural Revolution*. Cambridge: Cambridge University Press.

Young, Stephen C. (1992) 'The Different Dimensions of Green Politics', *Environmental Politics*, 1(1): 9–44.

Yuan Lijun (2005) *Reconceiving Women's Equality in China: A Critical Examination of Models of Sex Equality*. Lanham, MD: Lexington Books.

Zimmer, Louis B. (2011) *The Vietnam War Debate: Hans J. Morgenthau and the Attempt to Halt the Drift into Disaster*. Lanham, MD: Lexington Books.

Index